Remake, Remodel

D1235088

Remake, Remodel

Women's Magazines in the Digital Age

BROOKE ERIN DUFFY

UNIVERSITY OF ILLINOIS PRESS

Urbana, Chicago, and Springfield

Library of Congress Control Number: 2013951561

For Mom, Dad, and Michael

Contents

Preface
and Acknowledgments

As I think back on my early encounters with media and popular culture, I find it difficult to pinpoint the first time I watched a certain TV series, read a particular book, or tuned in to a new radio station. Yet there is one media moment that remains indelibly etched in my memory: the first time I thumbed through the glossy pages of *Seventeen* magazine. It was during a visit to my grandparents' house shortly after my twelfth birthday, and the archetype of youthful femininity that appeared before me no doubt reflected and reinforced my pre-teen angst. Indeed, I recall a flurry of emotions as I read through that early '90s issue of *Seventeen* again and again; with the benefit of hindsight, I can identify this as a powerful cocktail of envy and inadequacy, hope and aspiration. And so began my close, albeit conflicted, relationship with women's magazines.

In the years that followed, as I transitioned into and through adulthood, I exchanged my copies of *Seventeen* for the latest issues of *Cosmopolitan*, *Glamour*, and the now-defunct *Mademoiselle*; subscriptions to *InStyle*, *Marie Claire*, and *Elle* came a short time later. I faithfully relied upon these glossies for formative guidance in matters of fashion, beauty, fitness, and relationships; at the same time, I began to sense a widespread disapproval of the genre. My initial exposure to this critical perspective came in the form of an undergraduate course on the political economies of media, which located women's magazines within systems of patriarchal capitalism, asymmetrical power relations, and a gendered culture of consumerism. Gloria Steinem's "Sex, Lies, and Advertising" and Ben Bagdikian's *The Media Monopoly* struck a particular nerve and encouraged me to think critically about the unseen forces that shaped the content of *my* magazines.

During graduate school, readings in media studies, sociology, feminist criticism, and cultural studies enabled me to develop a more holistic and nuanced understanding of women's magazines by situating the genre within particular historical, sociocultural, and economic contexts. I also learned to position myself within this complex matrix of academic traditions as a self-identified feminist media researcher. The use of this label, however, remains heavily contested. I agree with Liesbet van Zoonen that studying women (or a women's genre, for that matter) is not enough to make one a feminist scholar.[1] Rather, I align myself with this approach because I believe that constructions of gender (both mediated and nonmediated) must be negotiated within and through larger forms of social, cultural, and political power. It is against this backdrop that I have conducted numerous studies of the women's magazine industry—including the one from which this book emerged—which critically examine industry dynamics, roles, discourses, and texts. Yet my personal connection to women's magazines endures, and I continue to read them for a combination of advice, enjoyment, relaxation, and escape. These seemingly disparate activities often bleed into—and at times nourish—one another.

I am by no means the first to acknowledge the inherent challenges of enacting the dual researcher/participant role. Contemporary feminist scholars have offered candid and reflexive accounts of their experiences studying gendered forms of popular culture, ranging from women's magazines and novels to beauty pageants and soap operas.[2] In the introduction to *Women's Worlds: Ideology, Femininity and the Woman's Magazine*, the authors acknowledge that their enthusiasm for the project "stemmed from our mutual pleasure in reading women's magazines themselves, tempered by the knowledge that this pleasure is by no means pure, unambiguous or unproblematic. . . . For all of us, of course, women's magazines have been a continuing presence in our lives but as feminists they have become an obvious subject for analysis and criticism, a staple topic for consciousness-raising groups."[3] Other scholars of women's magazines have similarly confessed to the "unfeminine pastime of at least occasional magazine reading," being a "feminist who was a 'closet' reader," and growing up "informed by *Seventeen* and *Mademoiselle*."[4] These revelations (we might imagine them divulged in a whisper) signal a larger tension that has both propelled and impeded feminist media studies, namely what is known as "the uneasy connection between the pleasures of popular culture and the political aims of feminism."[5] The relationship between power and pleasure (or feminism and femininity) remains a contested one, and scholars such as Angela McRobbie, Dawn Currie, Ien Ang, and Joke Hermes have made commendable attempts to bridge this divide. Let me be clear at the outset that this book does not provide a theoretical intervention into a debate that is perhaps irreconcilable. Rather, I find this to be a "productive tension" within which to locate this book; it is, after all, a product of my simultaneous and, at times, contradictory subject positions as a critical feminist scholar, longtime magazine reader, female, and participant in gendered forms of consumer culture.[6]

Not only have my personal and professional relationships with women's magazines shifted shape over the last two decades, but the industry itself has been the site of a swift and striking transformation. Recent developments in media technologies, cultures, and markets have created a perfect storm for industrial change by raising the question, "What is a magazine?" This book finds answers to that question in a detailed study of the magazine industry that reflects the perspective of those who face the currents of change on a daily basis: women's magazine executives, print publishers and editors, digital strategists, writers, designers, and more. Many of these individuals are working tirelessly and thanklessly (in terms of added financial compensation) to remake the magazine amidst chaos and uncertainty. This involves continuously repackaging the magazine product to fit a dizzying array of websites, social media platforms, mobile devices, and emergent tablet forms. Yet magazine producers are also forced to remake their processes, including those practices that historically guided them in matters of content, audiences, advertisers, and more.

The process of writing a book such as this can also be described as an exercise in remaking: rethinking research questions, revisiting theories, reinterpreting findings, and reworking conclusions. Fortunately, I did not have to undertake these exhaustive processes alone. I am incredibly grateful for the support and guidance of countless individuals who helped to make this book possible. First and foremost, I would like to convey my appreciation to the magazine executives, publishers, editors, writers, and digital strategists who generously devoted their time and insight to this project. This includes Lisa Arbetter, Deputy Managing Editor at *InStyle*; Glen-Ellen Brown, Vice President of Brand Development at Hearst Magazines; Brianna Cox Brunecz, former advertising sales representative at the *Knot*; Debi Chirichella, Senior Vice President and Chief Financial Officer at Hearst Magazines, formerly of Condé Nast; Joanna Coles, Editor-in-Chief of *Cosmopolitan*, formerly Editor-in-Chief of *Marie Claire*; Chuck Cordray, former Senior Vice President and General Manager of Hearst Magazines Digital Media; Sammy Davis, former digital assistant at Hearst who now oversees her own fashion journalism/retailing business, Sammy Davis Vintage; Suzanne Donaldson, Photo Director at *Glamour*; Mark Golin, Editorial Director of the Digital, Style, and Entertainment and Lifestyle Groups at Time Inc.; Devin Gordon, Senior Editor at *GQ*; Justine Harman, Assistant Editor at *Elle*, formerly of People.com and *People StyleWatch*; Tom Harty, President of the National Media Group (Meredith); Brennan Hayden, Executive Vice President and Chief Operating Officer at Wireless Developer Agency; Jayne Jamison, Vice President and Publisher at *Seventeen*; Ellen Levine, Editorial Director of Hearst Magazines; Matt Milner, Entrepreneur-in-Residence at Hearst Digital, formerly Hearst Digital's vice president of social media and community and the founder of Answerology; Hannah Morrill, formerly of InStyle.com and now an independent freelancer; Martha Nelson, Editorial Director at Time Inc.; Steve Sachs, former Executive Vice President of Consumer Marketing and Sales at Time Inc.; Lavinel Savu, Assistant Managing Editor at *InStyle;* Emily Masamitsu Scadden, former Digital Assets Manager at *Marie Claire*; Vanessa Voltolina, former editor for *Folio: The Magazine for Magazine Management*, now at NBC Universal; Mark Weinberg, former Vice President of Programming and Product Strategy at Hearst Magazines Digital Media; Chris Wilkes, Vice President of Audience Development and Digital Editions at Hearst Magazines, who is also Vice President of Hearst's App Lab; and five contributors who wished to remain anonymous. I would like to extend a special thanks to one final interview participant, Howard Polskin, Executive Vice President of Communications and Events at MPA—The Association of Magazine Media. Howard showed great enthusiasm for this project and gave me the opportunity to participate in the 2010 American Magazine Conference, where I learned firsthand about the opportunities and challenges of redefining the magazine.

In addition, I am incredibly grateful for the graduate education I received from the University of Pennsylvania's Annenberg School for Communication. This project, which began as my doctoral dissertation, was both directly and indirectly shaped by many of the faculty-scholars with whom I had the great privilege to work during my time there. I owe my deepest thanks to my dissertation advisor, Joseph Turow, who provided essential conceptual and methodological guidance as this project developed from the first spark of an idea into its completed manuscript form. Indeed, over the last seven years or so, he has offered me sharp insight, intellectual clarity, encouragement when needed, and above all else, unwavering support. I am also indebted to the other members of my dissertation committee, Katherine Sender and Sharrona Pearl, each of whom afforded me invaluable feedback, thoughtful direction, and vital reassurance. These three individuals have served as models for excellence in scholarship, and I can think of no one else with whom I would rather work on a project of this scope. Thanks are due as well to the University of Illinois Press editorial board, and most especially to Danny Nasset for his enthusiasm for and support of this project. I am also grateful to the anonymous reviewers for the constructive feedback and productive suggestions they provided on an earlier version of this manuscript. During the production phase, Jane Lyle copyedited this manuscript with great care and a sharp eye for detail, while Jennifer L. Reichlin expertly managed the production process. Temple University doctoral students Rachel Jones, Maria Cipollone, and Yvonne Fulmore also helped tremendously during the final phases of manuscript preparation.

I would also like to thank the colleagues and friends who offered ideas, encouragement, and welcome distractions. This non-exhaustive list includes Mario Rodriguez, Angel Bourgoin, Jeff Gottfried, Piotr Szpunar, Caroline Leary, Elysia Lichtine, and Hector Postigo. Finally, I owe the deepest gratitude to my parents, Leslie and Dan Pilszak, and my husband, Michael James Duffy. They have provided endless hours of support and understanding as well as sentiments of faith in my moments of self-doubt. There are no words to adequately convey my deep-rooted love and appreciation.

Remake, Remodel

Questioning Media Identity in the Digital Age

In October 2011, as the news of Steve Jobs's untimely death sent shock-waves through the internet and technology communities, French telecom entrepreneur Jean-Louis Constanza posted a short video clip on YouTube as a tribute to Apple's exalted leader.[1] The opening scene, titled "This One Works," featured Constanza's one-year-old daughter playing with an iPad; the beguiled tot coos as the touchscreen responds to her every finger tap and swipe. In the following scene, "This One Does Not Work," she replicates these tactile movements on a print edition of the women's monthly *Marie Claire*. After poking and prodding the glossy pages with her tiny hands, the disillusioned child inspects her pointer finger to make sure that *it* still works (it does, of course). She is joyfully reunited with the tablet device in the concluding scene, "I've Had It. Off to the One That Works." Constanza's exposition of the iPad/magazine juxtaposition then fills the screen: "For my one-year-old daughter, a magazine is an iPad that does not work. It will remain so for her whole life. Steve Jobs has coded a part of her [operating system]."

The "A Magazine Is an iPad That Does Not Work" video was a viral sensation that generated more than four million YouTube hits and an unwieldy stream of viewer comments. Journalists and bloggers from the *Atlantic*, *Gawker*, the *Huffington Post*, and even *Parenting* magazine used the clip as fodder for debates about the generational and cultural shifts engendered by new technologies. To some, the video illustrated what "it really mean[s] to be a digital native" who knows only a world of instant gratification.[2] Others suggested that Constanza's video was merely a product of careful editing and sequencing. As one of the highest-rated YouTube comments read: "Your child is behaving like a normal one year old. The iPad has bright colours and flashing lights. Of course it's more instantly gratifying. . . . She's being tactile. You're being reactionary."[3] In either case, Constanza's magazine-as-a-broken-iPad metaphor shed light on the elusive nature of print media at the dawn of the twenty-first century. At a time when the boundaries between media industries are beginning to crumble, what distinguishes a magazine from any other medium or content provider that can be encoded as 1s and 0s? Put simply, *what is a magazine?*

Indeed, recent transformations in the technologies, economies, and markets of mass communication raise fundamental questions about the identities of different media. If a medium—be it television, newspaper, magazine, or radio—is abruptly hewn from its technological form (i.e., a screen, printed page, or radio tuner), then what identifies it as such? Although this question may seem overly simplistic or, alternatively, needlessly abstract, the stakes for the individuals who earn a living as professional content creators are very real. As they transition their processes and products into a digital media environment, traditional media workers face daunting challenges: rapidly evolving technologies, intensified deadlines, amplified workloads, and new sources of competition. Further, the identities of producers are ostensibly blurring with those of consumers, threatening to undo a bifurcation on which the mass media system has steadily relied. Popular narratives about interactive media suggest that low-cost production and distribution technologies provide audiences with unprecedented access to the cultural circuit. To some, these activities mark a refraction of deeply entrenched flows of information and communication. Media scholar Henry Jenkins, who has written extensively on the affordances of participatory culture, argues that the technologies and tools of the new millennium have helped to shift structures of power in consumers' favor.[4] Neologisms such as "prosumer," "produsage," and "co-creator" seemingly bespeak the euphoria surrounding digital media.[5] Other scholars are more critical of the consumer empowerment narrative and suggest that the boosterish promise of democratic participation is nothing more than a "corporate ruse."[6] Regardless of where one stands on the participation-as-empowerment/exploitation polemic, it is indisputable that media professionals are jockeying for eyeballs with a new generation of YouTube-created celebrities, MySpace-spawned singers, and bloggers–cum–political pundits. And this competition is quite fierce in the aptly named attention economy.

In addition, the way in which media workers define their products has implications for the content that gets created and circulated throughout the mediated public sphere. Certainly the accuracy and depth of information made available to audiences shapes their understanding of the social world. Yet the business logic of producing content for several media platforms at once may adversely impact content quality. Within traditional news journalism, anecdotes abound about how the race to break news online has led to sloppy editing practices and the electronic publication of yet-to-be-confirmed reports. CNN's so-called "Dewey Defeats Truman moment" in announcing the 2012 Supreme Court healthcare ruling and the premature reports of Penn State football coach Joe Paterno's death are but two examples. At the same time, government regulation has not evolved quickly enough to keep up with the fast pace of change within the digital media world. Laws and self-regulatory approaches that long guided media production processes are not easily translating into the emergent media era.

Taken together, these trends signal a sea change in cultural production that can be productively understood within the framework of media convergence. While definitions of convergence vary, most are oriented around two interrelated movements: (1) the coming together of the components of print, electronic, and digital media on a singular device, and (2) the blurring of boundaries between media producers and consumers.[7] Signaling the broader cultural applications, creative industries scholar Mark Deuze expounds that convergence takes place on many levels: "between different channels, forms, and formats, between different parts of the media enterprise, between the acts of production and consumption, between making media and using media, and between active or passive spectatorship of mediated culture."[8] In each of these cases, convergence implies the decline—or at least fragility—of traditional structures of information and communication. Media specialists are no longer the only ones creating professional-quality content; production no longer takes place exclusively in the workplace; and content is no longer tethered to particular media formats.

In light of the boundary shifts associated with media convergence, producers are ostensibly compelled to (re)define their industries, their roles, their audiences, and their products. Yet it remains unclear exactly how executives and producers are undertaking this redefinition without fully breaking from the past. Several other questions related to media identities in an era of convergence are also salient: What are the implications for how, when, and where media producers work? How do the cross-platform and interactive logics of production challenge the traditional categories of readers and audiences? To what extent do external pressures, particularly those from advertisers, shape these logics? And, finally, what is at stake for the content that gets distributed in various media forms?

Women's magazines provide a compelling site to examine these and other questions about how "traditional" media industries are transforming in a digital era of media. For decades, women's magazines were regularly published, print-bound guidebooks aimed at neatly defined segments of the female audience: working mothers, female fitness enthusiasts, sophisticated black women, and fashion-forward twenty-somethings, among many others. Crisp pages, a well-composed visual aesthetic, and an intimate tone were among the hallmarks of women's glossies up through the turn of the twenty-first century. During those halcyon days of publishing, each magazine also conveyed a "unique" personality articulated through its editorial voice. Faithful readers could tell from just a few lines of text whether the magazine conveyed the tone of *Vogue*'s illustrious editor-in-chief Anna Wintour or the "charismatic and charming" tenor of longtime *Glamour* editor Cindi Leive.[9]

Contemporary women's magazine producers are directly confronting the challenges of digitization, participatory media, and splintering audiences. Most publishers have seen consistently declining revenues as both audiences and advertisers migrate to free, immediate, and interactive platforms. Magazine websites have yet to draw the audience numbers of popular social media networks; according to the 2011 "State of the Media: The Social Media Report," Americans devote 22.5 percent of their time online to social media sites, with Facebook ranking as an easy favorite.[10] Although magazine-friendly devices such as the Android, iPad, Kindle, and Nook are being launched in rapid succession, executives have yet to develop viable profit models to temper their losses. As I show in the chapters that follow, these changes translate into uncertainty about the meaning of the magazine in the early twenty-first century. In fact, many key figures in the consumer magazine business have directly engaged with the earlier-mentioned question: "What is a magazine?" In April 2010, for example, a cadre of industry leaders gathered at the Time and Life Building in New York City for the "What's a Magazine?" conference, subtitled: "The answer used to be simple. You knew it when you saw it. But now what is it? [. . .] The answer will determine our future."[11]

Time Warner chairman Jeffrey Bewkes echoed this question more than a year later in an interview about the changing of the guard at Time Inc. After announcing the appointment of digital expert Laura Lang as chief executive of Time Warner's publishing subsidiary, Bewkes suggested that the new form of the magazine is form*less*. "What is a magazine if I'm looking at a tablet version of *People* and watching the red carpet at the Emmys? What's the difference between that and E! Entertainment Television? It's the same thing."[12] His quote indexes the complexity of the epochal shift occurring in the consumer magazine industry. As content spills off the printed page and across the internet, iPad/tablet, mobile, television, and retail industries, magazines are seemingly evolving from *objects* into *brands*.

Remake, Remodel: Women's Magazines in the Digital Age pulls back the curtain on the women's magazine industry to chronicle this fascinating evolution—and its implications for both producers and consumers of content. Drawn from my in-depth interviews with magazine publishers, editors, creatives, and digital experts; an examination of hundreds of trade and mainstream press reports; and attendance at industry events, this book tells the story of an industry straddling two seemingly different media eras. The notions of remaking and remodeling the magazine speak to the changes in both the products and the processes of women's magazines. To reckon with new and emergent media platforms—web, mobile, tablet, and more—producers continuously rethink, repackage, and redistribute media content (the *product*). The once-static print article gets transmogrified into an interactive feature for the iPad, a blog post on the website complete with a reader poll, and links and images on the magazines' Facebook and Twitter feeds. Yet the *processes* that underpin the remaking of the magazine are more complex, intimately bound up with longstanding production roles and routines, assumptions about the audience, and deeply embedded relationships with advertisers.

As I show in this book, the stakes of this dual-level remaking are being felt across the industry, superimposed on some of the more established demands of creative labor. To keep their jobs, magazine workers are forced to balance specialization with being Jacks-and-Jills-of-all-trades, face a loss of creative autonomy, and are entrenched in a professional culture in which social and gender inequalities may be exacerbated. At the same time, the ways in which magazine producers redefine their work are gradually yielding different approaches to offerings for audiences. This results in new definitions of quality and creativity across platforms as well as content increasingly created by and for advertisers.

Remake, Remodel is anchored both historically and contextually. Thus, some of the topics it addresses channel the unique history of women's magazines: the intimacy readers feel as part of imagined communities of interest, the social construction of publishing as an "acceptable" career for female workers, and (problematic) assumptions about the cozy relationship between editors and advertisers. Yet it also probes distinctly modern trends that fit within the cultural moment of convergence. This includes competition from fashion bloggers and the surreptitious ways producers court interactive consumer audiences on their web and mobile properties. The book thus attempts to negotiate continuities and changes at this juncture. The central discursive thread that weaves its elements together is identity, or perhaps more accurately identity challenges. Three particular identity constructions lie at the heart of this book: organizational identity, professional identity, and gender identity.

Questioning Organizational, Professional, and Gender Identities

As formats across the media and culture industries blur under the logic of convergence, definitions of "media" inherited from the twentieth century seem less and less relevant. In 2010, for example, National Public Radio shifted to the truncated moniker NPR to incorporate the organization's growing fleet of (non-radio) digital and mobile properties. Several months later, when News Corporation's Rupert Murdoch unveiled his iPad-only digital news service the *Daily*, some interrogated the extent to which it fit comfortably under the rubric of "newspaper." In a similar vein, the mushrooming popularity of e-readers such as the Kindle, Sony Reader, and Nook has prompted a slew of definitional inquiries and debates, such as, "If you can't lend an e-book, is it still a book?" and "[Should we] call it a book without pages?" Directing the focus to the problematic entanglement of television with digital screen technologies, media scholar Joshua Green published an article aptly titled "Why Do They Call It TV When It's Not on the Box?" Green was particularly interested in the application of traditional televisual frameworks to the forms and services of "new television projects," including internet TV and YouTube.[13] These queries are not merely semantic, but rather indicate how digitization is eroding the specificity, or unique cultural forms, of traditional media.

Beginning in the mid-twentieth century, film theorists and auteurs sought to classify forms of cultural production based upon reflections about their "essential character."[14] Such classificatory systems underlie media specificity theory, which puts forth the idea that a medium—be it painting, photography, sculpture, or literature—has intrinsic characteristics that differentiate it from other expressive forms. Not only is medium specificity applicable to the realms of high culture, but its premises also guide the work environments and processes of mass media industries. That is, newspaper firms, magazine publishers, TV studios, and the like tend to operate within what Henry Jenkins has called "medium-specific paradigms."[15]

Technological convergence threatens to upend these paradigms. Indeed, for twenty-first-century media producers, the business imperative to work across platforms makes it difficult to discern where one medium ends and another begins. Management researcher Gracie Lawson-Borders examined this conundrum in her study of three cross-platform news organizations: "The question that most media executives must ask is not whether their organization is a newspaper, TV station, radio, movie or cable company. The more pertinent questions might be: Are we in the content business? What are the complementary channels to deliver . . . content?"[16] A reorientation such as this is not as easy in practice, as it forces media executives and workers to think critically about *who they are* and *what they do*.

Sociologists have mined issues such as these using the organizational identity approach. First proposed by organizational theorists Stuart Albert and David Whetten in the mid-1980s, organizational identity speaks to what members believe is "central, distinctive and enduring" about their company, later rephrased as "who we are as an organization."[17] The myriad writings published on organizational identity over the years illustrate how this construct is both constitutive of and constituted in corporate strategy, culture, practice, forms of dress, and ritual, among others. And although the initial theorization stressed the significance of the individuals working within an organization (how they define themselves), subsequent writings argued that organizational identity also incorporates the beliefs and behaviors of external agents.[18] In the case of media industries, executives and employees *as well as* consumers, advertisers, and competitors contribute to organizational identity constructs.

Curiously, many media scholars have overlooked the significance of this approach; a noteworthy exception is Liesbet van Zoonen. In studying journalistic cultures in the mid-1990s, she positioned organizational identity between structures such as time, space, power, and the market, on the one hand, and, on the other, subjectivities such as gender, ethnicity, political view, and education.[19] What is particularly relevant for the present study is her contention that "hard" journalism has a different organizational identity than women's magazine journalism, indicating the need to study these industries discretely. Outside of media studies, Mary Tripsas has contributed one of the few existing case studies of a company whose organizational identity is being threatened by technological innovations in the marketplace.[20] She takes as her starting point the notion of "identity-challenging technologies," or those that deviate from the expectations associated with an organization's (in this case, a digital photography firm's) identity. Although new technologies may be productive for senior managers, she suggests that identity constructions are quite constraining, as organizational workers are unlikely to adopt what goes against firmly ingrained beliefs and practices. In particular, Tripsas notes how the blurring of industry boundaries raises critical identity questions: "The potential convergence of PDAs, cell phones, pagers, cameras, and MP3 players into a single device challenges the identity of disparate individual producers. These organizations may need to shift identity, but given the initial ambiguous framing of what the new product is, the desired future identity may be unclear."[21] This seems evocative of the situation in which many traditional print and broadcast media industries are finding themselves. Their longstanding, unique cultural forms are being uprooted by the shape-shifting technologies and cultures of digital media.

The contemporary logic of media convergence also challenges the professional identities of those who work within the walls of traditional media industries. At a conceptual level, professional identity has been conflated with both individual identity (e.g., personalities and collectivities such as gender, age, race/ethnicity) and organizational identity markers.[22] Although these categories can and do overlap, I loosely define professional identity as the practices, values, and division of labor tied to a particular medium (i.e., magazine culture, newspaper culture) rather than to a specific corporation (i.e., Time Inc., the New York Times Company). This definition captures the dominant perspective on the cultural industries, which positions individual creativity in contradistinction to organizational constraint. As such, it fits neatly within a larger dualism in the sociological tradition that, as Paul du Gay summarizes, "posits an essential structural antagonism between the identities and interests of 'labor' or 'wage earners' on the one hand, and 'capital' and 'employers' on the other."[23]

Within media industries, professional identities are constructed through the interplay of education/socialization, popular representations of creative industries in mediated culture, and the individuals who work in the industry themselves.[24] The professional identity of a magazine writer, for example, is shaped by her magazine journalism education; the guidelines of industry associations such as MPA—The Association of Magazine Media and the American Society of Magazine Editors; the social constructions of the profession that circulate in public culture; and, of course, the personal assumptions and experiences of current magazine professionals.

In many creative sectors, the contours of professional identity began to shift in the last decades of the twentieth century, impacted by the political-economic forces of globalization, neoliberalism, and post-Fordism. Since then, creative work in the so-called "new economy" has been characterized as deskilled, flexible, temporary, and underpaid.[25] With the rise of digital media, these trends have become more firmly ingrained in the cultures of media work as content creators are expected to channel their energies into a variety of digital technologies and platforms. In his 2005 study of convergence in the newsroom, sociologist Eric Klinenberg argued that sites of news production increasingly demand flexible laborers who are able to create content for print, television, and the internet simultaneously. These changes necessitate a reconfiguration of news workers' professional identities as they pursue strategies for reformulating work across different platforms.[26] Among the strategies are technological training and formalized attempts to indoctrinate professionals in the content strategies and styles of other media. In the years since Klinenberg published his study, news journalists have confronted a dizzying array of new platforms for which they must also produce content: Facebook, Twitter, Tumblr, mobile and tablet devices, and more.

The ostensible intrusion of audiences into media production processes is an additional challenge to professional identity constructs. As noted earlier, one of the central tropes in discourses of convergence and digitization is the blurred boundary between media producers and audiences, the latter of which has been vociferously hailed as the "newly empowered consumer."[27] Mark Deuze has argued that the structuring of the creative industries historically "exclud[ed] multiple-way communication or any kind of meaningful dialogue between media users and producers" and thus prompted "the operational closure of these professions."[28] Today, however, blogs, wikis, social media sites, and other forums for user-generated content represent a considerable break from the traditional, top-down model of communication. As a result, producers *qua* producers must jockey with these sites for the attention of audiences. Examples abound of nonprofessional content creators whose audience base rivals that of the leading media voices. Of course, some media producers face a more substantial danger than the loss of audiences, namely the potential for unemployment as work gets outsourced to these (mostly) unpaid laborers.[29] Why buy the cow when you can get the content for free?

Although professional identity is a construct deeply entangled with social identity markers—gender, race, class, age, and more—scholars of media convergence have tended to sidestep these categories.[30] Gender, in particular, plays a pivotal role in the organization, processes, and products of media industries—in much the same way that it serves as "a mechanism that structures material and symbolic worlds and our experiences of them."[31]

Importantly, the definition of gender I ascribe to recognizes that it is not a natural fact, but rather a category that is socially constructed, performative, and constantly evolving.[32]

Conversations about the role of women in media organizations have been taking place for more than a century, but the rise of second-wave feminism in the 1960s crystallized concerns about gender inequity.[33] In fact, feminist critiques of organizational forms of male power were considered integral to women's liberation, and consequently, feminists sought out nonbureaucratic forms of assemblage for their own social movements.[34] Their concerns stemmed from a general sense of apprehension about the patriarchal structure of the labor market as well as from the narrower construction of media production as a "masculine" enterprise. This is not to say that women were fully excluded from the circuit of production; as I discuss more in chapter 1, women have historically been granted access to those media and cultural industries that considered it necessary to understand womanhood and femininity for commercial purposes. Cultural historian Kathy Peiss makes the case that throughout the twentieth century, women were employed by—and at times held a significant degree of power in—the women's press, advertising, cosmetics, and fashion industries. Yet in describing women's employment in these sectors as "a state of being, not a will to action," Peiss makes it clear that female admittance into these fields was not politically motivated, but instead substantiated the economic exploitation of femininity.[35] Put simply, the mentality was that women were the best ones to sell products and services to other women.

Despite this, numerous feminist scholars have sought to benchmark the role of women in media organizations by quantifying their contributions to the production of news, television, magazines, films, and more. The consensus is that there are far more male than female executives in almost every mass media industry, and the men enjoy far higher status. Summarizing the current imbalance, Carolyn M. Byerly and Karen Ross explain that media companies are typically sites "where men's ownership and creative control are still the norm everywhere, and where women have had a tough time gaining access to production, either as trained professionals or citizens." They add that masculine work cultures, sexual harassment, and the normalization of gendered work practices have further stunted the progress of women in contemporary media industries.[36]

Several other recent studies have gone beyond workplace gender composition to draw out the correlation between the diversity of media professionals and the diversity of media content. For instance, comparative studies of male and female journalists have found that the latter tend to emphasize social and humanitarian issues, suggesting variances in the agenda-setting function of news media.[37] Other writings have sought to examine gender-coded work environments. Reflecting upon this critical turn, Marjan de Bruin writes: "Counting men and women, identifying positions and mapping employment patterns is regarded as necessary and useful baseline data but it is also seen as only scratching the surface of the realities of media organizations. In order to learn more about what is actually taking place on the work floor, it is necessary to go beyond the 'body count' and to start looking at specific social practices, embodied in conventions and rules, formally and informally, based on history and tradition, sustained by people working in the media organizations."[38] To this end, while recent years *have* seen an upsurge in women entering print and broadcast media organizations, men continue to hold the lion's share of power.

Meanwhile, the rise of computing and the movement to post-Fordist working practices have coincided with new assumptions about gender relations in the media sector. Flexible work has become synonymous with female emancipation from patriarchal work structures: by "working from home," women can ostensibly combine work and childcare duties. Although this conjecture lends credence to narratives of female empowerment in the information age, a number of analyses have problematized this assumption with data about continuing gender imbalances in the new media sector.[39] In the early 2000s, Rosalind Gill concluded from her study of European freelance new media workers that "some of the mythologised and highly valued features of project based new media—informality and flexibility—are the very mechanisms through which inequality is reproduced."[40] More recently, Banks and Milestone contend that while there has been real progress for some female producers in the digital sector, gender inequality and discrimination endure.[41] These conclusions urge a critical reexamination of the interrelationships between gender, professional, and organizational identities in the contemporary media moment.

Studying Media Industries in an Era of Convergence

As a project in media industry studies, this book can be situated within a growing corpus of work that interrogates the changing nature of media production. This recent intellectual ferment is both noteworthy and necessary given the trajectory of media research up through the century's end. Traditionally, mass communication scholarship has been catalogued into a triad of industry-, audience-, and text-based studies, a compartmentalization that has reflected and perpetuated paradigmatic clashes over theory and method. Studies of media industries typically emphasize the sociological, economic, and institutional considerations that guide content creation; audience-oriented research foregrounds message reception and the potential "effects" upon audiences; and, finally, textual studies home in on the content itself, including its opened-up spaces for message polysemy, and even subversive resistance.[42]

Although analyses of audiences and texts have far outnumbered those of production, several important sociologies of news organizations surfaced during the 1970s and 1980s, shedding light on the assumptions and practices that informed decisions about "what news is." Researchers such as Gaye Tuchman and Herbert Gans went inside newsrooms to talk to journalists and observe their roles, routines, and relations *in situ*.[43] This methodological approach confronted the difficulties of inference, or the fact that other empirical traditions overlook the "complex articulation of differing influences and constraints . . . embedded within the moment of production."[44] Several other key studies focused on the world of entertainment, most notably the realms of music and fictional television programming.[45]

By the 1990s, however, media production studies were eclipsed by political economy of communication, a tradition that shifted attention to macro-level power relations embedded in ownership and regulatory structures. The growing influence of cultural studies during this era also figured into the communication field's movement away from production research, especially in light of what Elana Levine aptly described as "the cultural studies bias toward analyses of texts and audiences."[46] Writing in the early 2000s, Levine encouraged cultural studies scholars to undertake production studies in order to generate "new insights and heretofore unrecognized connections between media production, media texts, media audiences, and the social contexts within which they circulate."[47] Accordingly, the last decade has witnessed an exciting revival of production-oriented research, much of which draws upon political economy and cultural studies without wholly conforming to either approach.

These contemporary interventions into the cultures of media production operate under various names, including "production of culture," "cultural economy," "cultural industries," and "creative industries."[48] Not only do these titles reflect different disciplinary roots, but they are also embedded in larger institutional and political projects. For instance, the shift in the UK from "cultural industries" to "creative industries" has been linked to policy initiatives and a "conceptual shift" with respect to the political economies of arts and culture.[49] While debates about these approaches will likely persist, they have been confounded by the recent uptick in writings that place media production at the center of discourses on culture-producing organizations. This includes a series of books and articles by communication scholars interested in mapping the future terrain of media production studies.

While Timothy Havens, Amanda Lotz, and Serra Tinic propose a mezzo-level "critical media industry studies approach," Jennifer Holt and Alisa Perren's edited collection offers different methods of studying media industries to account for transformations in technology and audience power, in addition to more sweeping changes such as the rise of neoliberalism and widespread revolutions in global policy and culture.[50] Additionally, the recent edited book by Vicki Mayer, Miranda J. Banks, and John T. Caldwell puts forth ideas about how to "move beyond the unproductive segregation of cultural studies and political economy" by looking at cultures of production across the media landscape.[51] Collectively, these works stand as evidence of the growing attention to production-centered research while laying out methods for critically examining organizational processes, the working lives of media producers, and the implications of group and individual decisions for media content.

A likely explanation for this heightened emphasis on the cultures of media production is the fact that so many longstanding assumptions about producers—and their relationship with audiences and texts—are beginning to unravel. John Hartley, one of the leading voices in the creative industries paradigm, insists that the entire field of media industry studies needs to be invigorated by the incorporation of audiences as agents in the cultural circuit. "Whether user-created content is critiqued as a corporate ruse or celebrated as an opportunity for 'digital democracy' . . . the fact remains that the rise of self-made media poses important questions for 'media industry studies.' A rethink of the metaphor of 'industry' is in order, to include all the agents involved in the system, not just inherited corporate structures. It is also time to abandon the assumption that causation and communication flow one-way only, and to take seriously the agency of the critical-creative citizen-consumer within an overall system in which major enterprises are also at work."[52] To this end, there is an emergent body of literature that uses the framework of cultural convergence to examine the shifting values, activities, and ideologies of today's media workers. Much of this work focuses on the field of journalism; for instance, recent studies have explored how cross-platform production, the rise of citizen journalism, and new demands on timing are influencing the news industry and, more broadly, public discourse.[53] Less attention has been devoted to convergent practices within particular creative and entertainment sites; however, book-length studies by Mark Deuze, Vicki Mayer, and John Caldwell, among others, have helped to elicit understanding of the industrial practices and labor forces underpinning the contemporary advertising, television, film, and video game industries.[54] What weaves these works together is an intrinsic concern with how the processes of media production and the nature of creative labor are evolving in a convergent era of media and culture.

Remake, Remodel draws upon political economy, cultural studies, sociology, and feminist studies of the media to explore the changing nature of production within the women's magazine industry. Like other scholars who work within the broadly conceived framework of cultural production, I take a mezzo-level approach that foregrounds the processes of media production rather than macro-level structures or micro-level issues of reception. In this way, my understanding of production is closely aligned with Mark Deuze's conception of media work, which includes "the complex process of making media, the organization of work, the role of new technologies, the interdependence of issues such as creativity and commerce, and the translation of increasingly precise market orientations to the differentiation of productivity."[55] However, I also depart from contemporary perspectives on media industries in two significant ways. First, I do not agree that we should abandon traditional assumptions about distinctive media industries in favor of an all-encompassing view of media production. Relatedly, and as I make clear throughout the book, I do not believe that new tools and technologies for audience communication are as revolutionary as techo-utopian discourses suggest.

The decision to enter into these theoretical and methodological conversations from the context of the magazine industry is in no way inadvertent. In part, this decision is based on the tendency of convergence scholars to overlook the consumer magazine industry as a rich site for analysis.[56] Such neglect is indicative of a larger gap in the media field where academics tend to make normative distinctions that privilege the production of hard news within a public-service orientation. David Abrahamson, who has published extensively on the history and modern state of consumer publishing, made the woeful claim at the 2008 State of Magazine Research conference, "Magazines remain second-class citizens in the journalism academy."[57] The alleged dismissiveness toward magazines is quite unfortunate, especially given the role of the industry in laying a solid groundwork for the mass media that emerged over the course of the twentieth century. Described as "the first truly mass medium in the United States," magazines provided guidelines for creating entertainment and informational content, appealing to advertisers, and commodifying niche audiences—trends that were later copied or expanded upon by other media organizations.[58]

A caveat of sorts must be added to clarify the positioning of *women's* magazines within the academy. Although this genre, too, tends to reside outside the margins of "journalism studies," teens' and women's glossies have occupied a central place in feminist media thought and empiricism since the 1970s.[59] I trace the simultaneous and intertwined evolutions of feminism and magazine studies in a subsequent chapter; however, it is important to acknowledge at the outset that the *women* of women's magazines are critical to the arguments and findings of this book. After all, women's magazines constitute a genre that is gendered in content and context—embedding both producers and audiences within a feminized space. As identity politics lay at the heart of recent transformations in media technology and culture, this project aims to advance our understanding of media production *and* gender in an unfolding digital economy.

In order to capture the perspectives of and impact on contemporary producers, I draw upon in-depth interviews with more than thirty magazine executives, editors, publishers, writers, and digital specialists across the women's magazine industry.[60] They represent some of the top titles and divisions at three of the largest publishers: Hearst, Condé Nast, and Time. I was fortunate to have the opportunity to speak informally with other magazine producers as a participant at the 2010 American Magazine Conference. Of course, I acknowledge the potential limitations of all of these responses; they must be couched in the framework of what Katherine Sender describes as the "pitch." This refers to the fact that media professionals are often steeped in an industrial culture of "selling ideas to sell products," and this orientation may influence how they present themselves and their work practices to outsiders.[61] The "pitch" may be especially pronounced in the women's magazine industry given the genre's oft-criticized constructions of female subjectivities.[62]

Putting this book together also involved a comprehensive search and analysis of trade articles and mainstream press reports published over a five-year span.[63] I drew upon hundreds of articles from *Folio: The Magazine for Magazine Management*, *Adweek*, the *New York Times*, and the *Wall Street Journal*, among others, in order to learn about such topics as the response of media producers and advertisers to new production and distribution platforms; debates about the distinctiveness of print; the extent to which magazine producers are incorporating content from consumers or are fearful of it; the roles and routines that may reflect the cross-platform logic; and descriptions of new business models and work cultures. These sources helped me gain a more holistic understanding of the changing nature of magazine publishing. However, as Anna Gough-Yates cautions, trade press accounts are not "neutral reflection[s] of 'what went on,'" but instead provide insight into how "practitioners [seek] to represent their production processes and practices to one another."[64] The accounts offered by interview participants and contained in the trade press are not the only sites of discursive modification. This book is also shaped by my own subject position as a researcher/participant in the magazine industry, a dual enactment of roles that I reflect upon in the preface. As Joseph Turow reminds us, "No matter how solid is the empirical research that forms the basis of the investigation, it must be admitted that the investigator's conclusions about the society, institutions, and organizations are always inferred, not seen."[65] I hope this does not make the analysis and conclusions ring hollow, but rather provides a self-reflexive lens through which to understand the following story of the economic, professional, and societal implications of media convergence in the early twenty-first century.

This story is organized in a way that reflects the defining components of the women's magazine genre: history, production, audiences, and content. Before examining precisely how producers are remaking their processes and products, it is first necessary to address the issue of what a women's magazine is—or, perhaps more accurately, what it *was*. Chapter 1, "Making the Magazine: Three Hundred Years in Print," finds answers to this question within a history of women's periodicals that spans several centuries. Since at least the nineteenth century, women's magazines have been shaped by broader sociocultural forces that have collectively contributed to their construction as magazines *for* and *of* women. By this, I refer to the fact that women have played an essential role in the genre's history as both consumers and producers of content. The past of women's magazines has also been defined by the creation of imagined communities of interest, the increasing specialization of titles, and the symbiosis of the magazine and advertising industries. These historically meaningful attributes of the genre provide the necessary backstory for understanding industrial shifts that are now unfolding.

Chapter 2, "Transforming the Magazine: From Print to Bits," fast-forwards to today in order to provide a bird's-eye view of the changes taking place in the economies, technologies, and markets of magazines. Trends that emerged in the late twentieth century—concentration of ownership among publishers, technological advancements, and the nichification of audiences—have since become firmly embedded in the magazine world. Meanwhile, the activities of magazine producers, audiences, and advertisers are drastically changing in this digital age of media. Today, most magazines circulate in digital, mobile, and tablet form while maintaining a vibrant presence on a growing number of social media sites—Facebook, Twitter, YouTube, Tumblr, Pinterest, and more. While these shifts are collectively upending the definition of magazines, they are not being felt evenly across the women's magazine industry. To this end, chapter 2 also looks at localized changes within the three publishers examined in this book: Hearst, Condé Nast, and Time Inc. Although each of these companies produces several women's fashion, beauty, and/or service titles, their organizational structures are becoming quite varied as they reorient departments, positions, and routines to address contemporary industry challenges.

With these historical, gendered, and contemporary contexts in mind, chapters 3–6 closely examine the identity-related shifts taking place inside the women's magazine industry. These chapters focus on the real and discursive sites where boundaries are said to be blurring under the logic of convergence: within workspaces, between producers and consumers, and across media industries and platforms, respectively. Chapter 3, "Production Tensions: New Positions, Routines, and Gender Roles," explores how convergence-related transformations are redefining what it means to be a magazine producer and how this differentiates those who work in magazine production from other individuals, organizations, and industries involved in the production of culture. To "work" in women's magazines today can mean a multiplicity of things. As I show, positions are being rethought, departments are being realigned, and traditional assumptions about magazine work are unraveling. These changes are leading to increased demands on workers, interorganizational tensions, and a professional culture that tends to favor certain types of people. Indeed, as digital specialists (many of whom are male) are brought into the industry, individuals with more traditional orientations and skill sets may be phased out. I thus interrogate whether this emergent professional culture has the potential to reproduce gender hierarchies and other social inequalities.

A different magazine production dynamic is described in chapter 4, "Rethinking Readership: The Digital Challenge of Audience Construction." Women's magazine producers have long understood the commercial imperative of constructing audiences, dividing them into demographic (age, race, gender, education level, income) and psychographic (hobbies, lifestyles, attitudes) categories. In an era of media convergence, however, such traditional means of segmenting audiences are becoming less relevant. Magazine creatives, for one, do not seem to have a clear sense of who the audience is for magazine brand extensions; nor do they know the extent to which this overlaps with the print readership. Such uncertainty raises the basic question of how they create content for an amorphous audience who may come to magazine websites through search and syndication. This often engenders a negotiation between attracting a large web audience and a loyal brand audience.

Relationships between magazine producers and consumers are evolving in more ways than one, and chapter 5, "Inviting Audiences In: Interactive Consumers and Fashion Bloggers," reveals the extent to which the producer-consumer boundary may be dissolving. Against the backdrop of an era of participatory media, producers are "inviting audiences in" to numerous spaces that they have carved out within magazine-branded properties. Community chat rooms, virtual programs, and user-generated contests engage audiences while supplanting the work of professional content producers. Although magazine editors maintain control over these initiatives, they have unequivocally less power over activities that take place outside industry walls, namely the rise of fashion blogs. After addressing how various industry insiders conceptualize fashion blogging, I explore industrial and organizational trends that seem to respond to this cultural movement. Together, these trends evince the ways in which media producers are responding to the consumer-generated era without losing a handle on their institutional goals.

What do these changes in the activities of producers and audiences mean for magazine content in its various manifestations? Chapter 6, "Off the Page: Medium-Specific Approaches to Content," provides an in-depth response to this question. It begins by framing the tension between medium-specific cultures and the rhetoric of cross-platform branding, leading to theoretical and conceptual questions about medium identity. I then discuss how producers' working patterns and assumptions vary across different media (web, magazine, and iPad) in three significant ways: the importance of the editorial voice, quality standards for editorial content, and expectations about the extent of advertiser influence. I discuss the latter in the context of a long history of murky relations between magazine editors and advertisers (the "church-state separation") and suggest important implications for media products driven by and for advertisers. Presumably, customized, marketer-friendly platforms such as the iPad serve as test beds for media/advertising relations within digital environments.

In the concluding chapter, I reinvoke the guiding question "What is a magazine?" to reflect upon the myriad ways in which contemporary producers are redefining their processes and products. Through a focus on reconstituted identities at the gendered, professional, and organizational levels, the practical realities of these shifts are made visible: magazine publishers are reorienting their businesses; executives are reaffirming traditional gendered hierarchies of value; the work culture for producers is simultaneously intensifying and becoming more precarious; offerings for audiences are based upon new—and potentially problematic—assumptions; and advertisers are playing a more direct role in matters of content. I hope, then, that this book provides a comprehensive, nuanced, and historically anchored perspective on the emerging culture of women's magazines at the dawn of the new millennium.

More broadly, this book aims to spark conversation and propel debates about the shape-shifting nature of creative labor. It seems too convenient to merely assert that "boundaries are collapsing" in an era of convergent media systems and practices. Instead, I show how producers are both allowing some boundaries to crumble and establishing new ones to preserve certain aspects of their identities. I use these findings to push back against the claims of collapsed hierarchies, consumer empowerment, and democratic participation that tend to configure convergence discourse. I also suggest some aspects of the creative industries that have been curiously overlooked and should be critically analyzed before the dust settles. Yet in order to see clearly into the future, we must first take a glimpse back into a history of women's magazines that began some three hundred years ago.

1

Making the Magazine
Three Hundred Years in Print

What are women's magazines? Their material attributes—sleek, glossy pages, vividly hued images, and consistent dimensions—no doubt distinguish them from other mediated forms of culture and communication. According to media scholar Lynda Dyson, magazines are carefully designed to meet the perceived needs of readers; for instance, the "feel of glossies connote[s] luxury and pleasure, despite the fact that their sale price is relatively low." Dyson also explains that their size and portability presumably encourage leisure-time consumption and pass-along readership.[1] Of course, it would be technologically deterministic—not to mention myopic—to overlook the immaterial elements that define the magazine. In the 1970s, Raymond Williams used the concept of cultural form to differentiate the technological aspects of a medium (in this case, television) from its social praxis and human affordances. Contemporary scholars have adopted Williams's idea to think critically about the socially constructed, intangible properties of a medium—the *magazineness* of the magazine, if you will.

Continuities in the cultural form and function of women's magazines can be traced to the American Victorian era—if not earlier. Indeed, the first magazine targeted exclusively to a female audience was the seventeenth-century London fortnightly the *Ladies' Mercury*, which promised to answer "all the most nice and curious questions concerning love, marriage, behaviour, dress, and humour of the female sex, whether virgins, wives, or widows."[2] By the next century's turn, women's magazines had become intricately woven into the fabric of Western social life, both creating and reflecting the political realities of early nineteenth-century women. Many of the features and approaches adopted during this era—advice columns, an appeal to feminine identity, fashion recommendations, and an intimate editorial tone—remain today. And while these factors helped to identify the medium, magazines were also defined by what they were *not*, namely newspapers and books. As magazine historian Margaret Beetham explains, "Unlike the essay-serial, [the magazine] mixed genres and had a variety of authorial voices, but unlike that other mixed periodical form, the newspaper, it carried no 'news.'"[3]

This is not to say that women's magazines have no symbolic connection to other forms of mediated culture. Quite the contrary: as the first truly commercial medium, magazines set an early precedent for the production, distribution, and financing of media content. Such guidelines helped to shape the course of the commercial mass media system that unfolded over the twentieth century. Some of the specific magazine practices that I discuss in this chapter—selling audiences to advertisers in order to offset the sales price, targeting narrowly defined sections of the populace, and blending entertainment and advertising content—were later appropriated and built upon by the radio, television, and internet industries, among others. The historical significance of magazines thus goes far beyond their material properties.

It is admittedly an oversimplification to group women's magazines together as a coherent and monolithic category without at least acknowledging their variances. Certainly an haute couture title like *Vogue*, a service publication like *Family Circle*, and a monthly self-improvement guide like *Self* depart from one another in their approaches to content, audiences, advertisers, and more. Even those titles nestled within the same subcategory (media research firms typically break the genre into "women's service," "entertainment/celebrity," and "beauty and fashion") rely on distinctive features, tones, and aesthetics to communicate their unique brand personalities to audiences (and advertisers). Hence, although *Martha Stewart Living*, *Good Housekeeping*, and *Ladies' Home Journal* fit under the rubric of what industry insiders call "service magazines," they are unmistakably different.[4]

Notwithstanding the nuances within and across magazine categories, I share the perspective of magazine and feminist media scholars who conceptualize women's magazines as a distinct genre. Not only is the genre concept a constructive analytical intervention into the realms of cultural production, it is also meaningful for those workers embedded inside the genre's culture. As David Hesmondhalgh and Sarah Baker explain in their recent book on creative labor, genres offer media workers "institutionalization and routinization in a highly uncertain interpretive production world."[5] The terms of genres, they add, are mutually constructed and continuously renegotiated. Women's magazines, then, are a distinctive media category formed through the assumptions and activities of magazine producers, audiences, advertisers, and those of us trying to understand them within a critical framework.

With regard to the latter point, I draw upon four decades of scholarship on women's magazines in an effort to flesh out the defining properties of the genre. This research follows a general trajectory that coincides with shifts in the academy and, perhaps more importantly, feminist political projects. It is thus not incidental that many scholars credit the second wave of feminism, and specifically the 1963 publication of Betty Friedan's *The Feminist Mystique*, with the emergence of women's magazines as a worthy scholarly topic.[6] Since then, media and women's studies scholars have pushed forward debates about gender, communication, commercialism, and power that collectively contribute to our awareness of what women's magazines *are*.

Magazines *for* and *of* Women

Any attempt to articulate the identity or meaning of the genre must start with the overtly gendered nature of the texts; they are, after all, "*women's* magazines." Yet in asking "Are women's magazines necessarily magazines *of* and *for* women?" Linda Steiner, a longtime scholar of gender and media studies, productively questions whether the signifier "women" refers to the readers, the producers, or both.[7] Much of the discourse on women's magazines takes for granted that these texts are created *for* female audiences. Historians have frequently used the gender of readers to set the terms of the analytical subject; as Margaret Beetham writes in the opening pages of her impressive sweep of nineteenth-century women's periodicals, "I define the 'woman's magazine' by its explicitly positioning its readers as 'women.'"[8] Popular writing on women's magazines also works from the assumption that the gender of readers (and not of producers) is what sets them apart from other cultural forms and genres.

The consideration that these periodicals are created exclusively for and targeted to female audiences has guided much of the critical literature on women's magazines over the decades, too.[9] Through various theoretical and methodological prisms, feminist scholars have addressed the role of women's periodicals in establishing guidelines for heteronormative femininity and domesticity, in conflating gender with consumerism, and in perpetuating unrealistic standards of beauty and physical perfection, among others.[10] Not only do these themes share a concern with the effect of magazines on *female audiences*, but they also note magazines' discursive role in fashioning notions of womanhood and feminine identity. Betty Friedan was among the first to denounce the problematic identity constructions circulating in women's magazines by staunchly arguing that their frequent domesticity tropes stunted women's "basic human need to grow."[11] As a former editor herself, Friedan was particularly critical of the fact that men made the majority of editorial decisions for women's magazines and often depicted women in polarized ways: as either housewives or careerists, who were respectively celebrated or condemned. This laid the groundwork for feminist analyses of the ways these texts socialized women and enforced an uneven distribution of power to reflect dominant sexual politics.

Throughout the 1970s and into the 1980s, scholars emphasized the significance of women's magazines to social identity formation, especially within what Marjorie Ferguson has called "the cult of femininity." For Ferguson, these periodicals forced women into oppressive roles based on socially constructed notions of the ideal woman.[12] Her contemporaries teased out some of these roles, discussing how magazines essentially trained women to be the "perfect mother, lover, wife, homemaker, glamorous accessory, secretary—whatever best suits the needs of the system."[13] Of particular concern to these scholars was the function of women's glossies in creating problems that could be resolved exclusively within the commercial sphere. By engaging in aspirational consumption—shopping for a new wardrobe, lipstick shade, or china pattern—women could theoretically assuage any anxieties they felt about their inner-directed personhood. From this perspective, women's magazines endorsed a (problematic) link between heteronormative femininity and consumerism. Later in the chapter, I return to this topic and explore the unique political economies of women's magazines.

The ur-narrative behind the works of Friedan, Ferguson, and their feminist contemporaries constructs women's magazines as a powerful ideological tool that readers accept uncritically. Yet by the 1990s, some scholars began to disparage such blanket assumptions, particularly the discursive construction of women's magazines as a "problem" for women.[14] If womanhood is not a singular category, some reasoned, why should we assume that readers interpret the texts in a singular way?[15] This individualist turn in the literature dovetailed with a methodological one; it was considered increasingly important to study readers' responses to magazines rather than to make inferences about their reception. Joke Hermes made an especially significant departure from earlier traditions by talking to readers about how, when, and why they used magazines. Her findings emphasized the pleasurable aspect of reading women's magazines while dispelling claims of their totalizing effect.[16] Thus, she showed how an individual can read a periodical for advice, escapism, entertainment, or even to criticize; the correlation between identity and magazines is not necessarily fixed.

While the move to studying magazine readers granted audiences a certain degree of agency and, perhaps, resistance, it did little to acknowledge the contributions of magazine makers. Much as in the larger field of media studies, then, the production of content was a mere afterthought. In the past decade, however, a handful of researchers have realized the critical need to study the production dynamics of women's magazines. Either implicit or explicit in these writings is the prominence of women in creating the content of and markets for women's magazines. Revisiting Linda Steiner's question "Are women's magazines necessarily *of* and *for* women?" it becomes clear that the gendered work culture of women's magazines is also among their defining features.

Since at least the eighteenth century, women have been involved in magazine production as contributors, writers, editors, and more. In fact, the magazine business was considered one of the few acceptable career sites for women in antebellum America.[17] Such popular acceptance was based on the fact that writing jobs could be completed in the privacy of one's home rather than in public workspaces, which were considered unfit for "proper" Victorian women. While countless females contributed to these early magazines, a few trailblazers rose to the highest ranks of the profession. Nineteenth-century writer Sarah Josepha Hale, for one, has been mythologized and celebrated for her transformative role in upending the gender composition of magazine journalism. Hale was appointed editor of *Godey's Lady's Book* in the 1830s after American publisher Louis Antoine Godey merged his namesake magazine with an existing women's title. During a tenure spanning four decades, Hale led *Godey's* to become the most widely read periodical of its day. Breaking with the patriarchal business model, she hired female writers and designers and regularly incorporated the creative contributions of readers. Within this context, scholar Amy Beth Aronson credits Hale with opening up spaces for middle-class women to serve as agents of change.[18]

Later in the nineteenth century, legendary magazine publisher Cyrus Curtis appointed his wife, Louisa Knapp, editor of a one-page supplement titled "Women at Home," which grew into the still-strong *Ladies' Home Journal* (at the time called the *Ladies' Home Journal and Practical Housekeeper).* Knapp Curtis published articles on topics she felt were relevant to American women in the early years of industrialization, including "Mother's Corner,"

"Needlework," "Dress and Material," and "The Practical Housekeeper." Like Hale, she is credited with producing a women's magazine that was written predominantly by individuals who intimately understood the issues and challenges of nineteenth-century womanhood: other women.

Another prominent female figure in the early magazine industry was Ida Tarbell, the famed writer and activist who was largely responsible for launching the muckraking movement during the Roosevelt era. As one of the few college-educated women in *fin-de-siècle* America, Tarbell called out the injustices of monopolistic enterprises with her report on the Standard Oil Company. Her revelations of the unethical practices of Rockefeller's company were published as a nineteen-part series in *McClure's Magazine* beginning in 1902, signaling the emergence of investigative journalism. Although Tarbell was not involved with women's magazine production per se, she did recognize the great potential of female writers in the industry. In her 1887 article "Women in Journalism," Tarbell identified some key female journalists while issuing a clarion call for other women to join the profession, which offered "large opportunities for doing good, for influencing public opinion, and for purifying the atmosphere of the times."[19]

These triumphant tales of female magazine pioneers spotlight the role of women in shaping the contours of the magazine industrial complex. However, other historical studies challenge—or at least complicate—these narratives of female agency. For one, some of the "female" editors and senior contributors were actually males writing under pseudonyms. Arnold Bennett, for instance, who served as editor of *Woman* in the late 1890s, often wrote under the moniker of Barbara, Marjorie, or Marguerite.[20] During this same era, the male editor-in-chief of *Modern Priscilla* adopted the feminine name "Miss Beulah Kellogg."[21] This surreptitious strategy implies a complicated negotiation whereby men understood the value of female personae who could connect with readers, yet they were unwilling to part with some combination of their economic and cultural power.

Accordingly, other writers identify the early twentieth century as the moment when it became widely acceptable for women to enter the publishing field. A confluence of factors—including the economic growth of the magazine industry and political projects such as the women's suffrage movement—opened the door to female writers and editors at various levels. Prominent female editors of this era include Gertrude Battles Land of *Woman's Home Companion*, Edna Woolman Chase of *Vogue*, and Elizabeth Jordan of *Harper's Bazaar*.[22] The number of female journalists also grew considerably during this time. Unfortunately, a disparity between the mostly female staff and male senior executives continued to mark the industry. Correspondence from fe-males working in the industry in the early to mid-1900s reveals unfavorable working conditions: they were paid less, experienced gender-based harass-ment, and received pejorative treatment from male colleagues.[23]

With the second wave of feminism came heightened concerns about the production and consumption of mediated culture—especially women's magazines. A particularly remarkable protest event unfolded in 1970, when more than one hundred women stormed the office of *Ladies' Home Journal* editor John Mack Carter to condemn depictions of females that came from the magazine's overwhelmingly male staff. As feminist scholar Bonnie Dow explained, "For eleven hours, protestors demanded an all-female editorial staff, childcare for employees and an end to advertisements on makeup and appliances. . . . They targeted every characteristic that defined women's maga-zines at the time."[24] Although Carter did not immediately resign, he did allow the feminists to contribute to an issue of *Ladies' Home Journal* that year. By 1973, Lenore Hershey had stepped into the role of editor-in-chief of *Ladies' Home Journal*, and her three successors were also female.[25] Whether it was economically or politically motivated, more women than ever before began to enter this profession.

By the 1980s, women had gained access to some of the highest positions on both the editorial and publishing sides of top-selling titles. During an interview conducted in 1993, *Glamour* magazine's then editor-in-chief, Ruth Whitney, provided a snapshot of the composition of the women's magazine industry: "The staff at *Glamour* is almost entirely female. The editorial staff numbers more than sixty and another forty that comprise the business area. . . . At Condé Nast itself, working conditions and attitudes have changed. There were no women publishers until really quite recently; it might have been as recent as five years ago. The publishers of *Vogue, Self, Mademoiselle*, and *Vanity Fair* are all female."[26] Whitney's mention of women's progress in "the business area" is noteworthy; the publishing side of the magazine in-dustry, which handles business, ad sales, and marketing matters, has been markedly male-dominated.

More than a decade later, in a survey of Australian women's magazine editors, Kayt Davies found that 93 percent of editorial staffers were female.[27] Although I was unable to find a comparable study of American publishers, a quick peek at a few magazine mastheads reveals similar demographic pat-terns. For example, the masthead from a 2006 issue of *Cosmopolitan* shows that the editorial staff was almost entirely female; the exceptions included senior staffers from the art and production departments. The three executive publishers were also female, although a handful of men were listed on the publishing side, including business, advertising sales, and finance directors and managers.

The rhetoric deployed throughout the industry is similarly favorable about the role of female magazine producers. At a 2009 "Top Women in Magazine Publishing" event, Patricia B. Fox, senior vice president of operations and general manager of the Healthy Living Group at Active Interest Media, remarked, "Magazine publishing, more than many other fields, has long been a great career for women." Similarly, books on gender and media set the publishing industry apart from other male-dominated creative sectors by emphasizing its inclusiveness and opportunities for female advancement.[28] Yet the limitations of such claims need to be acknowledged. While women may have reached the top of the hierarchies within publications, those who oversee these organizations are typically men. An article published in an online business journal several years ago noted: "Behind the scenes at many of the nation's top magazines are innumerable women working on the editorial and sales side of the business. Yet, considering the amount of women in these positions, the top spot of publisher, chairperson, or CEO, remains one dominated by men. Short of the success of Cathleen Black, president at Hearst Magazines, or Ann S. Moore, chairman and CEO of Time Inc., the pickings are slim when it comes to women."[29] This statement should raise even more concern given that Black and Moore have since left their leadership positions. In 2010, Black stepped down as president and chairwoman of Hearst to become chancellor of the New York City Schools; she left that position just three months later. Moore, Time Inc.'s first female CEO, retired in 2010 after eight years at the helm. Their immediate successors were both male. In addition, a report by VIDA, an independent organization for women in the literary arts, showed a significant gender disparity in the bylines of top-ranked magazines.[30] To be fair, these studies were not exclusive to women's magazines (and the VIDA study focused on "intellectual" titles such as the *New Yorker* and the *Atlantic*). Yet collectively, these statistics index the significance of incorporating gender identity in a production-oriented study of women's titles.

Articulating and Reaffirming Identity

The women's magazine genre is defined not only by its central placement within gendered circuits of production and consumption, but also by its role in constructing and articulating identities according to carefully sliced audience segments. That is, "magazines do not try to be all things to all people," but rather appeal to specific groups of individuals organized into meaningful social categories on the basis of characteristics such as gender, age, hobbies, and interests, among many others.[31] For instance, *More* is geared toward "smart, sophisticated, forty-plus women interested in fashion, health, beauty, travel, and self-reinvention"; *Health* is designed for "smart empowered women who know that healthy equals happy"; and *Marie Claire* positions itself as a vital resource "for the woman of substance with an eye for style."[32]

The tactic of developing and producing titles for precise segments of the population was set in motion more than a century ago, when advancements in transportation and printing, coupled with climbing literacy rates, led to a rapid rise in magazine circulations. Seeking to capitalize on this trend, editors aimed to differentiate their titles from others in the market with distinctive departments and features. Magazine historian Mary Ellen Waller-Zuckerman notes that by 1912, the group of leading women's magazines dubbed the "Big Six" (*Delineator*, *McCall's*, *Ladies' Home Journal*, *Woman's Home Companion*, *Good Housekeeping*, and *Pictorial Review*) each had a unique style and character. Thus, while *Pictorial Review* offered readers fashion and society material, *Ladies' Home Journal* was "edited for the socially conscious, intelligent homemaker."[33]

The targeting strategies of magazine producers grew more refined in the mid-twentieth century, linked to larger developments in the political economies of mass media. In particular, the proliferation of television sets in postwar America forced publishers across the industry to break with their traditional approach of targeting the masses. As advertisers reallocated their budgets to the new visual medium, many publishers responded by developing "niche" publications that appealed to specific groups of the population—and the advertisers clamoring to reach them. These specialty titles superseded a litany of general interest magazines that met their demise in this era: *Life*, *Look*, and the *Saturday Evening Post*, among others. Of course, the television industry would face a similar fate several decades later with the rise of niche cable channels.

In the wake of the Golden Age of Television, the "Seven Sisters" emerged to replace the "Big Six." This group of the leading mass-market women's magazines at the time (*Better Homes and Gardens*, *Good Housekeeping*, *Family Circle*, *Ladies' Home Journal*, *McCall's*, *Redbook*, and *Woman's Day*) earned the nickname in part because many of the editorial staffers hailed from the Seven Sisters colleges.[34] Although each title offered a distinctive focus and tone, they maintained a consistent group identity. Yet as the twentieth century drew to a close, the "Seven Sisters" saw their circulations dwindle as more specialized titles crowded the magazine marketplace. Executives began to question whether this group identity had become a "liability," while editors sought to lure readers by giving their publications "a more individual look" and content.[35] Magazine scholar Anna Gough-Yates documented a similar shift in the UK as the women's magazine industry demonstrated "more pronounced and self-conscious strategies geared to construct not only the identities of the magazines' readerships, but also the 'personality' of the texts themselves."[36] Magazine producers thus attempted to set their titles apart in an expanding competitive set by emphasizing subtle differences related to demographic and lifestyle categories.

Notably, as Joseph Turow points out, the actuality of industrial change was intricately more complicated than historical narratives of media evolution imply; we also need to consider the systems of market specialization. "The basic change at work was product differentiation," Turow explains. "It involved systematic attempts by manufacturers to create slightly different versions of the same products in order to aim at different parts of the marketplace."[37] Across the consumer goods and personal care sectors, manufacturers discovered the potential of creating and selling products for specific "types" of people. As Turow and other scholars make clear, these specialized identity categories are not natural, but rather are industrially constructed by media and marketing executives. Magazine audiences are more than the "actual receivers [of communication]"; the term refers to what James S. Ettema and D. Charles Whitney describe as "institutionally effective audiences that have social meaning and/or economic value within the system."[38]

These industrial constructions also serve a purpose for magazines' faithful readers: they reflect and reproduce particular aspects of their identities. As journalism scholar Susan Currie Sivek noted, individuals read content that "speaks to a part of [their] personal identity." She continued, "I think that if you listed off all of my magazine subscriptions, you'd get a pretty good idea of what I'm all about."[39] Presumably, we can tell more about an individual who subscribes to *Allure* or *Good Housekeeping* than we can about someone who reads the *New York Times*, loves period dramas, or is a fan of John Grisham novels.

As specialty titles, then, women's magazines are bound up with feminine identity markers. But *how* do they communicate these real or aspirational identity constructions to readers? One of the most blatant ways in which they attempt to reach current—or, more likely, potential—customers is through their cover art. A magazine's visual aesthetic is carefully designed to appeal to specific types of individuals as they seek to be identified. "Like people," magazine journalists Sammye Johnson and Patricia Prijatel write, "successful magazines have personalities that reflect their philosophies, energy, wisdom and wit. The cover is a magazine's statement of its identity."[40] Often the image represents an idealized form of feminine identity: the perfectly proportioned model, the fresh-faced celebrity, or the "everyday woman" who has conquered her domestic/weight/family struggles and now "has it all together."

The textual cues are equally significant in beckoning readers. Cover lines— those pithy, seductive, even provocative phrases framing the chief visual— are designed to catch a potential reader's eye and communicate distinctions among audiences.[41] A few contemporary examples can help illuminate this point. The cover lines on the January 2012 issue of *Allure* that frame "it girl" Rooney Mara are presumably the topics designed to draw readers in: make-overs ("20 Head-Turning Before-and-Afters"), skincare ("Perfect-Skin Habits: Stop Wrinkles, Zits, Dullness and More"), and flattering haircuts ("Whoa! Sexy Haircut—and It Works on Everyone"). The cover of the January 2012 issue of *Woman's Day* is significantly different. Set against a background image of DIY paint-tipped vases, it lures readers to "Lose Those Last 10 lbs!" and "Save $100 on Groceries This Month." These cues symbolize and signal members of very different target audiences.

Intimate Communities

While the visual and textual language printed on magazine covers allow readers to make split-second decisions about the personality of a particular magazine, the matter inside the magazine ensures consistency over time. Over the years, the responsibility for differentiating titles fell to the editors-in-chief, who were encouraged to "infuse their magazines with their own personalities."[42] By utilizing some unique combination of tone, format, aesthetics, and features, editors-in-chief create and maintain the identity of their publications while establishing the magazine as an intimate imagined space.

The roots of this trend run deep in the genre's industrial history. Edward Bok, who was the son-in-law of Cyrus and Louisa Knapp Curtis and succeeded the latter as *Ladies' Home Journal* editor-in-chief in 1889, wrote in his 1921 autobiography that he "divined the fact that in thousands of cases the American mother was not the confidante of her daughter, and reasoned if any inviting human personality could be created on the printed page that would supply this lamentable lack of family life, girls would flock to such a figure."[43] After trying to no avail to find this intimate voice among a number of female writers, Bok used the pseudonym "Ruth Ashmore" to create the first *Ladies' Home Journal* confessional-style "Side Talk with Girls" column in 1889. After two weeks, his friend Isabel Mallon took over the feature; she continued to write under the name "Mrs. Ashmore" for more than sixteen years.[44] Bok seems to have realized early on the importance of having editorial staff members with whom readers could feel an intimate connection.

The intimacy rhetoric in women's magazines was amplified by social and cultural transformations in the Victorian era. Alongside the growth of Freudian psychology in the early twentieth century, advice began to play an instrumental role in shaping the contours of the (feminine) self. Eva Illouz notes how women's magazines of the time "avidly seized upon a language which could accommodate both theory and story, generality and particularity, non-judgementality and normativity."[45] This seemingly made it possible for readers to feel a familiar connection with magazine editors whom they most likely would never meet. An editorial excerpt from a 1919 edition of the British women's magazine *Peg's Paper* reveals just how conversational that tone had become: "It is going to be your weekly pal, girls. My name is Peg, and my one aim in life is to give you a really cheery paper like nothing you've ever read before. Not so very long ago I was a mill girl too. Because I've been a worker like you, I know what girls like, and I'm going to give you a paper to enjoy. Look on me as a friend and helper. I will try to advise you on any problem."[46] Editor "Peg" thus assures her "mill girl" readers that she shares an understanding of the lifestyles of working-class young women. Yet she promises them not only a sense of community but also expertise ("and helper") gained through her own lived experiences.

Contemporary writings also disclose how important it is for editors-in-chief to share characteristics with their target readers. As Anna Gough-Yates explains, press coverage in the 1980s and 1990s would often feature "intimate interviews" with those at the forefront of women's magazines; "the editor's claim to knowledge of her reader would be justified by an attempt to demonstrate her lifestyle 'fit,' and consequently 'in-tune-ness' with the tastes of the magazine's target readership."[47] Additionally, Kayt Davies's study of Australian magazine journalists revealed that two-thirds of women's magazine editors surveyed matched their readerships' demographics in age, gender, and income.[48] Magazine editors' expertise is thus constructed as identificatory and stems from their overlapping demographic and lifestyle categories with readers. Most of them use an intimate tone to address their readers, nurturing what Angela McRobbie aptly describes as a "close and intimate 'big' sister relationship" in hopes of retaining loyalty.[49] Monthly "Editor's Letters" are therefore penned in a conversational, even confessional, style and tend to close with a personalized signature; *Seventeen* editor-in-chief Ann Shoket concludes every letter with "XOXO—A."

Although magazine communities are structured around imagined relations with editors, it is the participation of readers that keeps these communities intact. As noted earlier, readers have long been encouraged to submit stories, letters, and requests for advice to their favorite magazines. In some cases, the sense of kinship afforded by magazines encouraged female readers to pursue pro-social aims.[50] Yet to other scholars, imagined community formation is among the most insidious features of women's magazines because it veils their commercial purpose. Ros Ballaster and her coauthors of *Women's Worlds: Ideology, Femininity and the Woman's Magazine* critique women's magazines for making gender "sufficient qualification for participating in the culture of the magazine." This system, they continue, essentially conceals the industrial nature of the magazine production process.[51] The recognition of women's magazines as "industrial" spaces points to their explicitly—and unapologetically—commercial nature.

The Consumerist Ideology

During Meredith Corporation's 2012 Analyst Meeting, National Media Group president Tom Harty, who oversees such iconic titles as *Ladies' Home Journal, Better Homes and Gardens*, and *Family Circle*, explained to shareholders the media conglomerate's longstanding focus on female readers: "Women are the driving force behind most decision-making as it relates to making purchases for their family, their homes, their health, and their personal well-being. Women already control seventy percent of household spending in the U.S., which amounts to $4 trillion. They are increasingly earning their own money and more, which means their ability to spend is only likely to rise in the future. . . . All this makes women extremely attractive audience[s] for our advertisers, and it's very important strategically for Meredith."[52] Harty's acknowledgment of the central positioning of women within the consumer economy helps to ground the perspective that women's magazines have been integral to the machinations of commodity culture. As commercially subsidized media products, women's glossies sell advertising space with the prospect that readers will purchase the products and services they see. Yet the function of magazines is not only to sell particular commodities, but also to create and perpetuate a larger consumer ethos. By circulating idealized forms of femininity, these texts ostensibly convey the notion that women can resolve their problems within the marketplace. As anti-aging foundations, volume-building mousses, and cellulite-reduction creams are sold under the guises of youth, beauty, femininity, and above all happiness, consumerism is presented as a way of life. It is in this vein that renowned journalist and feminist leader Gloria Steinem described women's magazines as vehicles to "mold women into bigger and better consumers."[53]

The indelible link between the advertising and women's magazine industries was forged in the wake of the Industrial Revolution, as manufacturers introduced new product categories and newly branded goods to the marketplace in droves.[54] Advertising professionals (most of whom were male) seemed to realize early on that as the primary household consumers, women were the coveted demographic—and women's magazines were an ideal conduit to them. This recognition dovetailed with a number of social changes, including the rapidly escalating population and the growth of leisure time among middle-class women.

As women's magazines became increasingly attractive to readers and advertisers alike, some publishers began to vigilantly pursue the ad accounts. The *Ladies' Home Journal*'s Cyrus and Louisa Knapp Curtis are often credited with cultivating the symbiosis of the magazine and advertising industries in the late nineteenth century. Helen Damon-Moore explains the extent of their impact so lucidly that it is worth quoting at length:

> Cyrus and Louisa helped to mediate the interaction of the growing consumer culture with notions about gender, providing in their magazine a forum for the intersection of these two significant forces. Many elements combined to propel the *Journal* into the mass circulation magazine ranks . . . [among them] commercial developments that included the rise of middle-class consumption and the demand for national advertising. Cyrus and Louisa Curtis were commercial pioneers who oversaw the intersection of gendered reading with the demand for a gendered advertising forum to create and develop the highly successful *Ladies' Home Journal.*[55]

As advertisers increased their investments in high-circulation women's magazines, innovative tactics were employed to make magazines especially amenable to commercial messages. For one, publishers began to juxtapose ads and editorial material on the same page, assuring advertisers that readers would pay attention to their messages. Some publishers would also assist advertisers with the creation of effective messages while simultaneously publishing editorials informing their readers of the value of advertising.[56]

Already, though, tensions were beginning to mount between the magazine companies' editorial and advertising departments. While early twentieth-century publishers gradually came to see themselves as being in the business *of business*, many editors clung tightly to their roles as advice purveyors who put the needs of readers first. Waller-Zuckerman identifies *Vogue*'s Edna Woolman Chase and the *Delineator*'s Theodore Dreiser as two editors who had to "battle their advertising departments to uphold editorial integrity."[57] These clashes can be situated within larger shifts in journalistic culture. In the 1930s, *Time* founder Henry Luce used the analogy of church (editorial) and state (business) to describe the ideal separation that should exist between these departments to ensure content objectivity in the print media. Although women's magazines visibly advocated this separation, the ground underneath this metaphorical wall would soon begin to quake.

In the postwar years, when income levels soared to unprecedented heights and consumerism and citizenship became indissolubly linked, the advertising function of women's magazines began to supplant their editorial, or literary, function.[58] Political economist Ben Bagdikian has documented in detail the implications of the redistribution of resources for magazine content. Rather than creating articles that would best address the perceived needs of periodical readers, magazine editors incorporated articles that would have a favorable impact on advertisers and their wares. The rationale, Bagdikian explains, is that articles on "genuine social suffering" or that "put the reader in an analytical frame of mind" would prevent readers from "tak[ing] seriously an ad that depended on fantasy or promoted a trivial product." Thus important issues were ignored in favor of "fluff" that would put people in a "buying" mood.[59] Similar critiques have recently been waged against almost every mass medium as private interests and commercial impulses ostensibly outweigh the public's informational needs.

In an effort to understand the social and cultural implications, both researchers and cultural critics have examined the systematic impact of magazine advertising on matters of content. Relying upon interviews with magazine publishers in the early 1980s, Stella Earnshaw noted that magazines' dependence on advertising revenue has two content-related implications: 1) editors create content that will appeal to increasingly segmented audiences that advertisers consider worthwhile, and 2) journalists feel compelled to create a "persuasive environment" within the magazine that will encourage a mentality of consumerism.[60]

Several years later, Gloria Steinem critiqued common magazine production conventions, including providing a "supportive editorial atmosphere" or using "complementary copy (for instance, articles that praise food/fashion/beauty subjects to 'support' and 'complement' food/fashion/beauty ads)."[61] One clear and familiar example is a recipe contained in the editorial section of a domestic magazine that calls for Duncan Hines cake mix, Heinz ketchup, or Perdue chicken—and appears adjacent to an ad or coupon for these products. Linda Steiner, a scholar of gender and journalism, explored the specific ways in which advertisers compel magazine staffers to fuel shopping patterns, namely by filling their magazines with the message that readers' problems and failures can be resolved with specific purchases.[62] More often than not, editorial advice for women included specific product categories or brands. Over the last two decades, examples of the encroachment of advertising on editorial matters have abounded.

To this end, while the women's magazine industry has changed with the ebb and flow of the times, many of its defining characteristics have remained stable for more than a century. Some of these qualities are solely material—the format, size, and aesthetic that physically distinguish magazines from books and newspapers. Yet their unique cultural form has contributed to social ideas about what these magazines *are*. That is, this genre has long been defined by its gendered nature (magazines *for* and *of* women), unique editorial voice, intimate community tone, and commercial imperative. Although production practices and routines have been instrumental in this definition, it is the interrelationships of magazine staffers (most visibly the editors who had authority and provided a "unique voice"), advertisers (reaching segments of the population through a magazine's niche and influencing content, both directly and indirectly), and audiences (communities of interest who saw their identity reflected in the magazine) who have kept this definition in place. Nevertheless, recent transformations in the magazine publishing industry are challenging traditional constructions of women's magazines.

2

Transforming the Magazine

From Print to Bits

The massive tides of change churning through the early twenty-first-century media landscape have had a profound impact on the women's magazine industry. But what exactly are these changes? To what extent can they be ascribed exclusively to digital innovations? Are they being felt evenly across the industry? And how have they created a perfect storm that has opened up the question of "What is a magazine?" Certainly, some of the salient industrial shifts—the movement to online production and distribution and the meteoric rise in free, immediate, and interactive channels for news and information—are largely due to the forces of digitization. Yet technology is only one part of a larger story about the magazine industry's recent transformation. In fact, many of the trends associated with convergence within the consumer publishing industry—including audience specialization, multi-skilled production patterns, and advertising/editorial interdependence—were set in motion during the last two decades of the twentieth century.

The consolidation of media companies that began in the 1980s was primary among the factors that set the traditional magazine business on a new course. As a series of rapid-fire mergers and acquisitions swept across the mass media system, the publishing industry became more concentrated and globalized. Vertically integrated companies such as Hearst, Time Inc., and Condé Nast significantly increased their share of the market by bringing smaller or independent titles under their corporate umbrellas. Consequently, these magazine behemoths were able to wield considerable power in the marketplace by luring advertisers with volume discounts. For example, to attract a large consumer goods company such as Unilever (whose products include Dove, Axe, TRESemmé, Lipton, and Hellmann's), Hearst publishers might offer a discounted rate if the advertiser purchases space across several Hearst titles, say, *House Beautiful*, *Harper's Bazaar*, and *O: The Oprah Magazine*. This system clearly incentivizes partnerships between advertisers and the largest of the publishing chains.

It was likely this logic that compelled Condé Nast to purchase *Women's Wear Daily* from Fairchild Publications in the late 1990s. As Roberta Garfinkle, then director of print media at the advertising agency McCann-Erickson, explained, "It makes advertising rates more attractive because Condé Nast can put *W* in with the rest of the package. That's the key. And advertisers will be drawn to that."[1] A few years later, Time Inc. added roughly one hundred titles to its international publishing roster with the acquisition of the British company IPC Media. Hearst undertook a similarly hefty acquisition in 2011 when it purchased more than one hundred magazines from the French publisher Lagardère, making Hearst the largest monthly magazine publisher in the United States and a viable contender in the women's market.[2]

This period of globalization and consolidation also saw the rise of magazines as branded entities. Indeed, as large companies began acquiring titles in already successful categories, they realized the crucial need to emphasize the unique brand identity of each title. A few of the most successful magazines even spawned brand spinoffs; for instance, the publishers of *People* launched *People en Español*, the now defunct *Teen People*, and *People StyleWatch*. This branding logic also, presumably, helped to attract advertisers who were presented with a seemingly infinite array of media options. As media industries scholar Joseph Turow explains, media companies aimed to placate restless advertisers by telling them they were not associated with a media *product*, but rather "with a media brand that many consumers saw as a badge signifying important relationships in their lives."[3]

While the branding rhetoric was communicated externally to magazines' audiences and advertisers, other significant changes were taking place internally and behind closed doors. As labor regimes became increasingly flexible across the creative sector, magazine workers were expected to diversify their skill sets. Specialty writing began to wane by the late 1990s as magazine workers were expected to have "broad skills and adaptable constitutions" that would enable them to work in a variety of environments.[4] Anna Gough-Yates explains that these new work patterns were especially pronounced within the women's magazine market. The publishing business, she explains, became decentralized as a way to foster "flexibility, internal competition, innovation, and a greater degree of emphasis on design and quality."[5] Thus creative workers were expected to remove themselves from professional silos and move fluidly within and across different departments.

Production processes were also transformed by widespread innovations in desktop publishing, which simultaneously increased print quality and decreased magazines' production costs. Typesetting specialists were no longer required, as writers could easily use word-processing equipment, and thus writers and editors were expected to expand their skill sets to include layout.[6] Technological developments also enabled staff members to access proofs digitally, eliminating the time lag associated with waiting for physical proofs. As Lavinel Savu, former editorial operations director of *InStyle*, who was promoted to assistant managing editor in 2012, recalled:

> When I first started in the industry during the 1990s, we worked on paste-up; we used to manually paste images and text on boards and send the composed layouts to the printer to get photographed and transferred to press plates. Going from that analog process to desktop publishing and computer to plate, where you can close a story in New York and have it on press in Wisconsin hours later[, was one of the biggest changes]. Reducing the lead time in the production cycle gives magazine makers more flexibility with deadlines and, in turn, more control over what kind of content they can publish as well as how precise, relevant and newsworthy that content is.

Additionally, computer databases were instrumental in allowing magazine publishers to understand their readers in more intricate and nuanced ways, and this data helped them to gain leverage in deals with advertisers. Media and popular culture scholar Matthew McAllister notes that in the 1990s, some magazine and newspaper companies were able to generate significant revenue by sharing their subscription lists (which frequently contained demographic and psychographic information) with advertisers. After compiling consumer data on eleven million subscribers to its then thirteen magazines, Condé Nast used that database "to help advertisers with targeted promotions and direct mailings."[7] At the level of distribution, computer networks led to the expansion of new systems with greater capabilities to target and market magazine titles in particular markets.[8] It therefore became possible to create several different versions of a magazine and direct them to particular segments. Subscribers in northeastern cities may get a different set of articles, and likely different ads, than subscribers in the American South.

Although many elements of the computer revolution were seen as a boon to the magazine industry, the internet posed a formidable challenge. Beginning in the early 1990s, most publishers feared that putting magazines online would "scoop" the traditional periodicals, providing consumers with little incentive to pay for the print-bound periodical. Those publishers who did turn to the web saw it as a vehicle for expanding the availability of subscription services. An article published in the magazine trade publication *Folio* in late 1993 informed publishers of the benefits of the "Electronic Newsstand" subscription acquisition system: "The service is open 24 hours a day, seven days a week, accessible through the internet, an online network available to about 15 million users, 10 million of those in the United States. Participating magazines provide a table of contents and several articles or excerpts so users can obtain a sense of their editorial make-up. If so inclined, readers can subscribe to a magazine by sending an electronic mail message."[9] In this passage it becomes evident how the initial emphasis was on the internet's accessibility (over phone and mail subscription orders) rather than its content offerings.

In the years bracketing the millennium, however, publishers began to realize the crucial need to create web content for the swiftly growing population of internet users. An article published in *Folio* in 1999, titled "Web Publishing: A Primer," captures this emerging culture of adaptability. Author Tim Miller urged magazine executives to take advantage of the medium's "interactivity . . . [by] creating new services, ultimately attracting and retaining new print subscribers." He added, "In the process, we can create new sponsorship opportunities and new ancillary revenues."[10] Although the end goal remained much the same—to drive print subscriptions—Miller's clarion call invoked the economic possibilities of the internet, including the potential for advertising partnerships. By 2008, most magazine executives acknowledged that online magazines should differ in strategy and content (e.g., immediacy and instant reader contribution) from print.[11] Unfortunately, finding a profit model to sustain the online content was—and remains—a daunting task.

What is more, drawing consumers to magazine websites in an era of ubiquitous content is no easy feat. As Chuck Cordray, senior vice president and general manager of Hearst Magazines Digital Media from 2006 through 2011, usefully explained, "We're not just competing against [other] magazine sites, we're competing against the Web period." He continued, "People don't say, 'I like this site compared to competitive sets in magazines,' they compare it to their best online experiences."[12] The online experiences Cordray references include not only corporate, top-down sites, but also a slew of bottom-up sites such as blogs, social media sites, and other Web 2.0 properties. According to a Nielsen report published in 2010, half of American's online time is devoted to social networking, playing games, and emailing.[13] It is not surprising that the more time people spend with social media, the less time they have for traditional, professionally produced media forums.

As digital challenges continued to escalate through the decade's end, they were compounded by the economic recession of 2008. One report estimates that magazines lost about one-quarter of their ad pages between 2008 and 2009, marking the worst decline in ad revenue in a decade.[14] Among teen and women's glossies, countless titles have folded or shifted to an entirely online model in recent years, including *Jane, Teen People, Cookie, Domino, CosmoGirl*, and *Modern Bride*. With such conditions as a backdrop, some media analysts have predicted the death of the magazine industry. One particularly bleak view comes from an anonymous magazine insider who refers to herself/himself as "the grim reaper" and tracks magazine closures on a site named the Magazine Death Pool (www.magazinedeathpool.com). A 2012 eMarketer report indicating that people are spending more time with their mobile devices than with print products seems to indicate that this downward trend is unlikely to reverse in the near future.[15]

The industry's collective responses to such threats fall along two main lines: celebrating the unique strengths of print and, concomitantly, repositioning magazines as cross-platform brands. Among the most extraordinary efforts to publicize the endurance of the print-bound periodical was a collaborative undertaking by leading executives at the five largest publishing houses: Hearst Magazines president Cathie Black, Meredith National Media Group president Tom Harty, Time Inc. chairman and CEO Ann Moore, Condé Nast president and CEO Charles Townsend, and Wenner Media chairman Jann Wenner (as noted earlier, Black and Moore have since stepped down). Launched in 2010, the "Magazines: The Power of Print" campaign included ads in nearly one hundred magazines to "promote the vitality of magazines as a medium."[16] One two-page spread from the campaign featured David LaChapelle's provocative photograph of a bubble-clad Lady Gaga, adjacent to the following text:

> Young people do everything online. Like order millions of magazines. Somehow, amidst their infatuation with Facebook, YouTube, Twitter and the like, young adults are still making time for another one of their favorite pursuits: reading magazines.
>
> Contrary to popular misperception, the phenomenal popularity of the Internet has not come at the expense of magazines. Readership is actually increasing, and adults between 18 and 34 are among the most dedicated readers. They equal or surpass their over-34 counterparts in issues read per month and time spent per issue.
>
> What's changed isn't people's affinity for magazines but the means by which they acquire them. Last year, nearly 22 percent of all new paid subscriptions were ordered online.

And just as the Internet drives magazine subscriptions, magazines drive Web searches—with nearly double the effectiveness of the Internet itself. Some might call it ironic. The medium that some predicted would vanquish magazines is actually helping fuel their growth. And vice versa.

Other ads featured similarly celebratory statistics, a veritable backlash against narratives circulating about print's impending demise.

Other individual titles have continued to foreground the unique materiality of print through eye-catching, tactile, even 3-D covers. Many of these initiatives involve advertising sponsorships. In 2009, for instance, Hearst's *House Beautiful* broke with the editorial tradition of keeping covers ad-free when it featured a pocket cover with a pullout paint chart sponsored by Glidden. Other companies have integrated digital components directly into their print-bound periodicals. Hearst partnered with Hewlett-Packard in late 2011 to provide personalized ads to print subscribers; ads in the magazine included issue-specific URLs and QR (quick response) codes.[17]

The other large-scale response of magazine publishers is the strategic repositioning of magazines as *brands*. Although a scattershot collection of magazines—including *People* and *Good Housekeeping*—have long referred to themselves as "brands," today's titles have fully penetrated the internet, book, radio, mobile, outdoor, and retail industries. In 2007, the Magazine Publishers of America, as MPA—The Association of Magazine Media was known at the time, vibrantly signaled this shift with a conference titled "The MagaBrand Revolution: How Media Brands Are Finding Success on the Printed Page and Beyond." More recently, according to a *Mediaweek* report titled "Magazine Hot List 2010," magazines were selected "by analyzing what each has done to expand beyond its core print business." As the report continued, "That's essentially the new golden rule of publishing: to no longer be simply a publisher. New business extensions are *de rigueur*, from the obvious Web sites and mobile apps to conferences, TV shows, book lines, even awards programs and retail extensions."[18]

Examples abound of this branding logic, particularly within the women's category. For instance, successful titles such as *Cosmopolitan* and *Glamour* now provide branded content over satellite radio and through programming such as the latter's *Glamour Girls* digital TV series. Several other magazines have spun off into the cable market, and this trend is likely to only intensify. In fact, Condé Nast recently announced the launch of an entertainment division centered on creating programming based on the publishing Goliath's "personalities, articles and general brands."[19] *Seventeen* has made considerable inroads into merchandising with its jewelry, prom, and bedding collections. *Seventeen* is also among the growing roster of magazine companies that sponsor regular events; other examples include *Self*'s "Workout in the Park" series, the *Glamour* "Women of the Year Awards," and the *Allure* "Best of Beauty" event. Outdoor retail spaces are another interesting branding outpost. In 2010, *Real Simple* opened a temporary holiday pop-up shop adjacent to the landmark Rockefeller Center; visitors to the "store" were treated to gift bags, makeovers, and holiday gift-wrapping. They could also purchase merchandise featured throughout the *Real Simple* "Gift Guide." The pop-up shop returned the following year with a number of co-sponsors, including L'Oréal and Citi.

Women's magazine companies' forays into online and digital spaces also reveal their concentrated efforts to resuscitate their magazine titles. In addition to continuously updating their own multimedia websites, most magazines offer audiences the opportunity to engage with their brands across what has been called the "social mediasphere." *Self* magazine's webpage (www.self.com) is a fitting site to examine the extent to which magazines are adapting to the rapid spread of social media. A banner on the homepage calls on fans to "Get *Self* Everywhere," and includes links to the magazine's Facebook, Twitter, and YouTube sites, each of which has an active following. *Self*'s Twitter feed is populated by posts from Editor-in-Chief Luzy Danziger and currently has more than 180,000 followers. *Self* also offers readers an iPad app, which the website describes as "your favorite magazine brought to you in a fresh, new format." Along with the standard magazine fare, the app includes fitness slideshows, how-to videos, a live ticker of useful events, and an interactive ingredient tracker.

A report by the digital communication agency Affinity has confirmed the importance of these types of social and mobile media ventures for magazine companies grasping for a financial lifeline. According to the report, the number of digital users visiting magazine-branded social networks reached an astonishing thirty million in 2011, marking a 5.7 percent increase over the preceding year. The same study found that the percentage of individuals accessing magazine content over smartphones, tablets, and other mobile devices grew 6.2 percent to thirty-five million.[20] To this end, the rise of tablet devices has been a vexing issue for those at the front lines of the magazine industry. When Apple launched its first-generation iPad in 2010, many scrambling publishers hailed it as a veritable knight in shining armor. Howard Polskin, executive vice president of communications and events at

MPA—The Association of Magazine Media, explained to me how the launch of the iPad "made everyone more forward-looking."

> It seemed like an ideal platform for magazine publishers to use because [of] its graphic display, the way it shows rich media, the way articles come to life, the way design looks, the way photos reproduce on an iPad. These are tremendously exciting. Plus, it seemed like there might be business models where magazine publishers could actually profit from it. That also underscored the fact that the app world was a world where magazine publishers could play. And then people could read the magazine on their iPhone, or their Android. That took advantage of the mobility of these devices because with a smart phone it's with you twenty-four/seven. You could in fact read magazine articles on it. You could hear sound and motions. So these were all positive things for magazine publishers.

Echoes of Polskin's enthusiasm have resounded throughout the industry, and many participants at the 2010 American Magazine Conference seemed hopeful that the iPad was a bellwether for the digital economy. A recent study of advertising effectiveness on the iPad was similarly auspicious; a University of Connecticut researcher found that compared to static print ads, interactive ads generate "stronger engagement, message involvement, and attitude toward the advertisements."[21] However, the actual impact on business models remains to be seen.

Today, the iPad has a phalanx of competitors, including Barnes and Noble's Nook, Amazon's Kindle Fire, and Google's Nexus, all of which cost significantly less than Apple's version. Although publishers have been buoyed by revenues from digital subscriptions on these devices, the contract process has been quite onerous. Early in the game, Apple and large-scale magazine companies clashed over details about digital sales, particularly Apple's system of requiring consumers to manually search through the App Store to purchase particular issues of a magazine (rather than obtaining them through a subscription). More recently, large publishers including Condé Nast, Hearst Corporation, and Meredith Corporation struck a deal with Amazon; yet the prices of many magazines on the Kindle Fire are set higher than the print editions.[22] As these delivery systems continue to take shape, publishers are confronting an even more substantial issue: how to transition print production models to the nascent mobile and tablet world.

The challenges and responses just recounted have had an incalculable impact on the producers, consumers, advertisers, and content of consumer magazines. Yet this effect has not been felt equally throughout different organizations, and in particular at the three publishers whose companies and brands I draw heavily on in the chapters that follow: Condé Nast, Time, and Hearst. Though each of these companies produces several women's fashion, beauty, and/or service titles, they vary widely in their historical traditions, patterns of ownership and control, profit models, and industrial logics. The contrast between them has become even more pronounced in the wake of the industry's evolving transformation from print to bits.

Condé Nast

The international publishing company that reportedly pioneered the shift to specialized titles was established in 1909 when American advertising manager Condé Montrose Nast acquired *Vogue*, then "a source of gossips, garnished with drawings and doggerel."[23] Soon thereafter, Nast integrated several other U.S. and British titles into his growing publishing fleet, including *British Vogue*. Condé Nast Publications was incorporated in 1922 and remained economically stable even amidst the financial turmoil of the Great Depression. Following Nast's death in 1959, media entrepreneur Samuel Irwin Newhouse took over, adding an impressive roster of titles to the company. Condé Nast moved from New England to its current headquarters in New York City in 1999, and Newhouse's son Si took over as chairman. The company remains privately owned, and the executive team currently includes CEO Charles Townsend and newly hired president Bob Sauerberg. On the digital side, Condé Nast hired its first chief technology officer, Joe Simon, in 2010.

Today, Condé Nast's magazine division is owned by Advance Publications; it also oversees the fashion and trade magazine unit Fairchild Fashion Group. Condé Nast's illustrious titles include *Vogue*, *Vanity Fair*, *Wired*, *Self*, *Allure*, the *New Yorker*, *GQ*, and *Architectural Digest*. Such high-profile titles are congruent with the prestigious image of Condé Nast, although the company seems to have fallen behind rivals Time and Hearst in subscription revenues.[24] According to *Newsweek*, Condé Nast laid off nearly two hundred staff members and cut budgets by 25 percent in 2009 in anticipation of an expected $1 billion drop in ad revenue.[25]

Despite these hardships, Condé Nast was considered an early frontrunner in the digital realm, launching the *Vogue* website in the UK and Epicurious. com in the United States through its Condé Net internet division. However, the company has struggled to balance its magazine websites with online-only properties such as Style.com and Epicurious. This struggle is reflected in ongoing structural shifts, as responsibilities for online content have changed hands on several occasions. Although Condé Nast had long separated the digital and print teams, the creation of Condé Nast Digital in 2009 was an effort to better coordinate them. In October 2010, the digital business was restructured again so that publishers would now oversee digital brands.

Two Condé Nast titles I draw upon in this study are *Glamour* and *Allure*. Launched in 1939, *Glamour* covers beauty, fashion, health, and relationship stories, as well as the occasional political issue. The mission statement contained in *Glamour*'s media kit best summarizes the editors' approach: "We're often optimistic, always inclusive, beyond empowering and can always separate the Dos from the Don'ts." The print magazine targets women ages 18 to 34, although the median age of readers has consecutively increased to its current 33.5. As of 2010, its total verified paid circulation was 2,314,020.[26] In addition to its website, the brand also includes a *Glamour* mobile app, a Google widget, an interactive TV initiative, the Glamour.com store, and a partnership with Match.com called *Glamour* Matchmaker. In September 2010, Glamour became the first major women's title to launch an iPad edition. Available for $3.99, the app included such special features as a how-to makeup video and a shopping gallery that allowed readers to purchase items directly from the title.

Allure, first published in 1991, focuses exclusively on beauty content. It has a circulation of 1,088,243; the average reader is 32.4, with a median household income of $70,735. A staple of the magazine is its annual "Best of Beauty" awards list—beauty reviews with the *Allure* stamp of approval. In 2010, the magazine developed an iPhone application that highlights the winning products and tells users where they can purchase them based on their location. This dovetails with the *Allure* online virtual store, which includes a searchable beauty product finder. *Allure* entered the iPad market in the spring of 2011, allowing readers to purchase single issues or subscriptions.

Hearst

Hearst Magazines is the namesake of newspaper magnate William Randolph Hearst, whose enthusiasm for automobiles led to the founding of *Motor*, the first Hearst magazine, in 1903. Throughout his lifetime, Hearst oversaw the creation, purchase, or loss of twenty different titles, including flagship *Cosmopolitan* (then a family magazine turned literary title). Today, Hearst Magazines includes U.S. titles *Esquire*, *Good Housekeeping*, *Harper's Bazaar*, *Marie Claire*, *O: The Oprah Magazine*, *Cosmopolitan*, and *Seventeen*; there are also some two hundred global editions linked to these titles. Although Hearst has long been thought of as standing in the shadows of both Condé Nast and Time, the company ascended to the number two position with the 2011 purchase of Lagardère, a company whose Hachette division includes haute fashion title *Elle*.[27] When longtime Hearst president Cathie Black, known as the first lady of magazines, stepped down in 2010, David Carey was appointed president.

Hearst initially entered the digital realm in 2004, when it signed a three-year contract with the women's content network iVillage to host and produce web services connected to such titles as *Cosmopolitan, Country Living, Good Housekeeping, Marie Claire,* and *Redbook*. Hearst purchased the websites back from iVillage in 2007, and they are now operated under the auspices of Hearst Magazines Digital Media, which is "dedicated to creating and implementing the digital strategy for Hearst's magazine brands and other sites which serve the company's consumer audience."[28] In explaining the transition from the iVillage model, Chuck Cordray told me, "At the time Hearst cut that deal [in 2004] . . . the belief was that online would not necessarily be an advertising medium. It would be great to sell subscriptions but not necessarily an advertising media. . . . During the course of that deal, the Hearst viewpoint on that, and the worldview on online advertising, changed very dramatically. So . . . it seemed much more important for Hearst to control the brands online rather than to have someone else do that." Now Hearst Digital oversees twenty-four websites and fourteen mobile sites for magazine brands, as well as digital-only sites such as Delish, Real Beauty, and social shopping site Kaboodle. They, too, have more than fifty applications and digital editions for Apple's iPad, iPhone, and iTouch products, including *Cosmopolitan*'s Sex Position of the Day app, Real Beauty's Instant Celebrity Makeover tool, and the *Seventeen* Fashion Finder app.

These services and programs reflect the proactive approach that Hearst seems to have taken to digital initiatives outside of publishing. To this end, it acquired Answerology, the niche Q&A site, in 2008, and the iCrossing digital marketing firm in 2010. In addition, the company has dedicated significant resources to research and development. Hearst's emphasis seems to have shifted to the app world with the development of a state-of-the-art App Lab. Under the direction of Chris Wilkes, vice president of audience development and digital editions, staff members from various backgrounds are working to develop mobile media content and synergistic partnerships. Wilkes told me that there are currently fifteen full-time staffers, as well as about fifteen others who "moonlight" in the lab.

Much of my analysis of Hearst focuses on two of its popular titles, *Seventeen* and *Marie Claire*. *Seventeen* was first published in September 1944 by Walter Annenberg's Triangle Publications; it was not until nearly sixty years later that Hearst acquired the title. Today, as the top-ranked female teen magazine, it includes fashion, beauty, relationship, and college advice targeted to women ages 12 to 19, with the median audience age being 16.5; the circulation is 2,029,281. *Seventeen* has made inroads into a variety of nonmagazine markets and industries through its myriad partnerships and licensing deals. Examples of these include the *Seventeen* eyewear, bedding, shoe, handbag, and jewelry collections, as well as the magazine's partnership with the television series *America's Next Top Model*. Moreover, the *Seventeen* web, mobile, digital magazine, newsletter, Facebook, YouTube, Twitter, and Pinterest properties and sites illustrate its prominent presence across the new media landscape.

Marie Claire, originally a French weekly, was launched in the United States in 1994 as the self-described "must-read for those who love style and adventure"; it now boasts a circulation of 1,015,053. Among its topics are fashion, beauty, career, health, and social commentary. The median age of readers is 34.5, and their household income averages in the mid-$80,000s. There are a number of interactive features on the *Marie Claire* website that enable readers to get customized information and advice: the Virtual Weight Loss Tool, the "Find Your Best Scent" program, the Virtual Hair Salon, and even a job search tool. Importantly, *Marie Claire* editors have been vocal about their interest in making interactive services accessible to their female readers. While she was still editor-in-chief, Joanna Coles told the *Huffington Post* that the magazine includes "a lot of pictures showing women and technology together because we want people to feel comfortable with technology."[29] Their A-to-Z fashion app has received glowing reviews, and they made headlines in 2011 with the launch of their iPad application featuring an innovative 3-D cover. *Marie Claire* also has a TV presence through its strategic partnership with Lifetime's *Project Runway*; since 2009, the winning designers have received editorial coverage in the magazine as part of their prize package.

Time Inc.

A subsidiary of mega-conglomerate Time Warner, Time Inc. is considered the largest magazine media company in the United States. According to the legendary tale of its founding, two zealous young news reporters, Henry Luce and Briton Hadden, resigned from their jobs at the *Baltimore News* in 1922 to establish *Time* magazine. Over the decades, Time Inc. grew to include well-known titles *Fortune* (launched in 1930), *People* (launched in 1974), and *Sports Illustrated* (launched in 1954). It currently oversees twenty-one U.S. magazines and more than twenty-five U.S. websites. Despite Time's stability, its executive office has been a place of tremendous change in the early years of the twenty-first century. In 2010, Time Inc. announced that Jack Griffin, a former Meredith executive, would replace Ann Moore as chairman and CEO. Griffin left that position six months later, along with chief digital officer Randall Rothenberg, whose stint there was similarly brief. In November 2011, digital expert Laura Lang stepped in as the new CEO despite having never worked in the traditional publishing business. Yet her tenure there was short-lived, for Time Inc. announced in 2013 that it would spin off its print magazine division into a separate company. *New York Times* reporter Amy Chozick saw the move as "as another clear sign that the industry was buckling under intense financial pressures." Indeed, the announcement came just weeks after Time Inc. revealed its plans to lay off a full six percent of its staff.[30]

At the time of this writing, the digital staff at Time is split into two divisions. The web team handles online content, search, and network operations; the other staffers work alongside print teams on design and user interaction. Time Inc.'s digital properties are faring well across the board, as the company's digital revenues account for 10 to 15 percent of the total advertising revenue.[31] According to the company overview, Time's websites have more unique visitors than any other publisher's, and its online network is one of the twenty largest online media properties. Statistics on its mobile offerings are similarly positive; the People.com iPhone app was even ranked fourth on Apple's list of the top paid entertainment apps. Like its competitors, Time is expanding beyond its core publishing properties. In addition to the acquisition of the StyleFeeder personalized shopping network, the company also launched the Axcess ad network, which brings together its various properties with enhanced behavioral targeting tools. Explaining the ad network concept, the president of advertising sales and marketing, Stephanie George, told *Folio* that it was a strategic response to the expectations of advertisers. "We're being asked for higher accountability in our media partnerships, digital budgets are expanding, and there's more trial going on in the digital arena."[32]

Time Inc.'s female-targeted publications include *InStyle* and *People*. With a circulation of nearly 3.6 million, *People* is a top-selling weekly with content that focuses on celebrity coverage and issues of human interest. Although it is not expressly a women's publication, its audience is more than 71 percent female, with an even higher percentage reading its *People StyleWatch* version.

The median age of print readers is 41, with an average household income of $68,882. The website, which has become a source for breaking news, was named "Website of the Year" in the Entertainment Category by MPA—The Association of Magazine Media.

Also part of Time Inc.'s Lifestyle and Entertainment Group, *InStyle* was launched in 1993 to provide readers with articles about beauty, fashion, home decor, entertaining, charitable endeavors, and celebrity lifestyles. The median age of readers is 35.1, with a household income of $83,598; its circulation is 1,783,864. The magazine also publishes two special issues annually: *InStyle Hair* and *InStyle Makeover*. In addition, the website is updated daily with fashion, beauty, and shopping content and features; visitors can also use the Hollywood Hair Makeover Tool or subscribe to *InStyle Mobile*, which comes in free and premium service options.

Suspended between a well-established past and an uncertain future, these three organizations—Condé Nast, Time, and Hearst—are facing the challenges of digitization head on. And though the most formidable challenges cut across companies, the ways in which they respond are quite distinctive, grounded in historical, professional, and organizational specificities. Some of these responses are the province of senior executives; others arise from within the organization. Thus, it is only by peering into the industry with many sets of eyes that we can fully understand how the magazine industry's change gets enacted through new positions, emergent routines, and reconfigured social hierarchies.

3

Production Tensions

New Positions, Routines, and Gender Roles

Joanna Coles, the fêted Hearst editor who was designated "Editor of the Year" by *Adweek* in 2011, commented during our interview, "One of the things that readers always want to know is what is it like to work at a magazine—what [are] the staff like?" It was partly such inquisitiveness about the women's magazine profession that inspired *Marie Claire* executives—including Coles, who served as the magazine's editor-in-chief from 2006 to 2012—to launch the reality TV series *Running in Heels* in 2009. Broadcast on NBC Universal's Style Network, the show centered on three young women interning at *Marie Claire*'s New York headquarters. Noteworthy scenes depicted Coles getting a finicky celebrity to pose for a "money shot" publicity photo, staffers working feverishly to make looming deadlines, and an intern "running in heels" in order to deliver a designer fashion line to Coles on schedule. As Lauren Ruotolo, director of entertainment promotions at Hearst Magazines, explained, "We want to tell the true story of women working in fashion. . . . [*Running in Heels*] will reveal what real life is like behind the shimmery curtain."[1] Indeed, the show provided an exclusive glimpse behind that "shimmery curtain" as it dramatized some of the less glamorous aspects of the women's magazine business: long hours, menial tasks, office frictions, and a distinctly hierarchical workplace culture.

Despite making significant inroads into contemporary popular culture, the series neglected to address the larger challenges confronting today's magazine professionals, including those related to the emergent logics of digitization, cross-platform distribution, and flexible labor. On one hand, a flood of nonprofessional participants (e.g., bloggers and citizen journalists) have entered the media marketplace, making competition for audience attention fiercer than ever. On the other hand, workers in traditional media environments are expected to be multi-skilled masters who can fluidly move content across media platforms. Both of these trends seem to amplify the movement toward "precariousness" in the creative industries, which according to media theorist James Curran involves "[decreased] job security, depressed wages, few employment rights, and long hours."[2] In light of this powerful mix of factors, today's media industries are a site of mounting tensions.

In the last half-decade, a great deal of ink has been spilled by researchers seeking to understand the implications of transformed circuits of production and consumption for professional content creators. In addressing the so-called blurring of roles between producers and audiences, many of these studies engage with questions of identity. The field of journalism studies is especially ripe with examples of this type of scholarship. Seth Lewis, for instance, locates the work and professional identities of journalists within an "ongoing tension between professional control and open participation in the news process."[3] More broadly, in his cross-industry study of media work, Mark Deuze argues that "the binary opposition between the social identities of 'production' and 'consumption'" is no longer relevant, as they are "mutually enabling and constitutive."[4]

Not only are emergent production and consumption practices reconfiguring professional and organizational identities, they are also foregrounding questions about creativity and constraint. Accordingly, many of the production-based studies of the news profession, including those mentioned in the introduction, explore how individualist impulses for news creation have been overpowered by organizational demands for standardized content.[5] The negotiation between creativity and constraint is ostensibly more pronounced outside the news sector, where artistry is emphasized within the production process. Vicki Mayer's detailed study of "below the line" TV producers (a budgetary term that describes the industry's hierarchical division of labor) explores how the notion of creativity essentially helped to structure this division by rendering invisible the creative actions of set assemblers, camera crews, casters, and other "below the line" producers.[6] In addition, the consumer magazine industry has been described as adhering to a value hierarchy of autonomy whereby magazine journalists can "operate with relative freedom as long as they produce results imbued with creativity."[7]

This chapter examines the implications of convergence-related shifts for the production processes, creative actions, and structure of the women's magazine industry. On both the editorial and publishing sides, executives and industry leaders are creating positions, redeploying responsibilities, realigning departments, and establishing routines that converge around new industry norms about content. Such changes are challenging the boundaries around professional and organizational identities. In some respects, longstanding divisions of labor are beginning to crumble, particularly between technical specialists and content creators. Yet organizations are simultaneously reinforcing certain boundaries that seem to reaffirm problematic assumptions about the gendering of new media work.

The Digital "A-Team"

In a media moment when magazine companies' web, tablet, and mobile properties are widely promoted, it is perhaps unsurprising that executives emphasized the need to fill their workplaces with technologically savvy staffers. Reflecting on the growing importance of digital specialists to her organization, Time Inc.'s editorial director, Martha Nelson, told me that in the early days of magazine websites, "The people who were running the website were not necessarily the top talent; it was often someone who was well-respected but wasn't necessarily going to move forward [in the] magazine." She contrasted that with today's magazine properties, which are now run by the "A-team, individuals who are both well regarded and highly compensated." Her Time Inc. colleague Mark Golin, editorial director of the Digital, Style, and Entertainment and Lifestyle Groups, made a similar remark when discussing his former editorial positions at two well-known print titles. "At that point, I don't think I could have told you who was running digital, if anybody was running digital at all." Not only do digital specialists play a central role in production and software design, they are increasingly contributing to content decisions. Hearst Magazines' editorial director, Ellen Levine, explained how digital positions that initially required technical expertise now often also require editing and reporting skills. She told me that while individuals on the digital team came to Hearst as "kings and queens of algorithms" predominantly involved with metrics, they now have a say in matters of content. This marks a seismic shift from the days when editors and production staffers remained in largely distinct professional domains.

In response to the organizational imperative of digital proficiency, magazine executives seemed to employ some combination of training existing staff members and hiring individuals from outside the traditional print media sector. With regard to the former, companies have dedicated considerable resources to educating print staffers in the technology, format, style, and tone of nonmagazine media: online, tablet, mobile, and more. Editorial workers representing both the print and online departments mentioned that they had undergone search engine optimization (SEO) training to encourage them to fill their articles with "search-friendly" terms. Moreover, a writer from *Glamour* said that *Wired* (another Condé Nast title) had sent over a representative to deliver a presentation on the utility of the iPad. These examples attest to the fact that print staffers are required to be fluent in—and create content for—a variety of different platforms.

Industry discourse reveals how this multi-skilled logic is affecting magazine professionals across departments and at all levels of the organization, from the budding editorial assistants to those in the top-floor executive suites. An article published in *Folio* in 2005, just before the digital floodgates burst open, noted the value of having technologically progressive leaders as executive officers: "there are CEOs suited to run a publishing business, and there are others suited to run a multi-platform, delivery neutral, community-oriented business. There is no doubt that finding senior execs who are Internet savvy, and Web passionate, as well as those who understand the content and events business, is not easy, but that is likely the profile that many companies are searching for."[8] It was presumably this mentality that, a few years later, led to a new generation of leaders at the helm of the world's top publishers: Hearst, Condé Nast, Time, and Meredith. Designated by media analysts as the summer 2010 "Velvet Revolution" in publishing, the changes included Robert Sauerberg's appointment to the presidency of Condé Nast, David Carey's movement from Condé Nast to head up the magazine division at Hearst, and Time Warner's announcement that Jack Griffin, the former Meredith Corporation executive, would step into the chief executive position at Time Inc. Griffin's replacement was Tom Harty, a longtime member of Meredith credited with 360-degree sales initiatives that involve cross-media integration and buys.[9]

Although these new leaders all had experience in print, media analysts suggested that their relatively younger ages would make them more apt to tackle the challenges of the digital age. "This is the changing of the guard from an older school to a newer school," said Justin B. Smith, president of the Atlantic Media Company. "It is quite remarkable that it took until 2010, fifteen years after the arrival of the Internet, for a new generation of leaders to emerge."[10] At the time, Harty was forty-seven, Carey and Sauerberg were both forty-nine, and Griffin was fifty.[11] The suggestion to incorporate young staffers also circulated throughout industry discourse and was a resounding theme at the 2010 American Magazine Conference for much the same reason: the presumption that younger generations are more technologically adept than industry veterans. For instance, keynote speaker Rishad Tobaccowala, the chief strategy and innovation officer of digital agency VivaKi, urged publishers to evolve to "attract the next generation of leaders," thus ensuring the industry's future.

Griffin stepped down a few months later, and in late 2011, Time Inc. went public with the announcement that Laura Lang, a seasoned marketing professional with experience in digital advertising, would serve as the new chief executive officer. In explaining the controversial decision to appoint an executive from outside of traditional magazine publishing, Time Warner CEO Jeffrey Bewkes commented on Lang's "understanding of digital and marketing, and strong relationships with the creative and advertising communities."[12] This movement away from traditional publishing skills reflects a striking reprioritization of the magazine business. At the level of publisher, responsibilities changed to such an extent that industry insiders felt that the title was less and less relevant in a cross-platform era. At the same American Magazine Conference, MPA president Nina Link noted that the term "felt like a description of a legacy business model. In our winter focus groups, participants eagerly pointed out that the title 'publisher' was being overtaken by more titles that span multiple media platforms, like 'brand director' or 'chief revenue officer.'" Title changes are of course meant to signal the brand rhetoric internally and to assure advertisers that the industry can accommodate new business models.

On the editorial side, the same sorts of semantically inflected changes were articulated as a means to reorient workers around various nonmagazine content spaces. At a *Folio* conference in 2006, Linda Longton, vice president of editorial for Randall-Reilly Publishing, said, "Editors who think of themselves as brand managers, rather than journalists, tend to seek out and embrace online strategies as well as other avenues—special issues, events, directories—that help their brand."[13] In 2007, John Q. Griffin, then chairman of the MPA, controversially suggested that editors-in-chief should be called "content strategists," a term that indexes the further encroachment of business on the editorial side. Of course, position title changes should not obscure the practical realities of the quickly evolving profession. Not only are print editors in command of an ever-widening range of magazine-branded material, they must also coordinate and at times oversee a growing number of employees with very different métiers.

These new responsibilities seem to signal a veering away from the longstanding professional identity construct of editors as tethered to a particular medium and set of production routines. My interview with Time Inc.'s Martha Nelson reaffirmed this. "The greatest editors have always been brand managers intuitively," she explained. She then clarified that "a true brand manager means that you have to do a lot of work to articulate what [the] brand is, what is your differentiating statement of value to consumers, what are your values, what is your personality, what is your look and feel." Logistically this brand work becomes ever more difficult to manage as distribution sites and institutional collaborations—licensing, advertising initiatives, cross-company partnerships—simultaneously expand.

Jacks-and-Jills-of-All-Trades

Inevitably, the progression from magazine as *object* to magazine as *brand* is having a substantial effect on today's magazine workers. Individuals holding top editorial positions indicated that their tasks had recently intensified, placing additional demands on their time. Lisa Arbetter, the deputy managing editor at *InStyle* and a magazine insider for two decades, told me that the position of magazine editor now requires a different mentality: "It has become about more than a magazine. It's about building a brand. At *InStyle*, we're working on digital extensions—web, mobile, video—and we are looking into doing TV. We also do a lot of event planning. We do books. We are looking into developing consumer products. . . . An editor today has to look at moving onto new platforms and into other areas. Brand building has become paramount. It's a lot of responsibility to nurture a brand." Arbetter described the pressure to always think across as many platforms as possible as a "juggling act." Similarly, Joanna Coles, who moved from *Marie Claire* into the top editorial position at *Cosmopolitan* in 2012, noted how the editorial process is dramatically different now than it was just a few years ago. "When we are in meetings trying to figure out what our next big ideas are, we always [think about], 'What's the iPad angle, what's the film angle, the web angle, here we can do a blog post on this.'" She added, "You have to think beyond just print now." These comments reveal sweeping changes in the creative process and indicate that editorial decision makers increasingly prefer content that will flow easily across media platforms. Though this shift is not inherently problematic, it has the potential to undermine conceptions of the magazines' identities if these decisions overpower those choices about what will best suit the perceived needs of readers.

Devin Gordon, a former editor at *Newsweek Digital* who is now a senior editor at *GQ*, spoke very candidly about the recent evolution of the magazine industry. Although his experience is not in the women's genre, his perspective offers a glimpse into Condé Nast's approach to editorial roles and routines. When I asked Gordon how his responsibilities were divided, he estimated that he devotes 75 to 80 percent of his time to print and the rest to digital. He admitted that his specific tasks on the web are "more vague": "I'm head of the editorial transition from the print magazine to the iPad edition. I run *GQ*'s Tumblr, which I started about two months ago and do every day in the minutes between whatever else I'm doing. . . . And then on the main *GQ* website, I just order up stories about sports, pop culture, politics, news, whatever I can. . . . And I'll write display for them when they need help. There isn't a job description, especially on the digital side, for me." Gordon's laundry list of responsibilities spans several platforms; yet as a member of the print staff, he told me that his priority lies with the print—the side from which his paycheck comes.

Although Arbetter, Coles, and Gordon represent senior editorial positions at different titles and organizations, they all acknowledged that the iPad editions would come under their purview, adding another layer of editorial responsibilities. The rationale is that by giving print staff members jurisdiction over the content, the editorial voice will be consistent in a way that seemed neither necessary nor possible online. Explaining the organizational logic behind this within Hearst, Chris Wilkes told me that the organizational system was considered a way to "break down the walls" between print and digital and more fully integrate the editors, or brand stewards. Others expressed a similar sentiment about the need to make sure that the iPad version was "on brand." Although Time Inc.'s Martha Nelson said that the senior editors were eager to work on tablet editions, she also recognized that this has become an essential part of their position requirements. "For their own career development," she advised, "They need to know more about the iPad."

There seemed to be less enthusiasm regarding the development of magazine extensions in the app world. According to journalist David Kaplan, who writes on the digital initiatives of newspaper and magazine publishers, the rise of app development is "wreaking havoc with traditional print production schedules and, in some cases, budgets. And, then there's the fear that even after all that blood-sweat, advertisers and readers will see the magazine apps as irrelevant." Kaplan quotes one anonymous executive who criticized the devotion of magazine resources to something that is of a "different format entirely" from the print magazine. As the source continued, "Consider the fact that iTunes doesn't even have a dedicated 'magazine section,' so we're effectively competing with *Angry Birds* and Flipboard at the same time."[14]

This comment captures the essence of traditional publishers, who fear that moving too far away from the identity of the magazine will hinder—not help—the brand.

Articles published in the magazine trade press described how some companies have imposed a new burden on editors by requiring them to edit both professional *and* nonprofessional, user-generated content. According to *Fray* editor Derek Powazek, "The role of the editor is probably the most changed piece [of the industry's movement to digital]. It's not this omnipotent decider of things, it's more like a camp counselor. [Editors are] there to encourage people to foster relationships."[15] This perspective is wholly antagonistic to the traditional professional identity of editors, whose primary goal is to oversee content rather than "relationships." This view did not get much traction among those I interviewed. However, with an eye toward the future, this "camp counselor" mentality may increasingly characterize the work of senior editors.

The multimedia mindset has implications not only for those in highly placed roles throughout the industry, but also for junior staffers, writers, and designers. Several individuals informed me that their day-to-day tasks had shifted in light of popular magazine brand websites, highly visible mobile apps, and new iPad editions. Vanessa Voltolina, who has experience producing both print and online material for women's magazines, believes that in the current moment of flexible labor, "magazine editors must be 'jacks-of-all-trades.'" She explained that her previous position at *Folio* necessitated that she divide her time between news reporting and developing content for both print and online. An editorial assistant from *Glamour* made a similar remark. Although she had exclusive responsibilities for print, she, too, was expected to contribute to the website. After telling me about her contributions to a series of *Glamour* blogs, she explained, "That was my way [of] becoming more involved with the web. I mean, it's something that I guess we'll get into, but we all know we should be doing it." She then added that the web team will occasionally assign her stories, indicating potential managerial clashes over her work priorities.

In addition, a health editor for a popular women's service title explained that over the last two years, her commitments had been reconfigured to account for the growth of the website. For example, she was assigned to produce a blog series, while her colleague (also on the print side) had the added task of filming exercise videos for the web. When I asked how the digital responsibilities get dispersed among the staff, she informed me that the distribution is based upon individual skill sets. "Our associate editor in print actually for the most part handles [the Twitter account]. . . . I think some of it is also just about who is media savvy, who is technology savvy." The expectation, then, is that members of the print team will contribute to new brand initiatives on the basis of their technological strengths rather than a formal description of the position.

These examples reveal the extent to which magazine staffers, particularly those affiliated with print, face intensified work pressures as they create and distribute material across a variety of platforms. The cross-platform mentality is both financially motivated and inscribed in organizational strategies. Debi Chirichella, who was chief operating officer of Condé Nast Digital at the time of our interview, commented on the digital division's hesitance to move people over to online because of revenue discrepancies between print and online: "Magazines are still able to support [a] much larger staff than you can with a website. But when the website is an add-on to your magazine, so-and-so spends twenty percent of their time or whatever. You end up with a lot more resources that the website doesn't really have to bear. It's borne by the magazine, so it's a little bit of an easier [situation]; you just have more resources behind it; but . . . for any website, it's hard to justify the economics unless [you're] being paid for a bigger piece." Accordingly, the size of online departments is directly correlated to each brand's share of revenue. To be fair, Condé Nast may be a bit of an outlier given the company's initial reluctance to move budgets to digital. Yet across the industry, many individuals' workloads are growing as financial strategists try to reconcile lower budgets with increased demands for content.

Another consequence of budgetary limitations is that magazine workers, both print and digital, are being asked to create content for brand partners and affiliates. *InStyle*'s Lisa Arbetter noted that members of her staff are encouraged to "think like marketers." An online editor for another Time Inc. publication informed me that her position sometimes entails producing features for corporate partners such as CNN, MSN, or Shine (a Yahoo! destination site for women). The purpose, she explained, is to "get links," or increase page views from visitors who follow hyperlinks back to the website. While she believed that readers enjoyed them, she emphasized, "It's more of a thing we do to sell, if you know what I mean." She was also asked to create content on the magazine website exclusively for advertising partners, a part of the job about which she seemed less than animated. "I like creating content that I know [the audience] wants, not what L'Oréal wants to put a lipstick next to," she admitted. Implicit in this remark is the tension between creativity and constraint that is often highlighted in media production literature. That is, organizational pressures to maintain revenue streams can overshadow individual assumptions about the needs of readers.

On the publishing side, too, magazines are "partnering" with advertisers by providing them with agency-like services. As *Advertising Age*'s Brian Steinberg reported, "Increasingly, marketers want deep integration with content, and they're finding that content producers themselves are often the best creative partners, making their threat to the agencies more tangible in recent months."[16] Thus, magazine producers are not just integrating clients' products into carved-out editorial spaces, they are literally creating some of the ads for them. *Seventeen*'s vice president and publisher, Jayne Jamison, spoke extensively about the role that her staffers play in the creation and execution of marketing campaigns. "We've gotten much more involved in marketing overall . . . becoming marketing [partners] for our clients and listening to their problems and developing very targeted solutions that our readers would respond to. . . . It's clearly a trend that our advertisers are saying to us, 'You know our market best, you know how to talk to this market best'; and let's face it, there are huge savings for them in terms of not paying an ad agency, creative fees. . . . Our rates are much, much lower." Like the magazines' editorial professionals, members of the publishing staff are also being compelled to assume new responsibilities, possibly without relevant training or experience. Although Jamison spoke enthusiastically about the changes, she did acknowledge the challenges, particularly the fact that it has been a difficult transition for people "who aren't used to really having to think creatively." Advertisers' clamoring for creative specialists may even impact the hiring process. Jamison said, "We want people to sell who have a marketing brain and people who are in marketing who can sell, so when we are hiring marketing people, we want them to be able to be in front of our clients because often they are selling the marketing programs." Those familiar with the advertising profession know that the creative and account-planning functions are quite distinct; it is thus noteworthy that ad representatives for certain magazines need to be able to wear both of these hats.

New Faces and Spaces of the Profession

Jamison's reference to new hires casts light on the second major structural tactic that magazine companies have had to employ in recent years, namely delegating new workers to contribute to and oversee digital initiatives. In some respects, this decision is a logistical one. Lisa Arbetter explained that her company appointed a web team because it became "unwieldy" for print editors to oversee so many aspects of the brand. In other organizations, the incorporation of new staffers is an acknowledgment of people's differing roles and activities, both of which are entangled with professional identity. From training to socialization to innate realms of expertise, print and digital specialists may have few professional overlaps. According to Mark Weinberg, the former vice president of programming and product strategy at Hearst Magazines Digital Media, "The print people are printing a magazine each month, and it's a lot of work, pretty much that's what they're equipped to do. The digital team is responsible for keeping an updated and functioning and successful website by both looking at what the print organization is creating month-to-month, and creating original digital content from that, but they are also looking at what else could or should be a part of the digital brand sites." This evinces the different timing schedules and routines that guide individuals in these roles. Weinberg's mention of "what they're equipped to do" suggests the dissimilar orientations of media workers. Hearst's Chris Wilkes similarly noted of print magazine producers, "There's different skill sets required for that; you're churning out a monthly product [that] requires really tight, disciplined management of deadlines, and it's a different type of individual." Significantly, Wilkes condenses professional and individual identities in suggesting that the "individual" is qualified for a particular role within the organization.

Change, they say, starts at the top. And since 2010, most magazine companies have appointed individuals to newly created executive positions. While Condé Nast incorporated a chief technology officer and a chief marketing officer into its corporate team, Time Inc. hired its first chief digital officer (although, as previously mentioned, he left shortly thereafter). In an *Advertising Age* article on the popularity of chief tech officers, Patrick Keane, former CEO of Associated Content and a digital executive within CBS, commented, "If you are not classically trained in the oeuvre of fast tech development, that's a hard thing to assimilate if you have been in the world of traditional media."[17]

The growth of mobile and tablet devices has also spawned a steady stream of new hires. For instance, Emily Masamitsu Scadden informed me that she used to work at *Popular Mechanics*, where she helped launch Hearst's first iPad title. In early 2011, she was appointed to the newly created position of digital assets manager at *Marie Claire*, where she assisted with the design and execution of the latter's iPad app. "It is a job that is evolving," she explained. "I get curveballs thrown at me all the time, where an industry is adapting to the different platforms. . . . It's all about knowing what's out there. . . .

There is a mix of production work, trafficking, making sure work flow is happening so that we are actually producing the layouts, the interactivities, the elements, and the assets that are going to be implemented in our digital version." Over at Condé Nast, a software developer recalled that he was the only one involved in application development when he joined Condé Nast Digital three years ago. Since then, however, they have brought many more people on board, which has allowed his own position to diversify.

The organizational logic of hiring specialists to oversee various content areas is abundantly clear: it puts experts at the forefront of new initiatives while allowing existing professionals to devote their energies to traditional roles and tasks. Yet coordinating staff members with varied interests and objectives is no easy feat for industry leaders who may find themselves uncomfortably wedged between groups with conflicting media orientations. The individuals I spoke with told me about various structural divisions they have utilized in an effort to streamline what may be a cumbersome production process. Hearst, for example, implemented a "matrix reporting structure" whereby individuals jointly report to print and web managers. Using the example of *Good Housekeeping*, Chuck Cordray, then the top digital executive at Hearst, explained that the Goodhousekeeping.com staff is physically embedded within the print department but reports to digital media. He continued, "They are in planning meetings for everything around issue planning, so they know what's coming up in print; they can work with the print team to say, 'Here are the extensions that would work online.'" The apparent success of this structure reveals the importance of spatial configurations in sites of cultural production, which can help forge consistent identities.

Interest in workplace configurations is not entirely new. In the late 1970s, Gaye Tuchman's sociology of news construction showed the function of office partitions and geographic separations in coordinating the activities within a newsroom.[18] More recently, Eamonn Forde noted that the political topography of music magazine production sites impacts the "socio-professional culture." For example, spatial relations between editors and staffers can be either opened or closed, with the latter reinforcing hierarchical patterns.[19] Such patterns are of particular interest to scholars of convergence since the organizational arrangement of multimedia departments can help or hinder the production processes.[20]

Indeed, several magazine staffers referenced the importance of centralized production spaces for editorial consistency. Hannah Morrill, senior beauty editor at InStyle.com, informed me that the company dedicates space within the organizational walls for freelancers to ensure that they speak in the "*In-*

Style voice." On a somewhat related note, Ellen Levine explained one of the tactics that Hearst employs to keep its content creators "on brand": "Rather than having the web editor sit off in New Jersey while we're here in New York, she or he is embedded with the editorial staff." This person, she continued, is able to review the story line-ups from print and often has a dotted line to someone like the print editor-in-chief. Levine's explanation indicates how the spatial structure within organizations is seen as a way to ensure a more consistent brand identity. Here, then, we can see two concurrent boundary refinements: internally, the boundaries between print and digital staffers are breaking down, while externally, a reinforced physical boundary inscribes various staffers in a communal brand space.

As a corollary, a lack of geographically defined boundaries, or inflexible internal boundaries, can cause frictions to erupt. As Hearst's Chris Wilkes explained of the different market logics guiding print and online workers, "We essentially created, whether it's a real or perceived wall, there is a wall between our print side and our digital side when it comes to the web." While some of these tensions may create unfavorable working conditions, others may be downright dysfunctional to the organization as they undermine historically rooted aspects of identity. A particularly significant problem is the tendency for people outside traditional editorial roles to have a say in content matters, a case of the proverbial too many cooks in the kitchen.

An editorial assistant from *Glamour* told me about the frustration she felt after one of her content recommendations was declined because "Condé Nast Digital doesn't want that." She continued:

> Once in a while, we'll say, "Why don't we do . . . quizzes or whatever. XYZ?" and our editorial director of the website will say, "Condé Nast Digital doesn't want us doing that anymore." And you're like, "Who is this monolith—who are they even to decide any ideas?" And it's very vague—I don't know who they are. I don't understand how crucial they are to our process. But they're like the *Wizard of Oz* [laughter]. . . . I mean, obviously a web editor knows exactly how they function, but they mention it in vague terms like that.

Devin Gordon made a similar remark about Condé Nast Digital, explaining that they are, "at least in my limited experience right now, . . . kind of this shadowy force that I know is there but don't really have any interaction with." This implies that print/digital interactions are particularly strained at Condé Nast, presumably an outcome of their continual restructuring.

Another interesting theme that materialized during my conversation with the *Glamour* staffer was the way she framed interactions with digital team members working on her floor. As she began, "We have one guy, I guess we call him our digital managing director, something like that, big and important sounding." Remarkably, an editor from a different publication made a similar comment about her company's explicit attempt to focus on branding through the creation of a brand group: "Our, um, . . . I don't know what his specific title is anymore, he's not the publisher anymore; I want to say it's like print director. There's a person now, on the business side primarily, but who oversees the print magazine and the website and anything else that we've done." Clearly she was struggling to define the title and position of this newly appointed brand leader. It is not incidental that she mentioned his affiliation with "the business side" and his role in overseeing print. I found these two instances to be strikingly similar; in each case, a female print staffer explicated management constraints established by a digitally oriented leader who happened to be male. I return to the gender dynamics and potential implications of this for the culture of women's magazines in the concluding section of this chapter.

By no means are these examples isolated; in trade press accounts and during the 2010 American Magazine Conference, many leaders sought advice on how to get print and digital staffers to work more cohesively. On the publishing side, there seemed to be a bit of finger-pointing going on; some individuals I spoke with blamed senior leadership for these tensions, while executives critiqued the inertia of ground-level employees. One advertising sales director, who worked at a Condé Nast title for nearly a decade, expressed her exasperation toward senior managers for a policy that prevented print staffers from peddling ad space on the magazine websites.[21] She confessed that the corporation felt like a "dinosaur" that, unlike "other top companies, [which] have integrated marketing and integrated sales," continued to keep their print and online sales teams separated. Consequentially, print ad sales people may discourage advertisers from package deals. She clarified:

> If someone comes in and wants [an] integrated campaign, we try to handle the online portion through a merchandising role, not really include the online property as much because it ends up siphoning off the money stream for us. If I sold the online portion as well and had my commission based on that, I would be more apt to want to include that. Whereas if I include them now, the way it's structured, they'll immediately set a very high threshold of the limit of where they can come in at an idea. . . . The first instinct, I think, is always to just keep it as print-only with whatever online properties I manage.

This situation is thus defined by intense competition among staff members in different divisions of the same title. This system economically incentivizes the self-preservation tactics of individual media workers, ostensibly preventing them from understanding the magazine and brand extensions as a unified entity.

Seventeen's Jayne Jamison suggested that it was the advertising sales representatives who clung tightly to traditional practices. "They are resistant to selling online," she told me. "They are resistant to things and to change, but it is the way we're moving, and I'm sure at some point every sales staff will be fully integrated, and there will not be silos." This perspective, that individual staffers are less willing to change, seems to make more sense from a professional identity point of view. That is, while managers may be willing to recalibrate notions of "organizational identity" to fit within a new technological paradigm, individual media workers may still cling to the practices and values woven into the culture of a particular medium. Change is easier in theory than in practice.

Conclusion

The changing economies and technologies of cultural production in the early twenty-first century necessitate a fundamental reconfiguration of media work. The concurrent trends of multi-skilled labor and consumer co-creative practices (the latter of which I discuss in chapter 5) have resulted in a further deprofessionalization of roles and positions within the women's magazine industry. However, the effects of this deprofessionalization are being felt unevenly across the industry, and decision-making power is firmly locked into traditional organizational hierarchies. The senior executives of magazine companies are often confronted with two work cultures: one that favors the training of staffers to be "Jacks-and-Jills-of-all-trades," and another that brings in new individuals to specialize in disparate aspects of media production in a convergent era.

Although these are by no means mutually exclusive, we can see how the former privileges the identity of the magazine or corporation over that of individual workers. The need for print editors—"brand stewards," as one informant called them—to distribute their editorial voice consistently across platforms may erode the distinctive identities of these magazine professionals. At the other end of the spectrum, bringing in new employees may endanger organizational identity, as these individuals work toward different organizational goals than their print-oriented colleagues. Tensions are already mounting over who controls the content, who the audience is, and what the role of each medium is in defining the brand.

For magazine executives, the decision about which workplace model to pursue is motivated by some combination of resources and assumptions about how to most effectively and efficiently produce multi-platform magazine content. These decisions have implications not only for the direction of the organization, but also for the people who earn a living within this business. Work in the creative industries has long been described as "precarious," characterized by temporary working arrangements, job instability, and long hours.[22] Yet the fast pace of change in today's media businesses means that these trends are intensifying, confounded by workplace reshufflings, new technologies, and the multi-platform media logic.

I want to consider, for a moment, how this change might be manifesting itself in shifting workplace cultures, and in particular through a changing industry demographic. A guiding conjecture for executives making hiring decisions is that young people are especially well equipped to oversee some of the popular online forums that magazines have expanded to, including social media sites such as Facebook, Twitter, and Tumblr. As previously noted, industry discourse stridently encourages magazine companies to embrace youth and nurture fresh talent. Such structural patterns may be characteristic of new media labor more generally, where workers are "notoriously young," in part because "the grueling work schedule inhibits family life, excluding older workers."[23] In discussing the role of "technology-savvy" staffers in moving content online, one anonymous staffer noted, "It's never been an old industry, in the sense that a lot of staffers are relatively young." This implies that in order to be technologically savvy, one must be located within a certain generational category. While younger people have certainly been exposed to computing and digital technologies for much of their lives, such generational suppositions have the potential to redistribute organizational resources in problematic ways. Arguably, the individuals who get displaced in the new media milieu are those most acculturated to the magazine brand.

What is perhaps more troubling is the potential for the industry's new organizational division of labor to fall along traditional gender lines. As I described in chapter 1, the women's magazine industry is a unique production site in which women were historically granted (a certain degree of) access. Recall that even before the Progressive era, magazine companies realized the significance of having magazine producers mirror their target consumers; by the 1990s, women held senior leadership positions at many of the category-leading women's titles. Unfortunately, the shift toward digitization has the potential to undermine the leadership role of women in the industry. Thus, if it continues to be the case that digital producers (many of whom are male) exert influence over matters of content, women may get elbowed out of their leadership positions. As the dust settles at this moment of unprecedented change, the gendered hierarchies of value within the industry may be subverted.

Although I have not yet systematically examined the gender dynamics of contemporary magazine producers, some themes that surfaced during this project reveal the possibility for problematic gender realignments. For one, several individuals I spoke with mentioned male staffers representing digital operations who wielded editorial control. The earlier remarks (i.e., "There's a person now, on the business side primarily, but who oversees the print magazine and the website and anything else that we've done") were from female print editors trying to understand the role of newly appointed (male) digital executives. Second, from the sample of individuals I interviewed, clichéd gender patterns were discernible. Most of the digital executives I spoke with were male; most of the editorial representatives were female. *Marie Claire*'s Emily Masamitsu Scadden was clearly an exception, but she, too, admitted that most of the people working on the technological/digital aspects of magazines production are men: "The reality of the tech world is that there are a lot of men. I came from a background where in addition to communication at UCLA, I also did a minor in computer science. I think a lot of times [the high proportion of men in technology] can overshadow some of the participation by women or women's publications." Finally, the near-simultaneous stepping down of Hearst's Cathie Black and Time's Ann Moore, both of whom were said to signify progressive female politics, may foretell a return to the traditional male-dominated leadership structure.[24]

While these cases are anecdotal, industry associations made corresponding pronouncements in terms of mounting gender disparities. A study published in *Folio* in 2010 revealed that men still earn higher salaries than women across almost every publishing discipline. For senior leaders, the difference in salary can be as much as $20,000.[25] With an eye toward the future, it will be important to monitor the gender composition of women's magazines; not only is this important for magazines seeking to keep continuity with the past, but it is also gravely necessary as part of a larger agenda toward achieving gender parity within cultural industries.

4

Rethinking Readership

The Digital Challenge of Audience Construction

"Never Drink and Text." This irreverent phrase was imprinted on an assortment of fuchsia-and-white-hued iPhone cases that were distributed to young women as part of Condé Nast's "Generation *Glamour*" branding campaign. Launched in the fall of 2012, the campaign targeted women in the so-called millennial generation, a highly coveted cohort that includes individuals born in or after 1980. Andy Spade, cofounder of the agency responsible for producing *Glamour*'s quarter-million-dollar campaign, offered his take on the millennial woman: "[She] is out there living in social media, influencing people with her opinions. . . . She shares her likes, she's tweeting, she's texting."[1] Perhaps unsurprisingly, the campaign had a vibrant presence across social media sites such as Pinterest, Twitter, and Instagram. The digital components of the campaign coincided with a series of changes to the print magazine, including a redesigned cover format, enhanced coverage of celebrities, and an increased emphasis on reader contributions. Acknowledging the critical role of market research in this brand overhaul, *Glamour*'s executive vice president and publishing director, William Wackermann, noted, "We did a ton of research into the millennials. . . . Why is everyone changing their nails? It's about self-expression. . . . women are interested in constant change, constant expression." Wackermann added, "She has a voice that's very distinct; it's a voice that's almost entitlement."[2]

As this example reveals, media executives strive to learn as much as possible about their audience members—who they are, what they do, and how they think, along with scores of other insights. Put simply, producers aspire to *know their audience*. Yet this strategic imperative is built upon the assumption that "the audience" is a real set of individuals, rather than a purely discursive construction. That is, media producers' ideas about audiences may be quite different from the ways in which individual members of "the audience" understand themselves.[3] Thus, while *Glamour* executives might see a particular reader as a college-educated Caucasian female who fits into certain age and income brackets, that individual may not consider those factors to be particularly salient to her own self-concept. Or she may feel that she has little in common with the millions of other young women who happen to fit within these same categories. As communication theorist Jay Blumler explains, mediated audience assumptions "often lack richness, complexity, or variety."[4]

Cultural theorist Raymond Williams called attention to the constructed nature of audiences more than five decades ago with his oft-cited declaration "There are in fact no masses, there are only ways of seeing people as masses."[5] Since then, the understanding that media audiences are industrially created and economically incentivized categories has gained considerable traction. Writing in 1994, media scholars James S. Ettema and D. Charles Whitney used the term "audiencemaking" to describe the processes through which media institutions and communicators define and delineate audiences; presumably, such assumptions help producers make sense of their daily work routines and products. Ettema and Whitney noted that audience constructions are often sites of contestation as various stakeholders—media producers, advertisers, government entities, and measurement services—vie to set the terms of audience categories.[6] Joseph Turow, Ien Ang, and Philip Napoli have also addressed the significance of metrics services in slicing and dicing, measuring and commodifying, and packaging and presenting audiences to advertisers.[7] Meaningful social implications emerge from such activities: by providing demographic, psychographic, and behavioral statistics on current and potential consumers, measurement techniques simultaneously reflect and reify existing social divisions.

Within the consumer magazine industry, research-driven audience segmentation is the *sine qua non* of the business. As I explained in chapter 1, editors and publishers of women's magazines have long targeted narrowly defined segments of the female populace—and advertisers clamoring to reach women in those neatly defined factions. These segments are based upon demographic factors (age, household income, marital status, educational level, and occasionally race) as well as lifestyle traits and behaviors. Niche segments may include fitness enthusiasts, aspirational domestic mavens, and soon-to-be brides. Those working in the industry draw upon surveys and other measurement techniques to understand these segments and craft detailed profiles of their "ideal reader."[8] With such profiles in mind, they can make decisions about their respective magazines' content, tone, format, and advertisements.

Readership research is not a novel concept; in fact, magazine professionals have been collecting data on their audiences for at least a century. In the early twentieth century, *Ladies' Home Journal* editor-in-chief Edward Bok utilized a rudimentary form of media research: he offered readers monetary rewards to answer such questions as, "What in the magazine did [you] like least?" "What did [you] like best?" and "What new features would [you] like to see started?"[9] Bok also developed a profile of the magazine's core reader based upon demographics; he imagined that her family fit within a particular middle-class income range of $1,200 to $2,500. An ad that appeared in *McCall's* in 1914 described the periodical as "a prosperous magazine . . . read by the prosperous women of the country; not all of them very rich, not all of them very poor; but the great middle class who are the real producers and buyers."[10]

Audience reports became more precise in the early twentieth century alongside the growth of syndicated measurement services such as the Audit Bureau of Circulation (ABC). Established in 1914 in response to the ad industry's growing demand for media accountability, the ABC provided circulation figures for national magazines and newspapers. Advertisers looking to buy space could choose a publication based on its independently rated circulation figures. This era also saw the emergence of publisher-specific tools for measuring audience demographics and behaviors. In his exhaustive analysis of market research within the Curtis Publishing Company, Douglas Ward explains that in the early 1920s, the company began to track "how long a magazine was kept in a home, how many readers it had per copy, how readership was broken down by sex and occupation, and whether advertising was read."[11] These developments signaled a monumental shift from *circulation* data to *audience* data.

A confluence of market-based changes and developments in research methods led to the establishment of more specialized research services, including Simmons Market Research Bureau (launched in 1963) and Mediamark Research Institute (launched in 1979).[12] Yet a more consequential shift was under way that would fuel the growth of audience research in unforeseen ways: media fragmentation. Philip Napoli explains that the fragmentation of audiences began with the expansion of satellite and cable TV in the 1970s, and it rapidly intensified in the decades that followed as media producers sought to provide advertisers with "greater efficiency and greater revenues" through more precise audience prediction and measurement tactics.[13]

Joseph Turow has documented some of the specific tactics that magazine publishers developed in the 1980s and 1990s in response to the fragmentation of media channels. At Hearst, executives used their expanding line of specialized titles to exploit subtle reader differences within and between generations of adult females. For example, *Good Housekeeping* editors and publishers set their sights on the so-called New Traditionalist, "a new kind of woman with deep-rooted values [who] is changing the way we live."[14] This approach helped to distinguish the magazine from other Hearst titles that focused on younger women pursuing careers outside the home. Hearst was not the only publisher to establish more narrowly defined audience segments in the last decades of the twentieth century. Meredith Corporation's Tom Harty reflected on the company's successful track record of audience segmentation activities: "Among big publishers in the United States, our portfolio is mostly focused on adult women. We have very strategically and deliberately expanded our audience over time by adding content and brands at . . . both ends of a woman's adult life, first, at the beginning, early stages of family formation and then during the period of her life when her children are grown and she is reinventing herself. Our singular focus on women kept us relevant to her and helped us and our brands remained vibrant with our consumers."[15] Harty's statement is indicative of Meredith's approach to audiences, whereby they highlight different life stages among female consumers. The presumption is that as women move through their lives, they will also progress through a predictable series of Meredith titles, from *Parents* to *Ladies' Home Journal* to *More* to *Better Homes and Gardens*.

If audience constructions are indeed bound up with larger shifts in media, culture, and society, then the transformations associated with digitization are no doubt reshaping the ways in which publishers think about audiences. This chapter examines shape-shifting approaches to audiences, particularly between producers for the print and digital products. While digital executives rely on advanced metrics to understand the behaviors of consumers, those in creative roles do not seem to have a clear sense of the digital audience—nor of the extent to which this fits within traditional conceptualizations. Such uncertainty brings up questions about how producers signal—and, more importantly, create content for—an amorphous group of individuals who might not mirror their traditional print audience. Readership must be rethought.

Measuring Audiences

Contemporary technologies allow marketing and media companies to learn infinitely more about consumer behavior. Against this backdrop, the magazine industry has made great strides in providing advertisers with more precise and timely audience metrics. In 2009, the Magazine Publishers of America (the original name of the MPA) circulated an update on an initiative they had launched three years earlier to improve the speed and accuracy of audience reporting.[16] According to the update, the movement to issue-specific and ad impact data (i.e., determining whether consumers were engaged in ads and/or took action on them by making a purchase) would make publishers "more accountable to advertising results and more comparable to metrics of other media."[17] Individual companies, too, have begun investing in specialized systems and databases to hone their information-gathering tactics. In 2008, Hearst Magazines rolled out a new customer database under the direction of Andrew Kirshenbaum, the director of database marketing. After explaining how the platform is able to combine demographic information about readers with transactional data, Kirshenbaum noted that this was a tremendous improvement over past systems, which "we used to pull off bits and pieces [of the data]."[18] A *Folio* report on this platform covered the advancements in more detail, including its utility for developing "cross-marketing opportunities using the information they have on prior purchase history and demographics," which is shared with the promotional team.[19]

This notion of "cross-marketing opportunities" was a resounding theme among the senior leaders I interviewed. Jayne Jamison of *Seventeen* spoke extensively about how the rise of metrics has changed the relationship between magazines and their advertisers by satisfying the latter's demand for accountability. "There's that many more details, and there's the post-buy analysis that you never really had in print that you have online, and you have with other elements like the iPhone, which is clearly measurable." By post-buy analysis, Jamison refers to an evaluation of advertising effectiveness *after* the campaign runs; with so many media choices, advertisers undoubtedly want to allocate their dollars to a platform with proven results. YouTube is another option for magazine publishers seeking to provide advertisers with real-time metrics. As Jamison explained, "It's . . . amazing to now create video content for our advertisers; we have about a million video views monthly on our site, so it's great because the responsiveness of our audience now is measurable online, and we know how many people click on everything and how many people took action on something. . . . For our industry, [engagement] has always been hard to quantify, and that's becoming easier actually now that we are on all these other platforms." As of early 2012, there were more than seven hundred videos on *Seventeen*'s YouTube channel. In addition to interviews with the magazine's cover models and a behind-the-scenes look at production, there are also cosmetic how-tos, DIY fashion tips, and features about dressing for one's body type, all of which offer tremendous potential for promotional material.

Also indicating the opportunities for audience feedback, Chuck Cordray, who was senior vice president and general manager of Hearst Digital at the time of our interview, told me that the most fundamental shift in publishing in recent years has been the upturn in metrics and accountability. "The ability to really track what users are doing, what consumers are doing in terms of advertising, is rising. And that is impacting how budgets are put together, where money is spent, and what advertisers are requiring as part of their media buys." While Jamison and Cordray come from very different positions within Hearst, they both view audience measurement as vital for attracting advertisers, a realization that reflects their own professional orientations within the organization.

Tools and tactics for "knowing the audience" are also imperative for editorial decision makers who are trying to determine what will best appeal to potential audiences. Some contemporary methods recall the survey techniques espoused by Edward Bok nearly a century ago. For instance, the October 2011 issue of *Shape* included a two-page questionnaire polling readers about their thoughts on the content and direction of the magazine. Conveying a conversational tone, the editors made their plea: "Okay, we admit it—we're dying to know what you think. Take a minute to fill us in: How are we doing? What do you want to see more of? It's your chance to help us shape *Shape!*"[20] The poll inquired about readers' favorite and least favorite sections, their sense of trust in the magazine's authority, their fitness and nutrition attitudes and behaviors, their desire to see "real" readers incorporated into the editorial material, and their demographics, among other topics. To further entice readers to contribute to the magazine's remaking, the survey noted that completed submissions would be entered into a promotional drawing (again harking back to Bok's survey incentives).

While *Shape* staffers relied upon direct audience feedback, there are other cases in which changes have been based upon *perceived* reader qualities and interests. As noted in the chapter introduction, *Glamour* instituted a series of editorial changes in 2012, adding new contributors, "hipper" features, and a heightened emphasis on celebrity news and pop culture, all of which are expected to appeal to a younger generation. "We felt like *Glamour* had become a little too formulaic," editor-in-chief Cindi Leive said. "If I'm bored, the reader probably is, too."[21] This example demonstrates how assumptions—or even anxieties—about the audience can prompt a reconsideration of some of the core elements of the magazine.

Some editorial staffers use the magazine website to try to gauge the potential success of features being considered for their monthly product. A junior *Glamour* writer disclosed that the print editor-in-chief frequently solicits reader input by assigning a print staffer to write a poll and submit it to the web team. While many of the polls available on the website may be a way to engage audiences, some may be quite useful for directing story formulas. For instance, "What's Your Biggest Beauty Goal for 2012?" and "What's Your Price Cut-off for Your Beauty-Related Gifts This Year?" might have provided the editors with story ideas and pricing guidelines for holiday gift recommendations.[22] Similarly, when I asked Justine Harman, former assistant online editor at People.com and PeopleStyleWatch.com, about the collaboration between print and websites at *People*, she explained, "We'll put a poll online and have all of our readers participate, and then put the results in the magazine. Kind of an untraditional moving people from the website back to the magazine, whereas usually it's the other way." The value to magazine producers is that they can get this information freely and almost instantaneously, helping them to make snap judgments about which story or angle to take. They can also print the results on the website, engaging users by allowing them to compare their own responses with those of other readers.

While polls seem to replicate traditional forms of market research, digital metrics track the behaviors of visitors to the magazine websites with great exactitude. According to one woman who requested that her publication not be named, there was a feature that their relationship and sex blogger would produce once a month under the title "Avert Your Eyes, Shy Readers." This was by far the most clicked-upon story, so they began using this sort of headline on the magazine cover and creating content around it. As she commented, "[Digital] is a faster metric for what sells, because you know right away." Time Inc. executive Mark Golin discussed how the content evaluation process has progressed over the years. Reflecting back on his career in print, he explained that researchers used to take a segment of the demographic and go through the magazine articles one by one. "Next to every photo, every piece of story, there was a little hand-pasted note that people [wrote comments on]." Now editors can "see how many people, and what people, went to particular articles and stayed on or left the site."

Publishers are also trying to capitalize on the growth of social media sites, particularly Facebook, Pinterest, and Twitter (a topic I return to in chapter 5). The targeting capacity of Facebook, for one, was addressed during a 2010 American Magazine Conference panel session, which featured a conversation between *Seventeen* editor-in-chief Ann Shoket and David Kirkpatrick, author of *The Facebook Effect*. Kirkpatrick described the popular social networking site as "the most targetable medium, bar none," given both user-provided information and inferential statistics. Other industry professionals are seeking out tools to aggregate data across these sites. Hearst's Matt Milner explained to me how his team uses HootSuite to "listen" to consumers in the social media world. According to the company website, "HootSuite is an essential tool for managing social networks by allowing teams to efficiently track conversations and measure campaign results."[23]

Despite widespread enthusiasm about the potential of digital monitoring and aggregating, a few individuals I interviewed were skeptical of the rhetoric and utility of these techniques. An online editor from InStyle.com was admittedly suspicious about the value of interactive digital components such as polls. In contrast to her publishing peers, she explained, "I don't think [online participation] is the key to the internet." Expanding on this, she said that a poll is not likely to attract hundreds or thousands of hits in the same way that a photo or feature might. Nor are people as likely to participate in the type of upbeat survey that InStyle.com would have. What is more, using online metrics to refine offline strategies is inherently problematic in that it presupposes that the same individuals constitute the audience for both print and online. This is not necessarily the case, as magazine producers provided widely variable responses when asked to identify the audience for their media properties.

So, Who's That Girl?

Print magazine editors and writers exhibited a clear understanding of the print readership and frequently cited figures listed in the media kits. A member of the *Glamour* editorial team offered her conception of the *Glamour* reader by reciting a phrase from an internal campaign: "Somebody who makes her own money, likes to spend it, is intelligent and on top of issues, but still cares about nail polish." This *Glamour* staffer was also well informed about the audience demographics, explaining that the median reader age has increased to the thirties despite the fact that much of the content seems to target women in their twenties. Other magazine professionals assumed that shifts in the audience reflected those in the broad media landscape. *In-Style*'s Lavinel Savu noted that readers are much savvier than they used to be. Similarly, Joanna Coles, former editor-in-chief of *Marie Claire*, expressed that women's magazine consumers are much more interested in technology than the public discourse suggests, a plausible explanation for why the title has progressively expanded to mobile and tablet devices.

Freelance writer and iVillage editor Vanessa Voltolina said that while the print magazine reader may be the same, producers need to expand the way they deliver content to her to remain competitive. "In the past, each [magazine] appealed to a niche female audience; now many are trying to be all things to her." She provided the hypothetical example of positioning a magazine as the place a woman comes to for fashion, to shop, and to get workout advice, all under the auspices of a single brand.

Although these individuals were able to articulate their understandings of the audience for print, many were unclear about how the print audience compared to the online audience. Some suggested that the online audience was younger, a logic based upon assumptions about age and technology use. For example, Hearst's Ellen Levine told me that she really did not know, but "Our sense is that the online audience for many of our magazines is different from the print audience for our brands. So, for example, they are maybe younger, by ten years or so." Similarly, when I asked an editor for a popular women's service magazine (she worked for the print publication but also blogged online) how she thought the audiences compared, she responded: "The web tends to skew slightly younger . . . probably about ten years younger on the website. The online reader isn't necessarily the print reader, and vice versa. We think of it as far as we still adhere to the basic . . . someone from our web staff can probably explain it better. But basically we still try to hit the basic tenets of the magazine." It is noteworthy that she defers to the web staff halfway through her response, signaling her belief that they would have hard data on online audience compositions. Also interestingly, this editor conflates the perceived age of the audience with other identity markers, noting how online content can be a little "racier" than that of print. After stating that some of the print readers were in their eighties, religious, and from the Midwest, she reasoned, "We'll be much more likely to cover a topic like sex on the web than in a print magazine. Something that's maybe going to [raise] eyebrows more than in print." In this instance, we can see how generalizations about the online audience—even without verification—can guide the content creation process.

Despite the overwhelming tendency to think of the online audience as younger than the print readership, one anonymous Condé Nast writer was suspicious of this assumption. She noted, "It's really hard to say what the demographic is. . . . I don't think we can generalize the way we used to by thinking a web reader is younger. I don't know . . . that information isn't available to me yet." She also motioned toward the digital team by saying that they probably had that information, as well as "all their email addresses and whatnot." Other individuals deflected this question, explaining that they were unsure or were "not the best person" to answer it. This is quite interesting given how central conceptions of the audience are for the editorial and advertising processes affiliated with the print publication.

Those appointed to magazines' digital teams showed an understanding of audiences that was clearly guided by online metrics and tracking activities. Hannah Morrill, who at the time of our interview was an online editor at InStyle.com, explained that the web audience was younger and also had less discretionary income than print subscribers. Her explanation was that some of the highest-ranked stories online (those in which the links received the highest numbers of clicks) are the "Under $100" features, which tend to do much better than the articles on luxury goods. Members of Hearst Magazines Digital Media's corporate team were similarly knowledgeable about the demographics of online audiences and offered interpretations of how they stacked up against their print readers. Chuck Cordray confirmed that the audience for their online properties was younger than the print readership. "Interestingly," he said, "for something like *Seventeen*, they are six months younger; for something like *Good Housekeeping* or *Popular Mechanics*, they run about ten years younger." Cordray went on to explain that there is little overlap in the audiences of the online and print properties. "Less than 5 percent of print readers go to our websites every month," he added. Not only is such a low number surprising, but it is also remarkable when compared with statistics from other publishers. People.com's editor-in-chief, Mark Golin, informed me that the print-to-online audience correlation for that title is closer to 30 to 40 percent.

While the previous discussion reveals tensions between constructions of print and online audiences, the launch of the iPad introduced another important variable into the mix. Some individuals believed that the audiences for print and iPad editions were one and the same; a member of the Condé Nast digital team explained that "people love that brand, and they'll read it in print or they'll read it on an iPhone or an iPad." Others, however, were skeptical of this supposition. Chris Wilkes, whose position at the forefront of Hearst's App Lab makes him especially informed on the topic, was working under a very different conjecture related to technological diffusion. Readers of magazines on digital devices, he contended, are "much more influenced by early adoption, bringing in these particular higher-end demographics that have disposable incomes to spend on these devices." This understanding, he explained, is guiding how the Hearst Digital team conducts audience research: "Most of the directional feedback we get from users isn't necessarily the actual users of these products right now, but also from usability research, where we bring in carefully selected panels of users and potential users of these devices and get their feedback on our apps, as opposed to just relying on what the early adopters want." Hearst's strategy attempts to anticipate audience behaviors by calling upon the opinions of potential users; however, this may have a tautological quality.

Search, Syndication, and the Unknown Audience

Recent developments in online tracking and consumer analytics have come together to trigger a new series of approaches to researching media audiences, including search engine optimization (SEO), content syndication and aggregation, web traffic generation, and more. While the lexicon of these audience-driving strategies seems complex, their outcome for magazine producers remains simple: to draw consumers to the magazines' digital properties. Discourses surrounding two particular activities—search engine optimization and syndication partnerships—illustrate some of the emergent challenges of constructing and signaling audiences.

The central premise underpinning search and syndication strategies is that many online audiences come to a particular website through the "side door," such as after clicking on a link that came up during a Google search or browsing through MSN. A 2010 article from *Wired* reported that close to 60 percent of all people find websites through search engines, and this number has likely grown.[24] SEO is the process of strategically using keywords to improve a website's search ranking. The first page of a Google search is indeed premier real estate, so it is not surprising that magazine companies are feverishly investing in SEO tools. Chuck Cordray explained why SEO is such a viable strategy for many publishers who are struggling to monetize their online holdings: "That ability to attract a new audience has been great in that the brand reach has gone up. There's very little duplication, and that's a lot of the reach for advertisers to be better."

Content syndication is a method of distribution whereby content written for one digital property gets circulated to a variety of affiliates with large audience bases. Web portals such as Yahoo! and MSN aggregate stories from an array of sources and organize them into categories like news, sports, entertainment, style, and travel. For instance, the top article in MSN's "style" section in October 2012 was a feature on "Sexiest Hairstyles for Fall," produced by *InStyle*. Below that was a link to "Five Beauty Tips to Steal from Beyoncé," produced by *Glamour*. Syndication deals seem like a win-win: web services receive ready-made content, while magazine publishers get access to potential audiences who will ostensibly click through to their website. Ashley Parrish, a former web editor at *Marie Claire*, explained to a *Folio* reporter that her magazine relied upon syndication partnerships to "distribute content out to larger pools of people and individuals who might not normally search for *Marie Claire* content."[25] Ideally, individuals will visit the *Marie Claire* homepage and find other relevant articles and features as they navigate through the site.

What tends to get left out of discussions about search and syndication is the potential for magazine companies to draw an unknown—or, worse, "undesirable"—audience. In response to Parrish's comment about enticing those "who might not normally search for *Marie Claire* content," we should consider possible reasons *why* individuals do not usually turn to this publication to meet their informational needs. Mark Weinberg, a former member of the Hearst Magazines Digital Media team, told me that the logic of SEO is based on a fundamentally different conception of magazine audiences:

> A website is consumed in a different way than an iPad application, and that's also consumed in a different way than a magazine might be consumed. And the behaviors of the audiences are different. The web audience doesn't behave the same way. . . . I would defy anybody who can find more than five people who could say on any given day, "I'm going to go to a specific site and see what they have on their website today." It just doesn't happen. What happens is people say, "I need to get this coffee stain out of my white shirt, I wonder what's the best solution?" They search for coffee stain removal, white shirt, and they get the *Good Housekeeping* Stain Buster guide.

Weinberg's narrative provides compelling evidence for why there may be a radical demographic difference between the online audience and the print readership. Hypothetically, while those outside a particular magazine's target demographic are unlikely to pick up an issue of it on the newsstand, they may find themselves immersed in the magazine's online content after a particular web search.

Weinberg also nodded toward the contemporary challenge of signaling audiences. "Ultimately what sells a magazine is pretty well understood right now and is not changing a lot, and what's selling a website is not necessarily its homepage." As I discussed in chapter 1, magazines traditionally beckoned their target reader through formulaic covers. As magazine scholar Ellen Mc-Cracken explains, "the cover helps to establish the brand identity of the magazine-commodity; it is the label of packaging that will convince us to choose one magazine over the competitors."[26] Although McCracken focused primarily on the cover's visual aesthetic, the cover lines are also instrumental in pulling in certain types of readers. In explaining how cover lines communicate audience distinctions, Joseph Turow recounts a discussion with a *Woman's Day* art director who said the cover lines were so significant in appealing to audiences that the company would develop them first, and then organize the content of the issue.[27] What this suggests is that one of the key visible markers of organizational identity—the cover—is much less relevant in the online world.

Another industrial implication of SEO is that guidelines for creating content, particularly headlines, are being revised in an effort to entice consumers who enter particular terms into search engines. Such "keywords" provide insight into the drastically new measures being undertaken to signal the audience. In 2009, the senior SEO analyst for Hearst Magazines Digital Media, Dan Rogers, told a reporter how they had increased online traffic 150 percent after integrating the Wordtracker keyword research tool into their content management system.[28] He gave a practical illustration of how keyword decisions are made within a women's fashion title:

> Fashion is a big part of what [women's titles] do, so early on we made the decision that we'd instruct them to run some comparatives on the keywords "fashion" and "style." In the print context they like to use the word style, but I stressed to them that style is somewhat nebulous in that it can mean a number of things. People's behavior online is different because when they are looking for content, they tend to be much more literal, because they have to be. The Wordtracker data showed us that seven-to-one, people were more likely to use "fashion" than "style" when looking for the kind of content we were promoting.[29]

This reveals the extent to which industrial analytics guide the processes of appealing to, reaching, and thus constructing the audience across various platforms. Although the variance between "style" and "fashion" may be minor, this example indicates how online metrics are influencing the content creation process. Matt Robson, who is Hearst's designated "SEO specialist," acknowledged some of the concerns of his peers. "Traditional publishers are reluctant to change their brands to be more demand-driven with less focus on exclusive content and more focus on meeting search demand."[30]

Relatedly, some producers indicated that they consider SEO initiatives to be an infringement on the creative process, with economic impulses outweighing concerns about quality. InStyle.com's Hannah Morrill informed me that her organization had recently invited a SEO specialist to the workplace to give a presentation on what makes a "searchable" story. Using the 2009 Hudson River plane crash as an example, the speaker noted that the *New York Times* website headlined its story "Pilot Is Hailed after Jetliner's Icy Plunge," and traffic to the site was unexpectedly low. In hindsight, she said, the headline should have been "Plane Crashes into Hudson," to pull in people who were searching for the story through Google. She then explained how the logic of search affects her own professional identity as a beauty editor. Whereas language in print is "flowery, punny, and clever," online language is decidedly straightforward, literal, and laconic. As a specific example, Morrill noted that in print, an article on fragrances would be written in colorful language and appear alongside a dazzling display of flower petals; online, the headline would read like a cover line, and the image would be a stock photo of a particular perfume brand.

Similarly, when I asked a Condé Nast editorial assistant about the process of creating content for different media, she recalled a recent presentation on the importance of using search-friendly terms in stories for the web. According to the company's guidelines, "It should have a number in it, and it should be as basic as possible, something like 'Ten Cute Hair Ideas.' . . . Because when people are Googling, it's all SEO." She then seemed to realize that the latter term might not make sense to someone outside the industry. She clarified, "What happens is someone out there Googles 'cute haircuts' because they want a cute haircut. And we come up first, we give you 'Fifteen Cute Haircuts for Fall,' 'Fifteen Cute Haircuts for Spring' . . . that kind of stuff. So that was [pause] interesting." Although this individual's description was expository, her tone seemed to disparage the role of SEO in sacrificing some of the creative essence—and perhaps the identity—of women's magazines.

Through an identity prism, we can understand why journalists and editors have been reluctant to embrace SEO approaches to content creation: they ostensibly lose control over creativity, delivery, and the beauty of language that has long defined magazine feature writing. This negotiation has been acknowledged within other sites of creative production. In addressing work routines in the television, recording, and men's magazine industries, David Hesmondhalgh and Sarah Baker usefully contend, "Attitudes toward audiences, then, are deeply bound up with questions concerning the quality of texts, and the quality of workers' experiences of production."[31] Sammy Davis, a former Hearst employee who left the company to launch her own online vintage fashion venture, seemed to capture this struggle on her LinkedIn site. Reflecting on the different business models driving print and online, she wrote:

> In digital media, what print lovers complain about most is a lack of quality content. And it's true: as we become more focused on page views and how to generate money, originality dies, and a site's content becomes watered down as much as a reality television show that runs for more seasons than the average length of a college education. As an aspiring magazine site editor, I firmly believe that content will keep a user returning to a site—but in a room full of a million voices with no one standing at the podium, it is my job as a content producer—and with the right experience, someday site editor—to use the web to attract the right people to my site's content.[32]

Davis's reference to attracting "the right people" is an issue that many magazines are grappling with. While the success of magazines has traditionally depended on their ability to target and reach ideal readers, the dissemination of digitally based metrics raises questions about how to productively define and attract audiences. If producers eschew time-honored standards in favor of SEO tactics, they could inadvertently dilute the organizational identities they have worked tirelessly to maintain—in the minds of both their audiences and their advertisers.

Some magazine executives acknowledged that the growth of SEO raises questions about whether to pursue audiences of quality or quantity. Hearst's Ellen Levine spoke very candidly about this during our second phone interview. She broached the issue by asking whether I had seen the *New York Times* article "The Dirty Little Secrets of Search," which exposed J. C. Penney's alleged "black hat" search optimization scheme. Treading into unethical waters, someone from J. C. Penney attempted to "cheat" Google by using false links to get the retailer to the top of the page on organic search results. According to the reporter covering the story, "There are links to JCPenney. com's dresses page on sites about diseases, cameras, cards, dogs, aluminum sheets, travel, snoring, diamond drills, bathroom tiles, hotel furniture . . . jokes and dentists—and the list goes on."[33] Levine noted the problematic trend of using search engine optimization for the wrong reasons: "Sometimes . . . to get a lot of people to come to your site, the editors have courted controversial points of view, and it will move them further up the line, but it also may damage the brand."

Levine gave a hypothetical example of how this may play out: "Let's say . . . one of the online stories is very graphic and specific about sexuality, much more so than you would include in print, much more so. And it was promoted online and drove a lot of new readers to your site. But that's not reflective of the print brand. It may repel the loyalists. Now, I don't know if that's long-term damage, but if it were cumulative, it might be problematic." Levine's cautionary tale raises a fundamental issue in terms of audience construction: Is it better to draw a loyal audience or a large one? While an organizational identity approach would suggest the former, the economic realities of the industry could lead magazine workers toward the latter as they try to increase the page views to seduce advertisers. Sammy Davis described the tendency of organizations to use SEO to draw audiences of scale with the clever term "Walmart traffic." As she defined it, "It's when people come to your site because maybe Gawker linked to you, but the people who read Gawker don't really care about vintage fashion. So they are on my site for like thirty seconds." The implication is that people who are duped into coming to a particular site are not likely to return, thus offsetting the numbers of one-time page views.

The ways in which Morrill, Davis, and Levine frame SEO are quite distinct; yet they collectively signal how new approaches to content may require a reconfiguration of audience categorizations. There is a somewhat different potential challenge for those individuals who work in digital departments, namely the reliability of metrics—or lack thereof. As I indicated earlier, audiences are social constructs dependent on fine-tuned metrics; this holds true in the online as well as the offline world. At a recent Technology, Entertainment, Design (TED) talk, USC professor Johanna Blakley noted that while new media companies are very interested in audience metrics, "they still need to figure it out." Speaking subjectively as a consumer, she contended: "When they're monitoring your clickstream—and you know they are—they have a really hard time figuring out your age, your gender and your income. They can make some educated guesses. But they get a lot more information about what you do online, what you like, what interests you. That's easier for them to find out than who you are."[34] What this means is that the information that producers share with advertisers about the online audience may not address the identity characteristics that underpin women's magazines: gender, age, income, and more.

Conclusion

Just as the boundaries around magazine producers are stretching to accommodate twenty-first-century demands, so too are the discursive lines demarcating magazine audiences. Producers on the editorial side, especially print writers and creative workers, struggle to articulate how the new brand audience (especially online) grafts onto the traditional readership communities for whom they have developed stories, features, and even covers. These individuals rely upon basic assumptions about age and income level to make sense of their business, yet this strategy could end up being a self-fulfilling prophecy whereby only these narrowly defined categories of "consumers" will return to magazine websites. Moreover, those executives on the digital side are relying upon new measures and metrics to develop a sense of who the audience is—and how best to reach them. Inevitably, there are still many things that companies do not know about their digital consumers. A reporter from *Mediaweek* commented in 2011, "For as trackable as the Internet is, Web publishers often know surprisingly little about their audiences besides what can be gathered from syndicated research or what they can infer from their own content."[35] This statement indexes the complexity of "constructing" the audience in a new era of information and entertainment.

The twin strategies of SEO and content syndication seem to capture this complexity. SEO and other digital tactics enable producers to know infinitely more about the activities and behaviors of visitors to the magazine websites. Yet such metrics are inherently problematic from an identity standpoint as they foreground the questions, What does it mean to producers if the audience you are attracting is not the right one? If magazines have been built around a definable audience for decades, doesn't this approach erode the idea of a magazine? In the coffee stain example provided by Hearst's Mark Weinberg, we can imagine how anyone might come across the magazine website (in this case, Goodhousekeeping.com) via Google, yet not necessarily feel any connection to it. As *Wired* contributor Michael Wolff explained of search logic generally, "many of these people have been essentially corralled into clicking a random link and may have no idea why they are visiting a particular site—or, indeed, what site they are visiting." He continued, "They are the exact opposite of a loyal audience, the kind that you might expect, over time, to inculcate with your message."[36]

Interestingly, then, there is an inherent contradiction in addressing magazine consumers in the twenty-first-century era of news and information: while knowledge is augmented at the individual level, it decreases at the aggregate level. Thus, while interactivity, customization, and data-mining activities give magazine publishers more granular data on who is interacting with the content, understanding these individuals as a cohesive group becomes tricky when people enter sites through the adjacent side doors of search and syndication. Nearly two decades ago, Ien Ang addressed a similar dialectic in her analysis of the television institutions' construction of "the audience"; although ratings services help guide programming decisions, they provide little information about "the dynamic complexity of the social worlds of *actual* audiences."[37] In the 1980s and 1990s, while viewing contexts of audiences grew more and more complex, technological advancements made it increasingly difficult for the industry to "bring their relationship to the audience under control."[38] In particular, tools that made it easier for audiences to customize programming (remote controls, DVRs) complicated traditional understandings of audiences as homogeneous groups of like-minded individuals. Writing in the early 2000s, Philip Napoli foretold a similar shift whereby changes in the new media environment were threatening to upend the audience marketplace by pulling apart what he identified as the "predicted audience," the "measured audience," and the "elusive and essentially unknowable" actual audience.[39] Both Ang and Napoli provide compelling evidence that advanced metrics do not translate into clearer audience conceptions.

The more you know, the less you know thus seems to be an apt way to describe the conditions of knowing magazine audiences in the contemporary moment. Such a high degree of uncertainty about consumption activities feeds back into the production process as content creators try to determine which formulas will attract "cross-platform" consumers. An unfortunate upshot is the winnowing of creative output. As Hesmondhalgh and Baker put it, "When creative workers care very greatly about the size of their audiences and try to anticipate what audiences might think, there might be a danger of workers losing contact with their own sense of excellence, with the standards internal to their chosen form of cultural activity."[40] As the target audience expands to anyone who enters particular search terms into Google, internal standards provide little guidance.

Importantly, producers' concerns about how to most effectively reach audiences tend to obscure the very real privacy implications of digital media metrics. Contemporary forms of audience feedback made possible by the online economy have been framed as panoptic, enclosing, and exploitative for the stealthy ways they compel audiences to freely provide economically productive data.[41] It is perhaps not surprising that this issue was scarcely mentioned by magazine industry professionals. Weinberg was one of the few who shared some of the societal concerns with the new era of digitization. Reflecting on the targeting capability of Web 2.0 technologies and especially Facebook, he told me, "I really fear for what will happen in the journalistic sense in this country when there's no money going into newspapers anymore. Because it's all leaking out, it's all leaking out." He continued, "Literally on your Facebook page you tell them where you live and what you're interested in—directly or indirectly. That's all I need to know, but there's a bunch of more stuff I can find out about you—as a part of how ad networks work—just that alone. So I know if you care about cars or cooking. And I know that you're—whatever city, whatever little city you actually live in. If you don't actually live where you went to school, I know that!" Of course, Weinberg understood the critical value of this information to advertisers, who can increasingly target people at the individual level. He rhetorically questioned, "Why would a kitchenware store choose to put a full-page ad in your newspaper or an insert in your newspaper, when [they] can target you as a cooking-interested person in a city where [they are] trying to sell the merchandise?" The problem, of course, is that consumers demonstrate little knowledge about how their online activities are monitored and shared with commercial entities.[42] Such discourses of privacy seem to fit within a larger duality that characterizes institutional rhetoric about the new media age: while the trade press often articulates interactivity as a strategy for knowing viewers, to external constituents the "consumer is king."[43] This tension is brought to the fore through new magazine initiatives designed to *invite audiences in*.

5

Inviting Audiences In

Interactive Consumers and Fashion Bloggers

In 2006, New York University professor and journalist Jay Rosen published a blog post titled "The People Formerly Known as the Audience," which heralded the integration of consumer audiences into media production processes. Speaking on behalf of consumer citizens ostensibly empowered by twenty-first-century technologies, Rosen defied an imagined throng of media executives: "You don't own the eyeballs. You don't own the press, which is now divided into pro and amateur zones. You don't control production on the new platform, which isn't one-way." Then, directly invoking the democratization rhetoric that frequently shapes convergence discourse, he continued, "There's a new balance of power between you and us."[1] To Rosen, the implications of new media technologies were especially profound for the newsgathering process. By collaborating, professional and nonprofessional "citizen" journalists could provide more accurate information, thus contributing to a better-informed Habermasian public sphere. Today, more than half a decade after his original post and in the wake of social media–enabled political movements on a global scale, Rosen's claim continues to gain traction.

Media practitioners and advertisers have cleverly hijacked narratives about the empowering potential of new media, often articulating technology as a panacea for consumer sovereignty. For instance, AdGenesis executive Michael Kelley voiced the popular "consumer is king" phrase during a 2011 panel on "The Evolution of Advertising."[2] This valorization of the audience is perhaps not surprising and can be understood as a discursive strategy that allows marketers to augment their own power to integrate—and learn about—audiences. It is in this vein that scholars and consumer advocates have critiqued interactive strategies as a marketing ploy or, more substantially, as labor exploited under the capitalist system.[3] Indeed, a decisive economic logic underpins participatory campaigns: by offloading creative work onto willing consumers, media and marketing executives no longer need as many writers, researchers, and other creative professionals on the payroll. These campaigns often create significant "buzz," the type of word-of-mouth interest that is considered paramount in an age of ever-fragmented media. The excitement generated by user-generated ad contests launched in conjunction with the Super Bowl—including those for Doritos and Pepsi—illustrates the very real ways in which nonprofessional participants can fuel the modern-day publicity machine.

Neither claims of audience work nor the techniques designed to encourage consumer productivity are entirely new. More than three decades ago, Canadian political economist Dallas Smythe conceptualized the audience as a commodity that is sold to advertisers in order to maintain the monopolistic system of capitalism. Audiences thus "work" by consuming advertisements—and ultimately consumer products—in their illusory free time.[4] Smythe's audience commodity theory sparked widespread discussion and critique among other leading political economists; Graham Murdock, Nick Garnham, Bill Livant, Sut Jhally, and later Eileen Meehan each contributed to the so-called blindspot debate.[5] Although intellectual fervor surrounding the audience commodity theory seemed to dissipate in the early 1990s, the opening of the participatory culture floodgates has led to a revival of interest in the laboring audience.[6]

Mark Andrejevic, Shawn Shimpach, and Christian Fuchs are among the contemporary scholars who have revisited and reworked Smythe's theory in an effort to conceptually accommodate the mechanisms of audience productivity within the interactive economy. Their work contributes to a larger body of literature that focuses on the nature of audience labor, which, according to an oft-quoted passage from Tiziana Terranova, is "simultaneously voluntarily given and unwaged, enjoyed and exploited."[7] Accordingly, the majority of contemporary writings on participatory culture, user-generated content, and audience productivity can be pigeonholed into one of two extremes: empowering or exploitative. In an assessment of this binary, digital media scholar Hector Postigo writes, "There appears to be an underlying tension between a free labor perspective and a participatory culture perspective that centers on what each believes will be the outcome of the overlapping and at times conflicting forces of participation and exploitation."[8] While Postigo finds a productive answer to this tension in the idea of "passionate labor," which involves structural conditions *and* participant subjectivities, other researchers have also tried to nuance these totalizing views of audience work.[9]

Despite the groundswell of attention to emergent discourses and practices of digital labor, certain social hierarchies have been overlooked, or at least sidestepped. Here I refer to the lack of explicit engagement with the role of gender in theories of digital/participatory media and labor power. This is a problematic oversight, especially given that the audience commodity (as fictitious as it may be) is recognized as gendered.[10] A noteworthy exception is John Edward Campbell's recent analysis of the iVillage network, the NBC-owned online community for women. He argues that the network is built upon gendered assumptions about consumerism. Accordingly, it encourages female participation in the "labor of devotion," or the interactive promotion of corporate brands. The labor of devotion capitalizes on advertisers' assumptions that when it comes to the online economy, "men loyally consume their favorite brands whereas women actively promote their favorite brands to other women."[11] Gender-based constructions of consumerism are thus cloaked in offers of community and sharing.

Campbell's work productively problematizes an emergent narrative about the empowering potential of contemporary media technologies for traditional hierarchies of gender. As feminist media researchers Carolyn M. Byerly and Karen Ross contend in their discussion of the shifting role of female audiences, "The level of interactivity that is enabled by technologies such as the Internet or digital television means that the viewer really can exert control over how she watches, listens [to], and reads popular media: finally, there is a reality to the rhetoric of audience power."[12] Although Byerly and Ross later nuance this Panglossian argument by noting how media owners and advertisers also gain from participatory practices, discourses of technology-powered feminism continue to flourish. Such arguments are not wholly different from Jenkins's articulation of the "newly empowered consumer," yet they are ostensibly more problematic in a feminist context that conflates participation and power.[13] By appealing to acculturated notions of gender politics, new media targeting women publicly deploy their commitment to female empowerment as further enticement for consumer audiences to contribute to content.

Certainly the changing expectations, technologies, and roles of (female) audiences in the digital economy are influencing the processes and products of women's magazines. This chapter explores the shifting dynamics of the magazine producer-consumer relationship within two different industrial contexts. The first section examines how producers are making their offerings for audiences more interactive by integrating commentary, advice, photos, and more. I put this trend in historical perspective by recalling women's magazines' tradition of "inviting readers in" (see chapter 1). The conflicting perspectives of producers at different levels and in different departments and companies show inflections in the meaning of audience participation within the branded spaces of magazines. Yet rather than see magazine interactivity as a fundamental threat to producers *qua* producers (a so-called dissolution of producer/audience boundaries), I explore how magazine producers and executives are trying to accommodate and even leverage the information provided by consumers.

The second section of this chapter takes a slightly different tack. Instead of focusing on the shifting producer-audience relationship inside magazines' textual spaces, I turn to an external force encroaching on magazine production, namely the rise of fashion blogging. After addressing how various industry insiders conceptualize blogging as a community and a practice, I explore industrial and organizational trends that seem to respond to this threat. This includes deflecting bloggers by publicly highlighting the unique skill set of magazine professionals or, conversely, incorporating these amateur-professional hybrids into the culture of the magazine. By examining these distinct forms of magazine producer-audience convergence, I argue that while there are external pressures to collapse boundaries between producers and audiences, the actual change is being vigilantly managed as producers seek to maintain their professional and organizational identities.

Interactive Consumers

Women's magazines have long created a shared sense of collectivity among readers, engaging them through personal, and at times personalized, advice columns.[14] For at least a century, editors have conveyed an intimate tone, encouraging audiences to feel a connection with producers whom they may never meet. Additionally, many women's publications printed the creative contributions of their readers and selected feature topics based on feedback provided during reader polls. Yet even with these occasions for participation, magazine readers were traditionally afforded few formal opportunities for interaction with other readers, and communication to producers was limited in many ways. Editorial power thus remained concentrated in the hands of the producers, who legitimized their role as experts within widely recognized domains of gender and femininity.

Today, however, magazine executives acknowledge—or even embrace—the broken-down binary between producers and audiences as they integrate

user-generated content into their branded online spaces. In 2007, even before Twitter and Tumblr were household names with massive numbers of
followers, an article in *Folio* advocated that publishers evaluate their Web
2.0 presence, because "the capabilities of online have put new emphasis on
user-generated content."[15] The following year, *Folio* convened a roundtable
on "Creating an Innovative Community," a how-to for producers hoping to
"leverage community, set rules, and make money." One of the panelists even
mused, "You've invited your audience to participate in the creation of the
experience, and that develops a much richer, stickier relationship between
the publisher and the audience."[16] In light of the explosive growth of social
media over the past few years, interest in (or perhaps concern with) the active audience has only intensified.

Within the women's market, exploiting social media opportunities seems
to be an outstanding business imperative as suppositions about gender, and
relatedly consumerism, guide the architectural landscape of digital spaces.
Brennan Hayden, the executive vice president and chief operating officer at
Wireless Developer Agency and a social media expert with a special interest
in publishing, explained to me, "[It is] well known that the female market
is the key to the kingdom in advertising, and women are interested in community." Because print magazines are not interactive, Hayden continued, it is
crucial for any publisher to add internet and mobile components. Similarly,
one executive who wished to remain anonymous asserted that while she is
skeptical about gender-based generalities, "Men are much more interested
in the gadget and the gidget. And women are not." She continued, "We just
came from a conference in London, where we also have a lot of brands, and
they found it to be absolutely true. The women want to be social on [the
internet] and get the information."

The trajectory of the narrative conflation of womanhood and online so-
ciability is predictably positioned within gendered discourses of technology. The developers of the internet were almost exclusively male, and it was
initially considered to be a masculine domain.[17] By the turn of the century,
however, some feminist scholars saw the internet as a female medium, and
fields such as "feminist internet studies" surfaced to take up debates about
the relationship between technology, women, and femininity. Yet as Liesbet
van Zoonen argued in the inaugural issue of the journal *Feminist Internet
Studies* in 2001, these thinkers began to "find themselves in an unexpected
and unsolicited alliance with Internet marketing researchers" who were interested in constructing the internet as a feminine space as part of the medium's
commercialization process.[18] Nascent online retailers clung especially tightly

to statistics indicating that women went online in search of community. As early as 2002, business researchers advised: "Since women enjoy the social aspect of shopping, merchants may wish to consider such features as chat rooms and threaded discussions to build a shopping community and reduce the solitary nature of online shopping."[19]

Since then, countless market research reports have recommended that online businesses incorporate a community component to draw female consumers, even if it means riding on the coattails of an existing social media platform such as Facebook, YouTube, or Twitter. For women's magazine producers, the incentive to offer community spaces and social sharing tools is overlaid with a desire to colonize consumers' social spaces. Thus, these initiatives not only help to immerse consumers in interactive brand spaces, but they also capitalize on the likelihood that females will share these experiences with others in their social networks.

Steve Sachs, a Time Inc. employee for nearly two decades who served as executive vice president of consumer marketing and sales from 2010 through 2012, provided a complementary perspective on the participation of audiences that underscored the willingness of consumers to share personal information. He explained that his job has been fundamentally affected by shifts in consumers' attitudes and behavior. "Five years ago," he recalled, "it was very hard to market to consumers through digital channels. Most people didn't respond to it, didn't like it, preferred to buy off of print ads, TV, or direct ads." Today, by contrast, people voluntarily provide information online, compelled by the twin benefits of convenience and customization. Sachs's comment speaks directly to the profound growth of the online retail industry over the years, fueled by clicks-and-mortar stores as well as internet-only shopping services. Yet his explanation also conveys a new impression of consumers: they *want* to receive microtargeted media and marketing messages—or they at least have come to expect it in today's online commercial culture.

Against this backdrop, we can better understand the ascendancy of the participatory rhetoric circulating within consumer magazine brands. A visit to any women's magazine website or application reveals the multitude of digital spaces in which audience members are "invited" to engage with both producers and other site visitors. I borrow this term from Derek Johnson, whose article "Inviting Audiences In" examines how TV producers are actively aiming to draw audiences into the interactive process through online contests, fan forums, and cross-media promotions.[20] In the case of women's magazines, this phrase takes on additional meaning given their tradition of inviting women in through reader contests and advice columns.

Glamour.com, for instance, allows audiences to comment on the various editors' blogs, email questions to different departments, and develop a personalized workout/eating plan through the "Body by *Glamour*" calculator. Cosmopolitan.com has an entire section devoted to the "Cosmo Community" (http://www.cosmopolitan.com/community/), where visitors can contribute to various thematic message boards, including "Dating and Relationships," "Working Girl," "Men, Men, Men!," and the general "Cosmolicious" forum. Within these sections, the scope of topics varies extensively, ranging from "My friend is having an affair with a married guy" to "Ex's mom's cancer returned . . . what to do" to "I want long hair." In this particular section, the advice comes not from magazine experts, but from other readers who have signed up to participate. This community section is grouped under "Secrets & Advice," and participants can choose their own user name. Of course, such offers of anonymity and secrecy help to deflect from the institutional reality of these sites: they are in the public domain.

The fact that online commentary sometimes becomes fodder for the print publication is made explicit on Allure.com. According to the website, "Our readers' emails inspire story ideas, alert us to new beauty trends, and keep us on our toes. We want to know what you think; write to us now!" In order to submit a comment, visitors must provide their first and last names and their birthdays, sources of information that are quite valuable to marketers and advertising networks. Gender, telephone number, and home address are optional.[21] The bottom of the form stipulates that "all submissions become property of *Allure*; they may be edited and may be published and otherwise used in any medium." We can imagine, then, how viewer commentary can be used as either content or direct—and free—feedback to both *Allure* producers and their advertisers. This speaks directly to an argument Mark Andrejevic offered in his study of the Television Without Pity website: "The promise of virtual participation in the production process . . . invites viewers to adopt the standpoint of producers, and thereby facilitates the conversion of viewer feedback into potentially productive marketing and demographic information."[22]

Some magazine producers have been very diligent about incorporating community spaces into their content in order to connect with readers. According to Ashley Parrish, former senior web editor of *Marie Claire*, "We make it very clear that there is a personality behind our brand accounts. It is about connecting with the community—asking them questions, responding to their queries and creating a conversation about the user, the brand and the content." [23] *Folio*'s Jill Ambroz added that these new tactics are "opening the lines of communication between readers and the publisher to gather new story ideas."[24] Parrish's comment, like the preceding example from *Cosmopolitan*, reveals the importance of the term "community" in conveying a welcoming, collective, and safe space for women.[25] Yet it should also be noted that these various forms of engagement translate into additional time spent on the website—and with the contextual advertisements.

Perhaps more notably, both Hearst and Condé Nast have recently launched highly publicized user-generated campaigns. In 2008, *Cosmopolitan* kicked off "*Cosmopolitan* Starlaunch: The Search for the Next Fun Fearless Female Rockstar." A musical talent search collectively sponsored by Nikon, Pantene, Cover Girl, and bebe, the contest invited hundreds of artists from across the country to upload their performance of an original song to YouTube. A panel of A&R (artists and repertoire) executives whittled the field down to ten semifinalists, and *Cosmopolitan* fans then voted online for their favorite. The success of the campaign was staggering. As *Folio* reported, "The program generated more than 500 auditions with more than 257,000 votes cast for the top ten finalists. The live finale featured a sold-out concert of more than 2,000 paid ticket holders and drove more than 1.9 billion media and press impressions."[26]

Two years later, *Cosmopolitan* launched the international "Fun Fearless Female" promotion, which encouraged women around the world to "be the star" of an ad campaign. The initiative was announced on the brand's YouTube channel with a video featuring then editor-in-chief Kate White, publisher Donna Kalajian Lagani, and former *American Idol* winner Jordin Sparks, among others. "Readers and users around the planet," Lagani said, acknowledging the increasingly global nature of the brand, could upload their photos on the website Cosmofff.com and "see themselves as part of the campaign." Viewers were depicted as "stars" after they added their photos to the *Cosmo* page at Facebook Connect. By letting ostensibly "real women" participate in the campaign, *Cosmopolitan* not only generated significant traffic to its social media sites, including Facebook and Twitter, but it also illustrated to individuals that they could participate in spaces typically reserved for musicians, models, and others employed by the creative industries. Yet in contrast to many contests that involve the production of commercials, jingles, or brand logos, there was very little imagination involved with the *Cosmopolitan* initiative. Although participants likely benefited from their participation (e.g., enjoyed the photo-shoot simulation), they did not provide much in the way of creative labor as it is traditionally conceptualized. Instead, the emphasis remained on the physical aesthetic despite the appeals to "fun" and "fearless[ness]."

Glamour, which incidentally is one of *Cosmopolitan*'s biggest competitors, has used similar themes to buoy its publicity efforts. The company's

2010 "Young and Posh" external ad campaign, for instance, included a user-generated component whereby readers were encouraged to upload their own photographs of denim, leopard, or citrus-hued styles to Glamalert.com. Featured reader selections appeared on the website flanking the typical shots of models. The democratization ethos was quite prominent in public discourse on the campaign. *Glamour* publisher William Wackermann told a *New York Times* reporter, "This is inspired by where the energy in the fashion market is. . . . It's the consumer, it's bottom up, it's a high-low mix."[27] One of my interviewees, an editorial assistant at *Glamour*, shared with me her understanding of the campaign: "[It's] sort of like how you the reader, you're influencing the magazine, you're young and posh. . . . Very new media; you're what's influencing *Glamour* magazine. A lot of this magazine is you. You are *Glamour*." It seems significant that both Wackermann and the editorial staffer conflate changes in the media environment with the way in which *Glamour* positioned itself to its readers and advertisers. Two years later, when Condé Nast executives unveiled their "Generation *Glamour*" campaign, the twin rhetorics of consumer empowerment and authenticity moved to center stage. In addition to the social media initiatives that I discussed in chapter 4, the campaign involved the launch of the website GenerationGlamour.com. Visitors to the site were encouraged to "represent [their] generation . . . [in] a new youth movement" by tagging their Instagram self-portraits.[28]

These enterprises are strikingly similar to user-generated ad contests sponsored by marketers, which offer audiences the potential for exposure while simultaneously capitalizing on their freely provided creations. As Michael Serazio explains in his study of contemporary guerrilla marketing techniques—or "advertising that tries not to seem like advertising"—many user-generated campaigns effectively stage a sense of agency. "Yet," Serazio makes clear, "the premise of viral marketing—and of the user-generated and word-of-mouth techniques of brand evangelism more broadly—is that you *are*, in fact, doing the work of . . . Honda, Burger King, or any other brand."[29] One pertinent example is a participatory contest that Dove developed and promoted by deploying a feminist rhetoric of empowerment in its call for commercial submissions. The polysemic nature of the contest enabled Dove to "simultaneously endorse the product, exploit participant labor, and give consumers a sense of power as individuals, as women, and as creative professionals."[30] These and similar initiatives are the progeny of a cultural moment in which audience attention is a scarce commodity and promotional messages get cloaked in the rhetoric of consumer control.

In early 2012, considerations of interactivity, empowerment, and labor were spotlighted when the venerable *Ladies' Home Journal* announced a noteworthy shift in its approach to content creation and distribution: beginning with the March 2012 issue, readers would provide much of the content for the print magazine. Attributing this change to research on the magazine's readers, editor-in-chief Sally Lee noted, "Usually content creation begins with an editor. We have content creation that begins with a reader."[31] The user-generated content comes from a magazine affiliate, DivineCaroline.com, which encourages users to submit contributions with the possibility of receiving payment. According to the site (which requires registration), "In addition to appearing here on Divine Caroline, your story could be published in *Ladies' Home Journal*, one of the country's most popular magazines! If your story is selected by LHJ editors, you may receive compensation for it. LHJ editors will be in touch with details if your story is selected."[32] Although I was unable to determine exactly how much contributors receive, this marks a break with the noncompensatory system of many other blogs. Many outside publishers were quite skeptical of *Ladies' Home Journal*'s new approach, yet it reflects changing ideas at the intersection of consumer control and editorial oversight.

While these examples provide a flavor of the ways in which female viewers are invited into production spaces, the larger picture that emerged from the interviews was more complicated, signaling tensions related to professional and organizational identities. Some producers articulated consumer participation as a redistribution of producer-consumer control, which had the potential to undermine the magazine's commercial authority. Others discussed the ways in which the information willingly provided by consumers serves as data for magazine companies and their advertisers. As I discuss in the conclusion, this tension may help us to revisit what has been called "the binary opposition between complicit passivity and subversive participation" within most theories of audience feedback.[33] That is, magazine consumers are afforded new opportunities for participation and public feedback, but an unequal distribution of power persists as producers seemingly utilize, or even exploit, this information.

As anticipated, social media executives expressed the most optimistic perspective on the role of user communities and participatory channels. Mark Coatney, director/media evangelist at Tumblr and a former correspondent at *Newsweek*, invoked the open dialogue rhetoric during his keynote address at the MPA Digital: Social Media conference in January 2011. "The whole point of the web is to give readers input. It is incredibly powerful for publishers. We want to be in these conversations and we want to be accountable to our readers. People respond when you play in their sandbox."[34] Coatney's optimism evidences the nature of the event (industry conferences such as this have been described to me by industry insiders as "cheerleading events") as well as his own career objectives. That is, Tumblr's business model is based on this style of accountability; Coatney therefore has a vested interest in attracting magazine publishers to his platform, ensuring its continued growth.

A social media guru and founder of the niche Q&A site Answerology, Matt Milner, former vice president of social media and community at Hearst Digital, mentioned the changing role of consumers several times during our conversation. When I asked him about some of the driving shifts in the twenty-first-century media landscape, he emphasized the weight of social media in giving consumers a communication platform. "I think the big picture is, there is a change in consumers, and the best that any brand can do, whether we are a media brand, is to try to embrace whatever change is happening." In this sense, Milner attributed much of the struggle of the magazine industry to consumers, who wield significant power and can assert new demands on the media industries. Although the corollary to this idea is that advertisers, too, are shifting placement strategies to reach these audiences, Milner was largely focused on the behavior of Hearst consumers. He added, "I think consumers have figured out they are the ones in control." This narrative reflects larger claims about the empowering potential of digital technologies; in practice, however, industrial control is not as easily relinquished.

To this end, Milner admitted that many magazine website editors have been hesitant to "[let] the brands get into the social sphere" out of fear that they will tarnish the magazines' reputations and those of advertisers. Certainly, it is more laborious to control the content provided by consumers, a responsibility that falls mainly on the shoulders of editors. This makes it harder to ensure that the content does not stray too far from the organizational identity of any particular magazine, which producers have historically held in place through exclusive control over published material. Relatedly, Milner admitted that some of his colleagues were wary about sending consumer participants to outside websites and brands to get information.

> A lot of times it goes against the brand to say, "Oh, there's a great article on Popsugar [a women's website focusing on fashion and celebrity] or there's a great article in iVillage [a women's blog that was formerly partnered with Hearst]." It seems sort of counterintuitive to want to send your traffic to your competitors . . . but that's what we're training our brands to do. . . . We get a fair amount of push-back on that one. [Editors will say,] "Are you guys crazy?" [laughter] "Yeah, we are crazy and still trying to do what's best for customers."

Milner's comment speaks to the challenge of magazine consumer expectations without the recourse of traditional methods of content control.

In fact, as consumer audiences are afforded increased access to magazine-branded spaces, producers must decide to what extent they will monitor those spaces—if at all. An examination of beauty reviews, a staple of many women's magazines, provides a glimpse into the struggles that magazine producers confront as they try to balance consumer trust and advertiser politics. As an example, I will draw upon a post from Glamour.com's daily beauty blog, Girls in the Beauty Department, titled "The Cheapie Little Bacne-Buster That's About to Become Your New Summer Skincare Must-Have."[35] The product they reviewed, Neutrogena Deep Clean Sport On-the-Go Cleansing Wipes, included a hyperlink that took visitors to the beauty website Ulta.com, where they could purchase the product. Although the *Glamour* staffers gave the product highly favorable reviews, the reader comments were at times quite critical. As one poster shared, "My skin care specialist told me that Neutrogena acne products are one of the worst things you can put on your skin because of the amount of alcohol in it. The alcohol dries your skin out tremendously. She only recommends their products for people with chronically oily skin. So, no, I won't be trying this out." Another reader agreed with the comment, while several others provided alternatives, including the tongue-in-cheek response, "Or you could just take a shower after you work out." It thus appears doubtful that these comments were monitored or edited before they appeared on the website. If they were, *Glamour* might be hesitant to publish negative reviews of one of its advertisers' products given the long-standing church-state relations discussed earlier in this book.

At the same time, the inclusion of reader quotes such as these within the editorial content of the magazine extensions raises the question of whether it is beneficial to gain viewer trust by creating spaces in the magazine for feedback—be it positive or negative. The bridal magazine and website brand the *Knot* is a perfect example of letting consumers participate to the extent that it doubles as a peer-to-peer networking forum. Although it is a commercial site that relies heavily on advertising, recent brides freely rave or rant about individuals and companies that played a role in their wedding. Brianna Brunecz, who was an account executive at *The Knot* for more than five years, noted that "credibility plummets" if reader comments are not published on the website right away.

However, we might imagine a scenario where an advertiser wants the comments framing its product to be carefully vetted for controversial content. *Seventeen*'s vice president and publisher, Jayne Jamison, for example, spoke at length to me about the interactive features that are available on Seventeen.com. When I asked her if she feared that consumer content would get out of control, she confirmed that the company does monitor its platforms for provocative content, which can be pulled down immediately. Incidentally, the Answerology platform that Milner developed and brought to Hearst (*Seventeen*'s parent company) has been positioned as a way for advertisers to avoid problematic adjacencies. As he told a trade industry reporter in 2009, "A lot of advertisers are concerned about inappropriate adjacency. . . . They're wondering what people are going to say next to their ads, but they trust brands like *Cosmo*, and Answerology allows them to be in the flow of what our users are doing."[36] This indicates that the rhetoric of consumer empowerment and democratization is fraught with tension for producers, who fear upsetting the delicate advertising/magazine industry balance.

A somewhat different strategy for dealing with potentially controversial content involves limiting user contributions to certain spaces carefully carved out by producers. For example, Hannah Morrill told me that InStyle .com's editors opted not to leave their "Beauty Product Reviews" section open to reader comments. "We decided people come to us for expertise; user-product reviews are not what we do," she said. Then, in a nod toward editorial-advertiser relations, she explained that things could easily get out of hand if "there are a thousand people saying they hate something we review." This suggests, then, that the fear that readers will write negative things about the products reviewed (and possibly advertised) in the magazine is a key factor in determining where viewer input is welcome—and where it is not. In this particular instance, disabling the user comment function serves two purposes: it reaffirms the boundaries between experts and ordinary people, while it also prevents the sticky wicket of having consumers post negative reviews of advertised products. The first is important for the professional identity of magazine creators; the second ensures that the advertising-editorial relation that defines the organizational identity of women's magazines remains intact. While the preceding examples illustrate how producers are responding to—and even working with—interactive audiences within magazine spaces, they are also forced to contend with a recent flood of amateur cultural producers who regularly produce fashion- and style-related images, information, and commentary: fashion bloggers.

Bloggers: The New Fashion Elites?

In less than a decade, fashion blogging has evolved from a scattershot collection of indie style musings into a burgeoning industry in which individuals with little or no training in fashion arts are rubbing elbows with the cognoscenti of the magazine industry. Indeed, many bloggers now enjoy the enviable privileges of traditional magazine editors: highly coveted tickets to Fashion Week events, lavish product freebies, and exclusive interviews with high-fashion elites. In 2011, Tumblr gave twenty-four of the site's top fashion bloggers the opportunity to attend New York Fashion Week, putting them up in a hotel and giving them access to backstage tours and a premier rooftop party.[37] One of the most renowned bloggers, Bryanboy, has been featured in countless newspapers and magazines and has the esteemed designation of "Marc Jacobs' favorite [blogger]." His position as an *America's Next Top Model* judge in 2013 further indexes the encroachment of fashion bloggers on traditional industry circuits.

The ascendance of fashion blogging culture fits cozily into a larger rhetoric about political-economic shifts in the fashion industry over the decade. The fact that haute couture designers such as Jason Wu, Vera Wang, and Norma Kamali now produce fashion lines for mass retailers Target, Kohl's, and Walmart, respectively, demonstrates the so-called democratization of style. As *Washington Post* fashion editor Robin Givhan proclaimed in an article published (not incidentally) in *Harper's Bazaar,* "The rise of the fashion blogger was inevitable. Fashion has evolved from an autocratic business dominated by omnipotent designers into a democratic one in which everyone has access to stylish clothes, anyone can start a trend, and the definition of designer—Donald Trump!—has become astonishingly malleable."[38] There are a number of plausible explanations for this movement, including generational differences, consumers' recession-conscious spending habits, and, of course, technologies that allow "anyone" to be visible in the mediated public sphere. Gesturing toward the latter trend, reporter Caitlin Brown commented, "Though often criticized for their lack of fashion education and credibility, the rising popularity of bloggers is allowing regular Janes like you and me to become part of the international fashion conversation."[39]

Digital communication devices that offer instantaneous access to fashion shows have also helped to fuel this democratization by significantly reducing the time from the runway to the real world. In announcing Style.com's movement from Condé Nast in 2010, the *Wall Street Journal's* Russell Adams said, "The internet has empowered shoppers to influence tastes and set trends, blurring the line between consumers and professionals."[40] The perspectives of Givhan, Brown, and Adams share a consideration of how technologies—and the digital zeitgeist—are allowing nonprofessionals to participate in media spaces formerly reserved for professionally trained cultural producers. The integration of nonprofessionals is not unique to the fashion industry; scholars have explored the democratization of other sites of cultural production, including films, news, and video game design. To some, this trend productively destabilizes top-down and bottom-up as fixed production heuristics, opening up fluid movement within and between these roles.[41]

Yet it is important to keep the perceived distinction between bloggers and professionals readily in mind; the former's assumed distance from the marketplace means that they are considered to be more authentic sources of information than paid magazine staffers. As Kathryn Finney, founder of TheBudgetFashionista.com, remarked, "If you're a junior writer at *Vogue*, you can't write a scathing review of Oscar de La Renta. Whereas, as a blogger, I have a lot more flexibility because my boss is me."[42] Assumptions about the transparency of blogs have nurtured in consumers a heightened sense of trust. According to a 2011 study jointly conducted by blogging and consumer research agencies, blogs are more than two times more likely than magazines to have inspired a beauty product purchase over the last six months.[43] A similar study published in 2012 indicated that blogs and newcomer social media site Pinterest have surpassed even Facebook when it comes to consumers' reliance on consumer recommendations for product decisions.[44]

Despite—or more likely because of—the presumed authenticity of peer-to-peer reviews, a number of advertisers have turned to fashion blogs in an effort to reach splintering consumer markets. An American Apparel executive who used the Fashion Hive blogger network to reach audiences enthused, "The blog culture targets an audience that regular online campaigns cannot—real people talking to real people. Bloggers offer an authentic word of mouth. . . . In addition to the conventionally recorded results, I'm really excited about the un-recorded aspects of this advertising—the fact that it's a discussion, not just yelling into a crowd."[45] The advertising opportunities on many blogs parallel those of magazine brands and include banner ads, newsletter sponsorships, events, giveaways, and more. The "Advertise" section of the Budget Fashionista blog, for instance, includes the same types of information found in traditional magazine media kits: audience demographics, circulation/page visits, and a rate card. It also boasts an impressive sixth-position search ranking in Google, along with some unique opportunities for advertisers: they can buy a sponsored post for $2,000 or sponsor a contest for $2,500.[46]

The flight of audiences to the blogosphere for fashion and beauty content highlights the business challenges for contemporary magazine producers. From an organizational identity perspective, discourses of blogger guidance and trust indicate the potential for Web 2.0 platforms to erode the central, distinctive, and enduring traits of women's magazines. This is layered upon the threat to the professional identities of well-known magazine editors and writers: their importance may be dwindling. As I discussed in chapter 1, the editor-in-chief traditionally played a fundamental role in defining the personality of the magazine and was largely responsible for marketing the publication through a highly visible public persona.[47] Today, however, the role of senior editors may be disintegrating as a new generation of trendsetters step into the limelight. As a *Financial Times* reporter asked, "What happens when following the fashion herd becomes wisdom of the masses? When 'citizen' journalists replace glossy magazines as oracles of fashion?"[48]

The relationship between fashion bloggers and magazine editors is tension-wrought, at least according to popular media narratives that pit them against each other in a proverbial war. Some professionals are quite dismissive of blogs, while others have criticized their undue recognition within professional circuits. For instance, *Vogue Italia* editor Franca Sozzani shared her view on fashion blogging in her editor's blog: "Why are they so credited? Why do they sit in front row? Why does the Chamber of Italian Fashion thinks so highly of them, so much as to provide them with a driver during the shows as it's happened during menswear? . . . These aren't people who have been working in fashion too long to end up criticizing everything, the shows, and they don't have a background in fashion so they are not conditioned by their knowledge or interests. Their comments are naïf and enthusiastic. They don't hold a real importance in the business."[49] To Sozzani, bloggers do not merit accreditation, as they have not undergone rigorous training in fashion design, styling, and merchandising. She also discounts their lack of experience, a nod to the fact that many bloggers are quite young and see blogging as a hobby.

Other industry veterans have suggested that bloggers are mere publicity darlings. As Vogue.com UK editor Dolly Jones said critically, "[Public relations] plants stories with certain bloggers who are influential. Those have a ripple effect. It's a really powerful selling tool."[50] Similarly, in an exposé on the surge of fashion blogging endorsement deals during Fashion Week 2012, *New York Times* reporter Ruth La Ferla contended that many fashion bloggers are no longer "showily outfitted swans . . . click-clack[ing] on the pavements, showing off a mash-up of vintage clothes, fast fashion and high-end labels in what used to be seen as a commerce-free zone." Increasingly, they are "billboards for brands," who unreservedly showcase the wares of neophyte designers while publicly promoting their own brand personae. The most recognizable bloggers can reportedly earn between $2,000 and $10,000 for one of these under-the-radar endorsement agreements.[51] These sorts of activities have generated skepticism among mainstream media, especially those in the women's magazine industry.

The opposing perspective, from the bloggers themselves, is that they provide readers with unique perspectives on style and beauty within a supportive, unbiased peer-to-peer community. The genre of "street style" blogging, in particular, celebrates the distinctive styles of everyday people in a way that seems to shun commercially created, mainstream styles. Further, bloggers frequently contend that they, too, are seasoned in the craft and can draw upon their own professional experiences to provide relevant information to readers. A member of the Independent Fashion Bloggers network described the work and commitment that goes into maintaining a site, noting, "For goodness sakes, some of us may be, even, you know, professionals."[52]

Given the clashing perspectives captured in contemporary discourses of fashion blogging and magazines, I was interested in how the individuals I spoke with understood the culture and practice of blogging. When I asked Time Inc.'s executive vice president for consumer marketing and sales, Steve Sachs, about his perspective on contemporary trends such as citizen journalism and blogs, he told me that while they did change the business, they were not considered a "threat." Instead, he said, "our job is to figure out where the opportunity [is] in changing consumer preferences." He then shifted the discussion to social media, particularly Facebook, which he considered "more important" than other forms of consumer-created content. While the growth of social media sites has certainly cast a shadow on some individual blogs, Sachs's equanimity toward them may reflect his involvement in other areas of publishing beyond fashion and beauty. In other words, because his professional identity as a marketing executive has very little overlap with individual fashion bloggers, this issue may not be particularly relevant to him.

Other informants were not as dismissive of or as critical about blogs as we might expect. Instead, most acknowledged the need to respond to the blogging culture, albeit for different reasons. Some individuals considered fashion blogs to be a competitive threat, in that they draw audience members' attention away from traditional content spaces. *InStyle* deputy managing editor Lisa Arbetter explained, "Women's magazines are competing with so many blogs that are covering the same fashions and celebrity news and carrying the same photos that we are. It forces magazine editors to think creatively. Packaging information and adding layers of service are where we excel and give readers something daily news producers cannot." Her concession that the fashion and celebrity blogs are "covering the same fashions and celebrity news and carrying the same photos" indicates that producers may on some level consider them to be an organizational identity threat. The latter part of this comment is aimed at the fact that many blogs provide continuous news updates, some of which are shared through social media platforms such as Twitter and Tumblr.

In a similar vein, Debi Chirichella, who was Condé Nast Digital's chief operating officer from 2008 to 2011, enumerated some of the reasons why it is more difficult for women's content producers to achieve the same online scale as men's and news sites. "There are so many places for women to get information: so many beauty sites, so many fashion blogs." She added, "The infinite shelf space of the internet just makes it harder because anybody can set up a blog and a lot of them do, so there's a lot more noise." Chirichella feels, then, that lowered technological barriers to entry are to blame for the onslaught of blogs. Her likening of blogs to "noise," though, signals a value hierarchy of content, where most blogs are on a lower tier than professional content sites.

From the perspectives of Arbetter and Chirichella, the fashion and beauty content market is fiercer online because of ubiquitous content coming from a variety of sources. However, others seemed to believe that there was something unique about women's fashion blogs. Justine Harman, who moved from People.com to an assistant editor position at *Elle* in 2012, noted, "If you peruse [a blog such as Fashionista], you see the emergence of the importance of these few voices in digital." She continued, "It's a very small, [tight]-knit group, and so, if you have the right voice and you have the right contacts, it's very easy to really communicate what you want to the powers that be in the fashion community." Instead of noting bloggers' closeness to the audience, as we might expect, Harman signals their distinctive relationship with the fashion community.

Additionally, Harman suggested that both the timing and the accessibility of the internet have been instrumental in the success of fashion blogging culture. Regular people, she explained, now have the chance to get fashion "brand messaging" much more quickly than before. "[Digital] gives even the most clueless shopper the sentiment that they are more clued in to what is cool and in fashion. . . . It makes fashion much more accessible." The timing of fashion is particularly detrimental to magazines, since their publication cycle was traditionally scheduled to coincide with the seasonal cycle of retailers. Fashion mavens eager to learn what is trending for the coming season may not want to wait until the eponymous spring and fall fashion issues hit newsstands.

Vintage fashion blogger Sammy Davis told me that "more and more women are turning to personal blogs for their fashion information, and turning away from the big dot-coms of the magazines." She felt that a key limitation of a contemporary women's magazine is its "nebulous voice." Her reference to voice is not insignificant; it has been argued that a magazine's voice is a central indicator of its identity.[53] Davis added that a lot of magazines are struggling because "they can't say the things that everyone can relate [to]. They are almost intimidating. People don't want to connect to them." On the other hand, she said that the strength of fashion and beauty blogs is the uniquely personal advice they provide to audiences—as well as the authenticity that goes along with it. Indeed, she assumed that "being 100% authentic" and listening to readers, rather than metrics, was one of the reasons the blogging community continues to thrive.

Davis's comment suggests that consumers may be less likely to trust professional sources because they are dependent on advertising and thus susceptible to economic pressures. As Cate Corcoran explained in an article in *Women's Wear Daily*, "Bloggers see themselves as truth tellers in a world where the truth is hard to come by." Corcoran cited one blogger as saying, "What we offer is a personal point of view. I love magazines, but they can come across as corporate."[54] Of course, some fashion blogs, too, are becoming progressively corporatized, nuancing the distinction between professional and amateur. This may indeed be the case with blogging networks affiliated with corporate sites. During my second interview with Davis, which occurred after she had signed a contract with AOL's women's lifestyle network Lemondrop, she referenced the benefits to advertisers in particular:

> Mostly from the point of view of advertising, it's really great because of the increased page views, so campaigns are going to be across the boards on AOL and embedded in the blogger' sites. Then we have the option of doing brand-sponsored posts. So say like [X brand], so we would style [an X brand] dress or something. But it's all up to us creatively. So that is where you get [the notion of a wall of] separation between church and state. The old-school way of things. We don't have to integrate the advertising into our blogs. But you get more money if you do. . . . However, we are not told what to do. You can do whatever you want. At least from what I understand, they don't make you post advertisers' products.

Davis's commentary is noteworthy on several counts. For one, it means that bloggers may negotiate editorial integrity with commercial pressures, a balancing act that traditional magazines have long performed. What is more, we can see how advertisers may turn to blogs for the precise reason that audiences supposedly consider them to be more trustworthy sources of information and commentary—the presumption that they are "authentic." Neither bloggers nor advertisers have much incentive to disavow this label; and for some bloggers (those who have achieved even modest success from advertising sponsorships), the ideal of blogger authenticity serves as a *productive myth.* That is, the themes of authenticity and autonomy that bloggers draw on conceal the fact that they are often embedded in the same commercial milieu as those institutional sites from which they distance themselves. This may help to explain why magazine workers and fashion bloggers perform a strange dance in which they sometimes critique and at other times celebrate one another.

Harman's perspective on the commercial impetus of online content was closely aligned with this view. She believed that the lack of professional standards on the internet meant that bloggers were more likely to accept financial and product incentives from advertisers. Harman's outlook is that the increasingly blurred church-state line in magazines is a logical upshot of the fashion blogging trend. When I asked her how this relates to the blogs themselves, she said that the ethics are completely different from those of print. "People come to expect the internet as to not be [ethical]. You have to take everything with a grain of salt that you read online." She then clarified, "That's not to say that the people who are responsible for the content online don't hold themselves to those standards. I just don't think it's expected."

What is particularly important about the perspectives of these current and former magazine professionals is that they reveal how fashion blogs not only serve as competition for the industry, but also seemingly erode the defining features of magazines. However, these individuals defined identity in different ways, including content uniqueness (Arbetter), form (Chirichella), and personal voice (Davis and Harman). Each of these harks back to some aspect of the historical identity markers of women's magazines.

Responding to Fashion Blogging Culture

Magazine producers both directly and indirectly indicated the strategies they are pursuing to shore up the boundaries around their profession while helping the magazine industry sustain its luster. Two particular strategies—publicly reaffirming professional expertise and incorporating blogging into their own brands—emanated from the cacophony of interview and industry discourse on blogs. Whether or not these responses to blogging culture are organic or calculated, they nonetheless fortify the boundaries around magazine brands and the personae that constitute them.

The first strategy among professionals is to turn the spotlight on their own expertise, shrewdly invalidating the convergence narrative that "anyone" can be a fashion/beauty/style expert. Examples abound of magazine professionals (typically the editor-in-chief) who allow audiences mediated access to their work lives, showcasing their inherent talent, their experience, or some combination of the two. As Tara Liss-Mariño, Katherine Sender, and I argue in our analysis of contemporary television depictions of media industries, such activities illustrate the reflexive responses of media producers facing threats of deprofessionalization. In describing the ways in which contemporary TV producers portray media industries, we contend:

> [Their depictions] emphasized that successful media professionals are hard working and uniquely talented, drawing on implicit and explicit references to producers' education and experience within their respective fields. . . . On one hand, this paradigm of the toiling creative genius opens up the seemingly impenetrable world of the media elite: it is talent and dedication (accessible to all, at least, in theory) rather than social status or connections that account for these characters' achievements. And yet the shows intimate that practitioners in these select industries have been admitted precisely because of their inherent abilities and unwavering perseverance. As a result, they stand above the flood of "ordinary" people in non-professional media roles.[55]

This implicit hierarchy of value seems equally applicable to magazine producers, who seek to publicly distance themselves from ordinary people-*cum*-fashion bloggers by emphasizing their own regimes and indicators of expertise.

Indeed, the past few years have seen a marked increase in reality TV programs devoted to top magazine titles, including *Marie Claire* (*Running in Heels*), *Seventeen* (*Miss Seventeen*), *Elle* (*Stylista* and *Project Runway*), and the rumored *Harper's* TV project *Fabulous at Any Age*. *Elle* was an early frontrunner in reality television, turning to the genre to spotlight its brand and its staff personalities. In 2004, then fashion director Nina Garcia appeared on the first season of Bravo's *Project Runway*. Although a *New York Times* reporter noted that "many magazine editors would balk at opening themselves up to the cameras," Garcia saw this as a way to "get the brand out there." Further, she felt that "regardless of the drawbacks—overexposure of certain editors and putting the less glamorous aspects of the business on display, just to name two—the power of television trumps any misgivings."[56] The *Teen Vogue* office also doubled as a reality TV set in the mid-2000s when MTV star Lauren Conrad began an internship there, which was documented on her reality series *The Hills*.

As I mentioned in chapter 3, former *Marie Claire* editor-in-chief Joanna Coles brought up *Running in Heels* during our discussion of the movement from a magazine to a brand. Coles was not hesitant to admit that the show was a way to draw in new readers during an adverse period of magazine publishing. It and similar programs showcase the hard work and stress involved with a position in the dog-eat-dog women's magazine industry. Unlike the traditional tropes of reality television, then, these depictions deflate the image of instantaneous fame. This narrative essentially erects a boundary between those who have access to this industry and those who do not, namely bloggers. Yet it also becomes apparent that this is a fast-paced, complex work environment that places intense demands on workers—a world far removed from the "leisure" realm of blogging.

The reality TV genre is not the only mediated site that showcases the magazine profession and highlights its impenetrable boundaries. *The Devil Wears Prada*, *Ugly Betty*, and *13 Going on 30* are among the fictional representations of the industry that have circulated in recent years. Yet perhaps the most striking example is *The September Issue*, R. J. Cutler's 2009 documentary about *Vogue* editor-in-chief Anna Wintour and her staff as they work tirelessly to produce the magazine's coveted September issue. Wintour is depicted as shrewd, inaccessible, and cold, and the staff and fashion designers' worship of her only intensifies the admiration of her within fashion circles. Showing Wintour in this light reaffirms why she is in a position of power with a cadre of individuals waiting for her every approving nod. The industrial culture is neither relaxed nor glitzy, but rather quite taxing on most of the employees.

Vanessa Voltolina, a former *Folio* reporter who now creates women's content for NBC Universal's digital properties, spoke to me about the crucial need for magazines to have a voice at this particular historical juncture: "It's a generalization, but as the market becomes populated with women's lifestyle magazines and websites, many [magazines] have either maintained or strived for a stronger voice. Often, a strong voice can help lead to a larger market share; without a strong point of view or differentiating content, you [a magazine] may be in danger of going under or having a very low readership." From Voltolina's perspective, the best way to beat market competition is to emphasize the editorial experience of experts, reaffirming their professional identity. The onscreen depictions of the personalities behind the magazines seem to do just that as they distance these figures from those who are not afforded televised access to the masses.

The second tactic used by magazine producers involves weaving blogs and bloggers into the fabric of the print magazine and, to a greater extent, the magazine websites. Many titles now require that editors-in-chief and other creative executives publish blogs on the website, adding a new layer of responsibilities and coordination to those socialized in the demands of print. In addition to its clear business logic, this change also helps to ensure that the personal voice of print and online components is consistent.

At the same time, many women's magazines are hiring high-profile bloggers to produce columns for the magazine brands; Wilson Lowrey and others have already explored this "amalgamation" in the context of news media.[57] Sometimes well-known individuals from the blogging community are asked to pen a single column. Most notably, *Harper's* asked blogger Tavi Gevinson, who was just thirteen at the time, to review its spring collection for the January 2010 print edition. That Gevinson has come to symbolize the blogger-versus-editor debate is not incidental; many magazine editors scoffed when this young woman was given a front-row seat at Fashion Week. Her incorporation into the magazine was, somewhat expectedly, described as a publicity stunt. In the men's fashion category, the well-known blogger The Sartorialist was hired to produce a monthly column for *GQ*.

In other examples, the assimilation of bloggers becomes part of a highly visible cross-media campaign. In 2009, *Seventeen* invited ten young women with top-ranked YouTube vlogs (video logs) to create beauty looks for the magazine. Editor-in-chief Ann Shoket publicly acknowledged that the young women were selected because they were already "'stars' on YouTube and thus brought to the table thousands of followers and millions of video plays." In addition to creating looks for the *Seventeen* website, these "Beauty Smarties" were encouraged to use social media—Facebook and MySpace—to "drive users back to the site."[58] Also in 2009, *Teen Vogue* published a piece called "Key Players," featuring a group of fledging fashion writers. The opening paragraph read, "They're not designers, stylists, or magazine editors—yet. The next generation of influential fashion forces is making its mark online with buzzed-about style blogs."[59] Implying that these teens may one day step into the coveted role of magazine editor only reinforces the narrative that it takes considerable work and a professional position to "make it big" in the industry.

Magazines' incorporation of bloggers reached new heights in 2011 with Glamour.com's launch of the "Young and Posh" fashion network, consisting of twenty-three popular fashion bloggers who produce regular content for *Glamour*. In announcing the initiative, the website noted, "We gathered some of our favorite personal style bloggers who spend their days making the interwebs a super chic (and oh-so distracting) place to be. For a daily dose of fashion inspiration, hang out with them every day here on Glamour. com!" Not only are the blogs hosted on a designated page on Glamour.com, but a link to the page is also included at the original blog URL. The boon to *Glamour* is quite apparent: these bloggers bring their own fan bases to the site, simultaneously increasing page views and reinforcing the brand identity of *Glamour* as fashion-forward. This fits within a larger strategy that publishers are being encouraged to employ as they adapt to a torrent of amateur creators. As media consultant Stephen M. Saunders contended, despite the fear of losing advertiser credibility, publishers need to realize that "if you build blogs into your network, so the Web 2.0 hope has it, the audience will come."[60]

The branding of this campaign as "Young and Posh" deserves critical reflection, too, particularly as this was part of a promotional effort to showcase the Glamour *identity* to audiences and advertisers alike. One blogger, not affiliated with the network, hailed the network on her own site for "bringing together the magazine and blogger worlds to celebrate fashion democracy—the belief that any girl with wit, personal style, and a camera can inform us about what is fashionable, that every girl has a voice where fashion is concerned."[61] This collaboration opens up a space for amateur producers while simultaneously confirming that the ultimate goal is to be affiliated with *Glamour*—as a reader or, more significantly, a magazine blogger. Again, the rhetoric underpinning this campaign is that a career in publishing is the ultimate marker of success.

Accordingly, several of the young women I interviewed told me that they saw their blogs and online contributions as a springboard to a career in the magazine industry. Recalling her former days on the job market, Justine Harman believed that creating and maintaining a blog would give her an edge over the competition: "For years, I tried to get a job at a magazine, probably in the worst time ever to try to get that job. I decided that for me to be a really strong candidate, I had to have an additional skill set that would separate me from everyone else. So I decided that digital was the wave of the future; I had to get on board or nobody [in the business] was going to look at me. I switched my mentality and [decided], 'All right, I'm going digital'. . . and [I] started the blog." Harman credits this experience, and the digital "buzzwords" it enabled her to add to her resume, with helping her to land the position at People.com/*People StyleWatch*. Another young woman I interviewed said that she, too, hoped to pursue a career in the women's magazine industry, an aspiration that had led her circuitously into digital publishing, blogging for a magazine trade paper, and ultimately writing women's content. The professional trajectory of blogger Sammy Davis is also telling. Although she transitioned from the magazine world to the blogosphere, she acknowledged that bloggers (herself included) will someday "move on to bigger and better things." These accounts suggest that there is a kernel of truth to the narrative that blogging can be a first step on the path to a magazine career. Whether purposefully or not, these instances also establish a hierarchy among women's fashion sources that positions traditional magazines on the highest tiers.

Conclusion

Participatory forms of media—user-generated content, digitally enabled communities, blogs, and more—are symptomatic of an era in which the tools and technologies of communication are ostensibly up for grabs. For magazine producers, the act of inviting audiences into branded content spaces can be both challenging and opportunistic. With regard to the former point, there is substantial risk involved with integrating consumers into the production process or, to echo Matt Milner's works, "let[ting] the brands get into the social sphere." Audiences may critique the content of a magazine or, worse, that of an advertiser, thus upsetting the delicate balance between the creators and receivers of magazine messages. At the same time, deploying the seductive participation-as-empowerment rhetoric portends great rewards. Magazine executives and producers can harness the information and creative contributions freely provided by audiences while publicizing their close relationship with these "real women."

In this context, consumer engagement in user-generated initiatives, community features, and contests becomes a form of "immaterial labor," which Maurizio Lazzarato defines as "the labor that produces the informational and cultural content of the commodity."[62] As this content spreads like wildfire through consumers' social networks, its value is amplified and enacted as the "labor of devotion."[63] That the consumers tend to be female makes these appeals doubly powerful—or, conversely, problematic—as this rhetoric becomes productively entangled with progressive gender politics.[64] This can be thought of as a reification of the deep-rooted relationship between gender, social relations, and commodity culture that I discussed in chapter 1. Importantly, I am not suggesting that participants in magazine-branded spaces are cultural dupes who blindly do the work of professional content creators; pleasure, socialization, expertise, and self-promotion are among the rewards of these activities. However, some individuals may not be fully aware of the economic incentives underlying their participation.

The question that seems to bubble up to the surface is this: How do producers *invite audiences in* without handing over the reins to their processes and products? One way is through the enactment of boundaries within content spaces. Indeed, we can perhaps think of the architecture of many interactive sites in accordance with what convergence scholar Eggo Müller described as "formatted spaces of participation." Rather than characterizing magazine texts as wholly open (read: democratic), this definition foregrounds how such spaces have their own routinized practices, institutionalized "with their own specific, cultural conventions and ideologies."[65] Some formatted spaces are clearly visible, particularly those on magazine websites that organize content according to thematic categories such as "beauty," "sex," "community," and "college life." These categories structure the types of contributions that are considered acceptable and those that are not—such as discordant topics that might dampen what Ben Bagdikian has referred to as the "buying mood."[66]

It could be argued that print publications have simultaneously invited people in and goaded them back into their traditional roles for some time. In her study of women's weekly titles in the late 1990s, Caroline Oates concluded, "The agenda . . . and the way they represent women, remain largely outside of the realm of the reader, yet the illusion of readers being allowed to participate in and even write their own magazine is an image offered by editors."[67] This argument is even more applicable today, when discourses of community, participation, and power circulate throughout various magazine platforms and within the larger media milieu. What is more, by exhibiting control mechanisms that bound participatory spaces, producers reaffirm their professional identities (as professional experts) as well as the identity of their organizations and brands.

Of course, magazine producers have neither the capacity nor the resources to wield control over all participatory forms of media, and the burgeoning culture of fashion blogging may be the clearest indicator of this. Fashion bloggers have the potential to erode magazines' unique position in this market (an index of organizational identity) as well as to supplant the expertise of prominent editors-in-chief (indexes of both organizational and professional identity). Yet discussions of "fashion bloggers" need to be sufficiently nuanced. By this, I mean that it is critical to distinguish prominent fashion bloggers from the endless mass of "ordinary" individuals who post on fashion, beauty, and service topics. There are perhaps only a handful of bloggers who have achieved the level of success necessary to pose a true threat to women's magazines; these individuals seem to exist in a unique liminal space between corporate professionals and average consumers.

Leadbeater and Miller's framework of "Pro-Am" professional-amateur hybrids is a useful way to conceptualize these thriving fashion bloggers. Pro-Ams, as they explain, are "innovative, committed and networked amateurs . . . working to professional standards."[68] It is likely that the Pro-Ams of the fashion blogging world are the individuals most likely to be incorporated into the magazines. While this integration might indeed be reciprocally beneficial, Mark Andrejevic raises the controversial idea that incorporation activities may be a form of enclosure. "The goal of enclosure is to capture productive resources in order to set the terms of access to them." In the digital age, he continues, "if information becomes an increasingly important source of value, then 'enclosure' refers to attempts to establish property rights over it and the resources involved in its production."[69] In the context of the fashion industry, magazine producers conceivably see the amalgamation of bloggers as a way to capture human capital resources while preserving the symbiosis between the fashion and magazine industries.

Taken together, these examples present a more nuanced view of participatory culture than that espoused by Jay Rosen in the opening of this chapter. Certainly, new entrants into the women's magazine industry are causing realignments in identity constructions: individual (gendered), professional, and organizational. Yet the overall impact on the boundary-defining activities of producers is rather modest in terms of power redistributions. This is not to dismiss the idea that recent technological and economic shifts have engendered significant organizational restructuring; to the contrary, they have. However, notions of sweeping changes in the media system and wholly opened-up professional spaces are exaggerated, or perhaps the result of misplaced convergence foci. As similar debates are taking place at the level of *media* convergence, it seems critical to address this issue in depth.

6

Off the Page

Medium-Specific Approaches to Content

The cover story of the May 2009 issue of *Publishing Executive*, a resource for magazine professionals involved in business management, print and e-media production, and audience development, featured an inaugural list of the "Top Women in Magazine Publishing." One of the honorees, Dwell Media president and publisher Michela O'Connor Abrams, issued a clarion call to her publishing peers: "Publishing is platform agnostic. The sooner any publisher recognizes that they represent a content brand that serves a community, the better off they will be. No publisher should be without a cohesive online, mobile, event and print content strategy. . . . Put your community at the center of your brand by tailoring and expressing your content on every possible platform."[1] From her perspective, two simultaneous strategies will pave the road to publishing success in the digital economy: the collapse of traditional media boundaries ("a content brand") and the unguarded embrace of interactive ("community") features. Magazine content, then, should flow effortlessly off the printed page and across online, mobile, and outdoor spaces. The religious symbolism inherent in the term "platform agnostic" is not incidental; by deflating the image of print as the supreme deity of the magazine universe, agnosticism offers an alternative to "traditional" media orthodoxies inherited from the pre-digital age. What Abrams fails to acknowledge, however, are the practical challenges involved with implementing a platform-agnostic approach.

In the face of emergent cross-platform and convergent media logics, producers confront many issues and questions that may unsettle their deeply ingrained cultural practices. For example, should the same type of content that gets created for the magazine *qua* magazine circulate online and across mobile and tablet formats? Or should content vary depending upon the platform for which it is produced? Can the norms and guidelines established for the print magazine stretch to accommodate new content demands? Or, conversely, should producers rethink traditional approaches to content, audiences, and advertisers? And, finally, what do the responses to such questions portend for magazine producers and consumers in the digital age?

This chapter finds answers to these questions by uncovering producers' explicit conventions and implicit assumptions about medium-specific content. Rooted in film and cinema studies, media specificity theory is predicated on the idea that each medium has "essential and unique characteristics" that differentiate it from other expressive forms.[2] This notion thus runs contrary to the current logic of convergence (blurring of different media), revealing tensions in terms of the organizational identity—central, distinctive, and enduring traits—of sites of production. Against this backdrop, I show how the practical realities of media convergence are much more complicated than contemporary narratives indicate. On the surface, magazine industry leaders appear confident about the opportunities for magazine content to move across digital sites and platforms. Yet behind this thin veil of optimism lie individual and organizational practices that continue to affirm the particularities of various media and, especially, the longevity of print.

I examine the apparent disjuncture between rhetoric and reality by focusing on three key media/platform variances: content standards, the centrality of a title's editorial voice, and expectations about the extent of advertiser influence on content. The distinctions between print and online are particularly compelling; in addition, tablet devices are being positioned as a tool that can elide medium-specific challenges while also serving as a test bed for advertising/editorial relations within digital environments. In the end, it seems that magazine content does not easily flow off the printed page, but rather swirls in the midst of many crosscurrents.

The Industry Rhetoric of Convergence

Media convergence describes the confluence of formerly separate technologies onto a single device; it implicates the crumbling of traditional media boundaries to make room for the ascendance of multi-platform media brands. "Convergence" and sister terms such as "platform agnosticism," "cross-platform," and "media brands" were frequently invoked during interviews and within accounts published in the trade and mainstream presses.

Yet the deployment of these terms was highly uneven; that is, individual magazine producers exhibited a high degree of reflexivity about the various meanings and applications of this new lexicon. This brought the tension between the reality and the rhetoric of media convergence into stark relief.

Industry associations, which according to sociologists Paul DiMaggio and Walter Powell provide organizations with models for change at moments of uncertainty, have swiftly and fully adopted the convergence rhetoric.[3] As early as 2005, the Magazine Publishers of America, as the MPA was called at the time, convened a panel on platform agnosticism; two years later, the "MagaBrand Revolution" conference encouraged producers to think of the magazine as a franchise instead of a medium. But nowhere was the rhetoric of convergence more central than at the 2010 American Magazine Conference. There, before an audience of hundreds of media executives, publishing professionals, and digital experts, MPA leaders unveiled the association's new name: MPA—The Association of Magazine Media. As MPA president Nina Link explained during the opening session:

> While many of us have print editions in countries spanning the world, digital technologies enable all of us to have a presence that circles the globe. Our footprint easily and instantly extends far beyond the borders of this country. . . . So, what should our new *identity* reflect in a world of continuing change?
>
> After much debate, we concluded that while media platforms and business models may vary, what remains constant are trusted magazine brands that provide curated content with strong audience relationships and communities of interest. We wanted to create a term that embraced magazines and all their multi-platform businesses, print and digital, present and future . . . a term that suggested the wider and deeper range of activities that our members were engaged in. So we coined the term "Magazine Media."[4]

From the perspective of the MPA, "magazine media" is a term that both captures and reflects technological and economic shifts that are propelling the industry into new markets *and* new content spaces. Link's pronouncement was presumably an attempt to reorient individuals and organizations around a new industrial identity that, while cemented in history ("what remains constant are . . ."), also marks a substantial break with the print-bound past. The complexity of redefining the magazine is thus redressed by the all-encompassing notion of "multi-platform businesses."

Like Dwell Media's Michela O'Connor Abrams, Link speaks in the new magazine language of *brands*, *platforms*, and *communities*. Yet the nuanced interpretations of these terms are noteworthy, bound up as they are with

individual assumptions and professional and organizational identity constructions. When I asked Howard Polskin, MPA's executive vice president
of communications and events, whether print magazines were considered
"platforms," he responded, "Magazines use many different platforms to reach
[the] audience. Magazine media means multi-platform." *Seventeen's* Jayne
Jamison brought up the issue of cross-platform advertising buys when asked
to comment on the biggest industrial change in the last half-decade: "[This
activity] is great because every platform has a different benefit, and that gives
advertisers the opportunity to really make an ad come alive with video and
things like [2-D barcodes] that can literally be put on a print ad and drive a
consumer right to a website. [They can also buy] something off of an iPhone,
and there's just endless opportunities that we didn't have seven or ten years
ago." While Polskin interprets "platforms" as an extension of the core magazine product, Jamison seems to conflate "platforms" with "media," signaling a
decentralized universe of media products (i.e., no single platform is favored).
Semantic inflections such as this are telling of executives' positioning of
magazines within the larger media world, and the term "platform" may be
particularly loaded.

Indeed, as media scholar Tarleton Gillespie argued in his analysis of discourses surrounding YouTube, "platform" is a structural metaphor that productively masks the commercial and political underpinnings of the service. In
particular, it enables media constituencies to "elid[e] the tensions inherent in
their service: between user-generated and commercially-produced content,
between cultivating community and serving up advertising, between inter-
vening in the delivery of content and remaining neutral."[5] In the context of
the magazine industry, then, "platform" may be a more productive term than
"medium" because it is seemingly more amenable to marketing influence.
An article published in *Mediaweek* (UK) in early 2012 casts additional light
on the strong commercial impulses underpinning the magazine-as-platform
rhetoric. As one magazine exec offered, "[Magazine companies] need a content strategy and a print plan that goes beyond the printed page. The use of
other platforms is vital for building deeper relationships with both readers
and advertisers." Yet the emphasis was seemingly on the latter, as industry
leaders enthused over new circulation metrics that provide advertisers with
evidence of "brand-reach across a multitude of platforms for the first time."[6]

Though the label "platform" may help to cloak the increasingly commercial
nature of magazines' digital extensions, their positioning as "brands" does
nothing to conceal the marketing orientation. Instead, this discourse seems
to embrace brands as a form of symbolic value in the post-Fordist economy

that draws on the "productive communications" of the consumer audience (see chapters 4 and 5).[7] Examples of the branding rhetoric abound. For instance, in discussing his appointment to the then newly created position of creative director of content extensions at Hearst, David Kang explained the mentality of "conceptually thinking about our magazines as brands. We're not wedded to the one product of the magazine."[8] Lisa Arbetter made a similar remark about the evolution of *InStyle*: "It's become more than a magazine, it's a brand." Addressing the industrial logic behind branding efforts, communications scholar Simone Murray writes, "Any media brand which successfully gains consumer loyalty can be translated across formats to create a raft of interrelated products, which then work in aggregate to drive further consumer awareness of the media brand."[9]

While Murray draws our attention to the financial incentives underpinning branding strategies (i.e., synergy and cross-promotion), the specific conditions and affordances of digital media are also critical. In his study of the changing cultures of production within the television industry, John Caldwell discusses how TV executives and producers are developing more pronounced strategies of brand building. No longer relying merely on logos (NBC's peacock) and signature programs, they are exploiting new opportunities for self-promotion and the cultivation of audience participation.[10] This aptly describes the marketing orientation of many magazine companies as they aim to move consumers through the various vestiges of the "brand."

The logic of branding is not without limitations, including its rationalization of advertising and editorial partnerships, a topic to which I return later in this chapter. Another limit is the sheer ubiquity of the phrase "magazine brands." Time Inc.'s Martha Nelson noted that "brand" is used so frequently that it becomes "kind of an empty word, or a word that is just good for selling, or a word . . . that makes people feel that they are thinking broadly and strategically, even if they aren't." To Nelson, then, the problem with the term "brand" is that it is superficial and has very little resonance with what is actually going on inside the companies. Other content creators did not explicitly articulate the limits of platform-agnostic and branding approaches, but instead enacted this through their professional roles, routines, and practices.

Content Standards

Despite the rhetoric of media convergence and the allure of platform-agnostic, one-size-fits-all production conventions, magazine producers steadily drew upon medium-specific approaches to content. I found this to be true not only with regard to the material attributes of different media (such as timing and spatiality), but also in terms of content "quality," articulated through editorial accuracy, coverage depth, and more. Producers seemed to attribute these deviations to the changing behaviors and expectations of consumer audiences; yet their industrial culture—including conceptions of magazine brand identities—also figured prominently in their emergent standards and practices.

Expectations of timeliness and efficiency are symptomatic of a twenty-four/seven era of information and communication; however, the print production cycle cannot accommodate either of these logics. The challenge of responding to the public's thirst for real-time information has been widely addressed within the context of the newspaper industry. In his study of convergent newsroom practices, for instance, sociologist Eric Klinenberg explained that the popularity of twenty-four-hour television news and internet news has "eliminated the temporal borders in the news day." This, he continues, has led to "an information environment in which there is always breaking news to produce, consume, and—for reporters and their subjects—'react against.'"[11] Although women's magazines have never pretended to be timely in the same sense as hard news sources, considerations of trends, social currency, and seasonality have long factored into their advertising and editorial decisions.

Contemporary magazine producers are rethinking these approaches in an effort to keep up with the fast pace of change in the larger media environment. One magazine editor contended that the real-time responsiveness of the internet makes the magazine website a productive space for content that is not completed before the publication's closing date. An event that coincided with October's Breast Cancer Awareness issue, for example, would need to go into the print issue over the summer; online, this information can go up almost instantly. For other producers, web and social media properties allow companies to react to current events in ways that are impossible with print. For instance, several Time Inc. executives suggested that *People* has achieved an enviable share of the magazine market because of creators' medium-specific approaches to timing. Martha Nelson explained that her team needed to fundamentally rethink the identity of People.com several years back. As she recalled, "Although it was originally a feature site, we decided it was going to be a news site which would power our digital business." By brushing up against the common discourse of content over form, *People* essentially creates two very different media products with distinct business logics. Mark Golin, who was editor-in-chief of People.com at the time of our interview, expanded upon this:

> The way we look at it is the website is a very different lean-forward experi-
> ence. It is brief, it is repeated often, in some cases our users come four or five
> times a day. And what people are looking for is the news that is happening:
> experiencing the news in real time; literally, getting to ride the real-time
> roller coaster. Then, oftentimes what will happen is over the week's time, the
> news is breaking the story that is happening online. Meanwhile the maga-
> zine is collecting everything that was gathered for online, adding additional
> details, and is ultimately kind of spinning this richer tapestry that guides the
> reader through the entire arc of the story, allows them . . . to really savor the
> magazine.

Approaches to timing, then, are guided by blanket assumptions about audiences and then embedded in production routines that successively repackage
and reroute content.

The spatial variances between print and online products were also acknowledged, but in surprisingly inconsistent ways. To some, the infinite shelf
space of the internet allows magazine websites to serve as overflow sites for
archived magazine content as well as for topics and articles that will not "fit"
neatly into the print product. One print editor told me that, in contrast to the
physical limitations of print magazines, there is always "room" online. Yet a
contradictory spatial logic also emerged, namely that content produced for
the web should be more condensed than content produced for magazines.
"What we are learning from the web," Hearst editorial director Ellen Levine
told me, "is that people want the information shorter than in print. Much
shorter!" Similarly, Hannah Morrill, formerly of InStyle.com, noted that the
online text must be much more concise and prosaic. While Levine's comment indicates that the behaviors of readers govern the depth of material
across various media, Morrill explained that the length of web content is
a consequence of search engine optimization guidelines (discussed extensively in chapter 4). Unfortunately, the incentivizing of search terms means
that some of the visual and verbal texture of the print magazine may be lost
in the jungle of algorithms and ranking rules. Mark Golin tangentially addressed this issue when I asked him to contrast web and print professionals'
work traditions: "As a magazine editor, I've spent a lot of time in big stories,
four- or five- or six-page features that you work on with editors and writers.
Online, you are skilled more around the two-to-five-paragraph story: the
fact[s], get to the point, wrap it up with a bang, and get it out. There's not a
lot of time to waste on artistry." Golin's reference to "artistry" points toward
some of the defining qualities of print magazines, including their in-depth
coverage and their imaginative language, both of which are limited online.

In addition to differences in the temporality, spatiality, and "artistry" of content across different media, editorial accuracy was also a vexed topic. By this I mean that individuals described, and at times critiqued, the fact that web content does not undergo the same rigorous editing process that print does. Vanessa Voltolina, who had freelanced in a variety of magazine companies involved in the beauty and lifestyle market, contrasted the two production cultures: editors and writers are "so careful when writing for print," she said, while the web "can sometimes makes people sloppy." Similarly, an anonymous print editor commented that stories can be put up instantaneously online, whereas there is a sense of quality-control assurance built into print editing. In these instances, the assumption is that magazines have a higher caliber of content because each individual spends more time reviewing and confirming details. Debi Chirichella, the former chief operating officer of Condé Nast Digital, explained that editing standards are directly correlated with staff resource allocations. The cost structure of print versus digital, she explained, "really throws the whole idea of creation into question. . . . The sort of quality content that . . . goes into a magazine, if you thought about translating that online, it just doesn't work." Thus, because the company cannot afford to have as many people assigned to online, print staffers who are already short on time are compelled to assume that responsibility.

These anecdotes about the quality and accuracy of magazine websites substantiate quantitative data published in a 2010 *Columbia Journalism Review* report on "Magazines and Their Websites." Among the findings was that "magazines with independent web editors in charge of content decisions are almost twice as likely to have a less rigorous fact-checking process for web content as print content, and almost three times as likely to have no fact checking at all for Web content."[12] While the implications of these conclusions for newsmagazines are quite evident, the fact that magazines have historically been identified as a trusted source of information means that accuracy in entertainment and service publications is also worthy of critical reflection.

Editorial Voice

In an aggressively competitive media marketplace, magazine producers must work tirelessly to set their publications apart in the minds of both audiences and advertisers. Some of the professionals I interviewed called upon these distinctions while articulating the unique brand identities of their respective publications. For instance, a *Glamour* staffer mentioned that her publication covers few sexually provocative topics, because "We're not *Cosmopolitan*."

Similarly, Justine Harman addressed the affordability and wearability of the clothes featured in *People StyleWatch*, where she worked through 2012, by stating, "We're not *Harper's*." In other instances, these distinctions were communicated via highly publicized branding campaigns, such as the "Generation *Glamour*" initiative discussed in chapter 4. Describing one of the magazine's earlier branding campaigns, "America's Sweethearts," *Glamour* editor-in-chief Cindi Leive remarked, "Clearly it's exuberantly cheerful, aggressively cheerful. This says very clearly that this is not a magazine that's trying to be *Vogue*."[13]

Establishing and maintaining a unique editorial voice—through content selection and arrangement, tone, writing style, and imagery—is therefore critical to the success of a publication. As magazine industry scholars Sammye Johnson and Patricia Prijatel contend, "A magazine with a well-defined voice not only offers the reader consistency and imagination, it also gives advertisers the opportunity to develop unique ads to match the magazine's voice."[14] Conversely, the absence of a recognizable editorial voice may be the kiss of death for a publication in an overcrowded media marketplace. When Hearst and the Walt Disney Company announced the shuttering of their short-lived *Lifetime* magazine in the mid-2000s, media analysts blamed the title's vague editorial philosophy. As *Mediapost*'s Michael Shields reported, "Media planners who spoke off the record indicated that the magazine had never really established a distinctive editorial voice." As one advertising specialist confided to Shields, "There are too many women's magazines as it is—they really weren't doing anything different."[15]

As I discussed in chapter 1, a magazine's voice often reflects the performative persona of the editor-in-chief. Not only must this individual provide readers with a consistent and identifiable tenor, but she is also responsible for ensuring that all members of the editorial team convey this same tone to faithful readers. Presumably, these charges become increasingly difficult as magazine content gets dispersed across a host of media products while new—and at times competing—voices enter into branded magazine spaces. Interestingly, it was two executives from Hearst Magazines Digital Media who provided the most critical reflection on the editorial voice—or lack thereof—across digital properties. Chris Wilkes, the vice president of audience development and digital editions, explained the contrast through the notion of "curation," a term that until recently was limited to the domain of cultural institutions—art galleries, museums, and libraries. According to Wilkes, "The magazine reflects the brand's true essences in terms of its beautiful design [and] expert *curation*; when you apply that digitally in a traditional sense like to the web, you eliminate some of these two critical things." Later he noted, "The vast majority of the pages consumed on our sites are individual article pages, not . . . curated or arranged in any way. They are just individual articles that users sort of bite off as they travel their way around the web." This comment indicates that editorial curation is a unique feature of magazines that does not translate well into the digital domain. Somewhat paradoxically, the term "curation" has recently emerged as a buzzword on the marketing scene to describe the customization potential of visually oriented social media sites such as Instagram and Pinterest. Wilkes's interpretation, however, seems rooted in a more traditional understanding of curation as a way to harness authority and expertise.

Wilkes's former colleague Chuck Cordray, who was senior vice president and general manager of Hearst Magazines Digital Media, echoed the importance of curation in describing the dissimilarity between audiences' print and web activities. Tying curation to larger ideas about medium specificity, he noted, "I think it really goes [to show] how people use, why they use, media differently. . . . You may sometimes have the same content, but you are choosing the form for a separate purpose. The form has some meaning." The claim that "the form has some meaning" is antithetical to the industry discourse of platform agnosticism. That is, it indicates the endurance of longstanding assumptions about print media. At first blush, the perspectives of Cordray and Wilkes may appear counterintuitive; although they both represent the digital side of Hearst, they conjure up something quintessential about the print product that is absent from the digital spaces in which they work. However, by discussing the current limitations of digital vis-à-vis print, they may effectively reaffirm their own status as professionals with identities that are distinct from those who work in print.

A more insidious threat to magazines' editorial voice and tone is structural rather than technological, an outcome of a creative labor force more flexible by necessity. In a cultural moment when content farms and pooled editorial are supplanting the work of hard news journalists once assigned to particular titles, it is not entirely surprising that the magazine industry is pursuing similar initiatives in an attempt to buoy falling revenues. Examples abound of industry outsiders (i.e., those who do not work for a particular publication) whose content is incorporated into magazine textual spaces, and vice versa. Pooled editorial, for instance, is based on the logic that "editorial teams fluidly organized can generate content useful in many related titles."[16] To this end, Debi Chichirella explained while at Condé Nast, the staff structure "has been very much across publications and websites because by and large, we're not at the point where we can afford dedicated teams for any individual site or product." Hypothetically, this means that you could have the same person creating content for *Glamour*, *Bon Appétit*, and *Wired*— three Condé Nast titles with quite distinct identities, audiences, and editorial philosophies—resulting in a winnowing of each magazine's editorial voice. Although the Hearst executive team allegedly assigns digital specialists to individual publications, the company frequently shares content across its inventory of titles. For example, women's titles and digital-only brands such as Real Beauty feature the exact same content library on the homepage with links to other Hearst sites. A visitor to the *Marie Claire* site who clicks on certain topics will be taken to *Seventeen*, *Cosmo*, or *Redbook* pages (all of which have very different audiences and brand identities). There were subtle gestures to other instances of shared content, particularly the fact that individuals without a formal connection may produce content for the web in light of resource constraints.

For internal agents (i.e., producers), these activities may effectively reinforce their affiliation with an overarching organizational culture; moreover, they may facilitate package buys (buying space in several titles at once at a discounted rate) among advertisers. Yet such institutional affiliations (e.g., Hearst, Time) are communicated to readers in only very modest ways. For instance, if I were to ask the readers of *Ladies' Home Journal*, *Self*, and *Marie Claire* to tell me which company publishes their magazine, I do not expect that many would correctly identify Meredith Corporation, Condé Nast, and Hearst, respectively.

In terms of organizational culture and identity, it can become quite convoluted when the individuals who create content for the website are not ensconced in the same corporate culture as those residing in the print department. This is particularly true in an era of flexible and contingent work arrangements, when creative labor is often outsourced to freelancers. In their multi-site study of creative labor, Hesmondhalgh and Baker show that despite the potential benefits of freelance work (e.g., flexibility and relative freedom), freelancers tend to lack a sense of solidarity with other creative workers, and some describe their experiences as quite isolating.[17] To this end, Hannah Morrill acknowledged that *InStyle* frequently incorporates freelancers into the same physical workspace to ensure editorial voice consistency. Yet even if freelancers and contingent workers are temporarily enclosed in magazine spaces, they are unlikely to feel the same kind of affinity to magazine culture.

One way to understand the potential implications of emergent labor patterns is to look closely at an event that took place at *Marie Claire* in 2010. In

October of that year, *Marie Claire* blogger Maura Kelly published a post on the magazine website that included scathing remarks about the lead characters in the TV series *Mike and Molly*, which centers on an obese couple who met at a weight-loss support group:

> The other day, my editor asked me, "Do you really think people feel uncomfortable when they see overweight people making out on television?" . . . yes, I think I'd be grossed out if I had to watch two characters with rolls and rolls of fat kissing each other . . . because I'd be grossed out if I had to watch them doing anything. To be brutally honest, even in real life, I find it aesthetically displeasing to watch a very, very fat person simply walk across a room—just like I'd find it distressing if I saw a very drunk person stumbling across a bar or a heroin addict slumping in a chair.[18]

Inevitably, the post became fodder for a variety of websites and even TV shows, most of which criticized Kelly's insensitivity. Yet it was Kelly's identification with the *Marie Claire* brand that was particularly problematic, especially when thousands of readers threatened to cancel their print subscription. As one critic wrote, "Perhaps, as a magazine that supposedly caters to women, *Marie Claire* would be better served by writers who don't use the magazine's website as a platform to publicly shame and berate women whose bodies are outside of one woman's ideal."[19] A senior staff member at Hearst shared with me her perspective on the incident:

> What happened was they had a couple of young web editors [who] edited it a couple of times, but they put it up anyhow without any input, or even if they got input, they were thinking it was freedom of the press: we pay her, and therefore we put out what she thinks. It was explosive . . . there were rallies and [such], and the problem was somebody internally here argued it was freedom of the press, and she had the right to do whatever she wanted, which, of course, when you pay somebody, that's just not true. You can edit it, but unfortunately somebody in the position to have influenced this stuff, if you can believe it, they actually thought it was freedom of the press.
>
> So when the uproar started, they didn't take it down. It should have gone down immediately. That would be the kind of thing that can damage your brand, and it did. Now, it wasn't bad enough to last forever. But I can tell you it was very problematic. . . . This woman is a paid blogger; therefore . . . she carries the mantle of the brand. Too many of those and you really hurt your brand.

Though an extreme case, this incident reveals the difficulties of having inconsistent editorial voices on magazine brand platforms. Such occurrences may become even more frequent with financially induced organizational changes (e.g., the amount of work done by freelancers, the number of individuals involved in the editing process). Not only does this example make clear the challenges of maintaining brand consistency across platforms, it also reaffirms my earlier claim that editorial standards and routines can differ significantly (e.g., the description of "young web editors" who had very little editorial input).

Advertising/Editorial Relations

The history of women's glossies that I traced earlier in this book revealed the deep and inextricable connections between the magazine and advertising industries. That editorial content and advertising messages have nestled so cozily together feeds directly into feminist critiques waged against women's magazines for constructing women as consumers above all else. Such criticisms are rooted in the concern that the "wall of separation between church and state" is nothing more than a convenient myth to be sidestepped in practice. However, the industry has instituted guidelines to ensure some level of distancing between the editorial and publishing sides.[20] As British academic Lynda Dyson writes of the contemporary world of publishing, "The professional ideology of 'objectivity' . . . has been shored up by institutional structures that have separated the editorial side of production from advertising and marketing departments in order to ensure that journalistic output appears untainted by the commercial aspects of the business." She suggests that this is true in the realm of hard news *as well as* within writing forms at the "softer end of the editorial spectrum"—such as women's magazines.[21]

Dyson goes on to explain that this structure is valuable not only to readers seeking objective information, but also for advertisers/marketers whose products receive "untainted" coverage in the minds of these potential consumers. In the United States, the standards codified by the American Society of Magazine Editors (ASME) serve as a guidepost for "best practices" among magazine editors and publishers. In 2011, ASME updated its guidelines to account for digitally based content, but the following four principles endured: "Every reader is entitled to fair and accurate news and information; the value of magazines to advertisers depends on reader trust; the difference between editorial content and marketing messages must be transparent; [and] editorial integrity must not be compromised by advertiser influence."[22] Of course, as magazine companies vie for audiences and advertisers in the aptly named attention economy, the relevance of these principles is up for debate. As one media expert noted, the ASME guidelines have been met with "skepticism about their relevancy, especially as magazines continue to scrap for every ad dollar they can find."[23]

My interviews revealed a certain degree of skepticism, too, which was embedded in medium-specific understandings of advertising/editorial relations. Several individuals reflected critically on the nature of editorial integrity within the print-bound magazine. According to a Condé Nast editorial assistant who wished to remain anonymous,

> I think Condé Nast's basic publishing model is that advertisers are featured in the magazine [content]. . . . Like *Vogue* only had twelve brands in every magazine because those twelve are advertisers. Again I don't think it is a secret. It's something that you just have to be very careful about because you don't want the same EXACT coat in an editorial that will be advertised several pages later, but it's definitely there. That's always struck me as incredibly shady, but what do I know about the fashion industry? I don't know how that poses extra incentives as far as advertising sales go, but it's definitely *interesting*.

This individual was seemingly struggling to reconcile the unspoken practices of the magazine business ("I don't think it's a secret") with her personal views on the culture of women's magazines ("always struck me as incredibly shady"). Even more striking were the comments from an editorial assistant for one of Time Inc.'s websites. When I asked her about the extent to which magazine companies feel threatened by the onslaught of consumer-led media, especially fashion blogs, she responded: "I definitely think there's been a new approach in magazines, perhaps at the detriment of the church and state separation between the business side and the edit side. . . . Magazines [must] have a business model that makes more sense . . . that can threaten the sanctity of editorial. . . . I do think the advent of the internet and all these online sites have threatened magazines and can ruin the quality of the magazine if [that line is] not toed gently." By invoking the "church-state" metaphor, this staffer nods toward the potential implications ("ruin the quality") of emergent business models for the *print* magazine.

Later in our conversation, this Time Inc. employee provided a salient example of the ways in which magazine editors are caving to pressures from advertisers amidst precarious economic circumstances. She explained that traditionally, when magazine editors wanted to include a particular product in an editorial feature (e.g., a black dress or red pumps for a fashion spread), they would submit product requests to numerous designers. Then, after deciding among the submitted products, the magazine would bear the responsibility of organizing and financing the photo shoot. Nowadays, in contrast, she said that magazine producers select from a stockpile of product images that designers and advertisers have sent unsolicited. The modified system saves the publishing company both time and money; yet it no doubt supersedes journalistic norms of editorial objectivity.

The similar perspectives of these two employees are noteworthy given their different roles, departments, and organizations. Yet their work statuses seem noteworthy, too: both responses came from young women who had entered the industry just a few years before our interviews took place. I found this surprising, as I expected this level of reflexivity to come from industry veterans who were socialized to adhere to traditional guidelines and were likely critical of unfolding media economies. This discrepancy can perhaps be explained by the fact that, unlike key decision makers, these industry neophytes are not as concerned with business imperatives and revenue streams as they are with content quality. Additionally, they may be more willing to critique industry-wide practices given that their professional identities are not structured by the marketing "pitch" that I described in the introduction.

I received a similarly frank assessment of the growing sway of advertisers when I spoke with Lee Eisenberg, who served as *GQ*'s editor-in-chief during the 1980s and was later hired to oversee creative and online extensions for *Time*. He explained that while there was "some permeability" in advertising/editorial content during his industry tenure, the commercial nature has gotten "far more intense," especially within the lifestyle and fashion categories:

> There are so many people who are considered "editorial" but who are fundamentally devoted to advertisers and prospective advertisers. Today you may see a story about a celebrity that focuses extensively on grooming products and the material possessions that celebrity uses. The story looks editorial, but it is clearly [showing] commercial products. There is not a complete *quid pro quo*, but if you are an advertiser today, you can easily see your products featured on virtually every editorial page in the magazine. Back then, the horrible thing was the "advertorial" [an ad in the style of an editorial]. No editor liked them, but at least the advertorial was labeled. But today [magazine] pages are so pervasively riddled with advertising that you almost don't need [advertorials] anymore.[24]

In Eisenberg's view, once-shunned practices such as complementary copy and advertorial features have now become standard fare within print magazines.

While the preceding comments reveal a growing sense of unease about the level of advertiser influence on the print magazine, such apprehension was barely detectable in discussions of magazines' online and digital extensions. As Hearst's Ellen Levine succinctly stated, "Advertising rules on the web are different." An example from the 2010 American Magazine Conference brings the degree of difference into stark relief. During a keynote panel featuring Meredith Magazine Group's vice president and group marketing director, Nancy Weber, and the vice president of media at Maybelline, Deborah Marquardt, the two executives gushed over their fruitful "partnership."[25] The collaboration between the cosmetics retailer and Meredith's *More* magazine, which targets women age forty and up, included a sponsored web series called *The Broad Room*, which was written by *Sex and the City* creator Candace Bushnell. Maybelline used the show to promote a new product, Color Sensational Lipcolor; in the screenshot of the series title, the word "boardroom" is crossed out and replaced with "broadroom," which is written in (presumably Maybelline) red lipstick. In describing the partnership, Marquardt quipped, "Candace Bushnell was a real puritan for church and state, but she came around." Here, then, Bushnell's original position seemingly harks back to a quaint time of puritanism, which by necessity has been replaced by the ethos of capitalism.

At the 2012 Meredith CEO Analyst Meeting, Liz Schimel, National Media Group chief digital officer, talked about some similar initiatives that the company is pursuing with its other magazine properties: "To make e-commerce really work, we are making the ability to shop from our content sites very seamless. We are allowing editors to easily create and integrate content for commerce opportunities. We are extending our reader plus visitors' experience into commerce-enabled programs and we are capturing very critical purchase data about our consumers and their shopping habits."[26] Not only does Schimel openly admit that editors are forced to cave to pressures from retail partners, but she also acknowledges the extent to which these activities facilitate the consumer data-gathering processes. Meredith is not alone in the push toward e-commerce; competing publishing companies are also launching retail sites aligned with their magazines' editorial philosophy. In late 2012, for instance, Hearst executives announced the creation of an online initiative called ShopBazaar. Owned by *Harper's Bazaar*, it features products directly from the magazine. Carol Smith, the company's publisher and chief revenue officer, described it as a "true content-to-commerce venture," and explained, "This is our brand moment. We will be a brand you read and a brand you shop."[27] The boundary between editorial and advertising seems all but forgotten on the web.

In the nascent tablet market, meanwhile, conventions and practices related to advertising are only beginning to take root. Already, though, it seems that producers are much more willing to accept sponsored and commercial content. During an interview with a digital marketing reporter, *InStyle* publisher Connie Anne Phillips explained, "Digital platforms are increasingly attractive to advertisers who demand accountability and want compelling, innovative programs that make consumers pay attention."[28] Examples of such "innovative programs" abound. In March 2011, for instance, *Glamour* announced the launch of an original reality series created for the iPad that gives viewers the opportunity to buy clothing worn by the characters directly through Gap.com. As *New York Times* media decoder reporter Jeremy Peters wrote: "The idea behind the series was to integrate a sponsor's products seamlessly into *Glamour* content—something far more difficult to do in the print magazine for both logistical and ethical reasons. *Glamour Girls* is first and foremost a vehicle for product placement, something Condé Nast makes no bones about."[29] Another Condé Nast title, *Vogue*, enabled MAC Cosmetics to sponsor its first iPad issue, letting readers buy beauty products directly through the application.[30]

Interview informants provided similar accounts of interactive advertising initiatives made possible by the iPad. One Condé Nast staffer noted that ads take visitors to a site where they can buy the products. She added, "same thing with all the clothes in the magazine and the nail polish. You tap on the picture, and it takes you to the store to buy the item. I think that they *have* to. . . . It makes the purchases so easy." Similarly, Emily Masamitsu Scadden noted that the iPad allows *Marie Claire* to incorporate features such as 360-degree fashion coverage or the opportunity to buy a product directly from the digital version. When I prompted her to tell me more about this, she continued, "We try to make everything that's possible to be bought online clickable. . . . [It is an] interesting space to me and intriguing to see what online retailers are doing as they enter a glamorized catalogue market."

There are a number of possible explanations for why expectations of advertising/editorial relations on digital platforms differ from those of print. The most obvious one is that publishers seek to recuperate the costs incurred by new systems of digital production. A panelist in the 2010 American Magazine Conference session "Life after the iPad: The Changing Content and Device Eco-System" explained that it requires 20 to 25 percent more production effort to go from print to a format that has both horizontal and vertical layouts. As Condé Nast's Debi Chirichella remarked, "There's challenges [on the iPad], and what we're trying to do is counter those challenges by adding a lot more functionality to the advertising, making the advertising itself more valuable to the advertisers." Certainly, the integration of promotional messages directly into editorial spaces is a value-added service for advertisers on the prowl for innovative ways to reach consumers.

Publishers may also be more willing to collapse "church-state" boundaries as they seek to stay afloat in an increasingly competitive online environment. Emily Masamitsu Scadden mentioned that the growth of e-commerce sites such as Net-A-Porter (an online luxury clothing and accessories retailer that "looks" like a fashion magazine) is changing the contours of the women's fashion market; women's magazines need to counteract these changes. Hearst president David Carey indicated that this was the case when he commented during a recent interview, "[Net-A-Porter] is a kind of fashion magazine of the future. We have to find a way to respond to that."[31]

Other explanations for medium-specific advertising conventions include the fast pace of change, design modifications, and the fact that "fewer strong conventions have taken root."[32] That print standards are largely institutionalized whereas online ones are not was alluded to in a number of interviews. Matt Milner of Hearst Magazines Digital Media shed light on the extent to which tradition and editorial integrity are intricately bound together. Using the example of *Good Housekeeping*, he noted, "When you have a legacy business like that, something that's been around for a long time, it just takes a certain shape as far as being an institution, and it is less easy to do experiments and experimental things with that brand." Milner contrasted the "roots" and "legacy" of *Good Housekeeping* with some thriving digital-only properties, including Hearst's former partner, the iVillage network. Such brands, he insisted, "don't have to worry about editorial integrity in the same way that print brands might still have to or *think* that they still have to." In this instance, it is not direct pressure from advertisers that leads to specific practices, but rather the distinctive production cultures of print and online.

Conceivably, this lack of institutionalization may explain why the digital-only properties of many magazine companies do little to camouflage their promotional aims or bracket off advertising content. An example is Real-Beauty.com, an independent editorial site run out of Hearst that aggregates story content from women's sites such as *Cosmopolitan* and *Marie Claire*. Mark Weinberg, formerly of Hearst Magazines Digital Media, informed me that site was created through their "long-term partnership with Procter and Gamble as the sponsor for all our brands." He continued, "We developed our Real Beauty site [in a way] that would deliver on the objectives of marketers and deliver the kind of qualified audience that would be interested in the information about their products that they were advocating." Sponsored posts are one example of "deliver[ing] on the objectives of marketers." He provided the example of questions organized into forum topics such as blonde hair or skin problems: "the audience can have this exchange of posing questions . . . and the community can answer that, but also sponsors can answer that question." Sponsored posts can be considered a stealth advertising tool, particularly if the viewer is not aware that the information is being provided by an entity with a vested interest in the response.

Conclusion

The evolution of the women's magazine industry over the course of the twentieth century and into the twenty-first has been profoundly shaped by the interests and activities of three key factions: magazine producers, audiences, and advertisers. Collectively, these groups have contributed to what we might think of as the unique cultural form of the women's magazine, defined by its depth, frequency, permanence, specialization, editorial voice, and more.[33] Today, however, as we move further into a media era configured by convergent technologies and roles, these properties are becoming less and less relevant. Cultural practices and industry conventions centered on "monthly editions," "in-depth features," and "editorial curation" do not seem to translate well into the digital domain.

It is perhaps too convenient to blame technological affordances for the distinctions between media platforms, specifically print, web, and tablet. While media-specific technical properties no doubt play a role in emergent processes and products, I believe there is something more fundamental at work, namely firmly rooted assumptions about what defines a magazine. Indeed, despite the rhetoric of platform agnosticism, many producers continued to work from within what Henry Jenkins has called "medium-specific paradigms."[34] As Oliver Boyd-Barrett, a political economist of mass communication, productively argued, "Media practices are ingrained with media genres, such that it can be said that practitioners are 'spoken by' genres as much as they develop them, and while genres do change, adjust and evolve over time, there is unlikely to be a simple one-to-one correspondence between the evolution of genres and the evolution of rationales for media practice."[35] Therefore, transformations in media technologies are not necessarily in step with media practices, and insular work cultures and patterns may further impede this change.

What surfaces from this analysis is the fortitude of medium-specific logics, particularly among those working inside the industry. According to social theorist Peter Dahlgren, "media logic points to specific forms and processes that organize the work done within a particular medium."[36] Mark Deuze contends that Dahlgren's approach allows scholars to overcome the problematic notion that media workers in different industries are guided by different assumptions. Contrarily, I interpret media logic as an approach that accounts for continuing distinctions in media content despite the rhetoric of blurred media boundaries and cross-platform content.

Not only do notions of media logic structure the activities of media professionals, but they also shape the content consumers receive across various manifestations of the "brand." Subtle and blatant variations in content include distinctions in quality/accuracy, consistency of the editorial voice, and guidelines for advertising material. The latter is particularly problematic—especially if consumers continue to expect a certain degree of editorial integrity from trusted magazine brands. The examples recounted in this chapter suggest that advertiser influence is much more acceptable in digital environments. Or, to borrow the words of one online merchant, "Combining retail and editorial is natural from an economic standpoint and natural from a consumer standpoint."[37] This approach may have a ripple effect, extending beyond the narrow realm of magazines to establish a twenty-first-century model for interactive informational and entertainment content.

In light of such findings about content variations across media platforms, it seems useful to reconsider the broad framework of blurred boundaries. While a convergence mentality indicates that content easily traverses media boundaries, producers showed signs of apprehension—if not resistance—to this "platform agnostic" approach. Some of this hesitation may reflect a desire to protect professional identities (e.g., one's position and responsibilities as a print editor); however, expectations about what a medium "is" remain central to the content creation process. Consequently, many magazine workers are finding themselves wedged between production cultures inherited from the twentieth century and the cross-platform, interactive, hypercommercial logic of digital media.

Conclusion
Remaking the Magazine

This study of the women's magazine industry was driven by a seemingly simple question: "What is a magazine?" Yet this question is in fact anything but simple, bound up as it is with pervasive concerns about the stakes of "new media," broadly conceived, for the processes and products of contemporary culture industries. In mourning the ostensible demise of print culture, magazine journalist Virginia Heffernan eloquently captures the tension between traditional and emergent media forms and cultures.

> What is a magazine? . . . If you're holding one, you can turn the page. But it's very possible that you're nowhere near a turnable page now. You're reading on a computer or a hand-held device, even though this column was intended for a magazine. . . . That creates some dissonance. Magazine-making is a twentieth-century commercial art, with time-honored conventions, protocols and economics. But the effort that goes into making a print magazine—lighting photo shoots, designing layouts, affixing page numbers—produces little value for those who find its elements deracinated on the Web. If you're reading these words online, why should you know, or care, that they are meant to follow an illustrated cover, a table of contents and some feuilleton pieces?[1]

Not only are technical and aesthetic publishing customs less and less relevant in this contemporary media moment, but audiences (and I would add to this, advertisers) may have little affinity for "time-honored conventions" inherited from the magazine industry's halcyon days. The convenience, customization, and cost of content (or, more accurately, the lack thereof) in an era of ubiquitous media are just as appealing to magazine audiences as they are daunting to magazine producers.

It is for this reason that I have explored the transformations associated with digitization and participatory culture from the perspective of those individuals who confront these challenges on a daily basis: women's magazine executives, print publishers and editors, digital strategists, writers, designers, and more. Many of these workers are continuously re-producing the magazine product to fit a dizzying array of websites, social media platforms, mobile devices, tablets, and more. Yet they have also been forced to remake their processes, including those that historically guided them in matters of content, audience construction, and advertising. To think both critically and comprehensively about this dual-level remaking, it seems productive to return to the identity constructions that have been woven throughout this project, namely organizational identity (the central, distinctive, and enduring aspects of a company), professional identity (the practices, values, and division of labor tied to a particular medium or culture), and gendered identity (the social construction of gender within organizational and professional contexts). Though these indexes of identity are intertwined, each offers a different lens through which to revisit the vexing question, "What is a magazine?"

At the broadest level, the evolution from magazine as *object* to magazine as *brand* represents a conundrum for magazine companies as they struggle to reach a consensus about "who we are as an organization."[2] With content moving across nonmagazine technologies and platforms, some organizations are visibly breaking from their historical roots as "publishers." This identity shift is especially apparent in industry rhetoric, such as the earlier-mentioned rebranding of the Magazine Publishers of America as MPA—The Association of Magazine Media, a move that both reflects and shapes magazine companies' investments in nonmagazine technologies in a globalized context. Although this rebranding makes the industry seem more progressive to outsiders (and particularly to advertisers, who may need to be reminded of the continued viability of magazine brands), terms such as "platform," "brand," and "cross-platform" do not necessarily map onto internal production activities and priorities. In a book on the perceived redefinition of television, Amanda Lotz argues that the convergence of digital technologies raises questions about the language of "screen" technologies. For example, she queries whether YouTube and the like are "best categorized as 'television,' 'video,' 'computer,' or perhaps even just as a 'screen technology.'"[3] In case it is not immediately clear why such linguistic nuances matter, art historian Anna Brzyski explains that "new terms . . . have a power to instigate and channel cultural production by giving phenomena particular shape. In other words, they not only describe but also proscribe behavior, strategies, and ways of talking and thinking about art."[4] The distinctions Brzyski alludes to thus go beyond linguistics to encompass the differently constructed culture, forms, and content of mass media, all of which get implicated in the production of the media forms. Put simply, for content creators, it *matters* whether the medium is a magazine or newspaper or website.

Organizational identity shifts are also articulated through leadership and staffing restructuring. Indeed, the fact that digital strategists have transitioned from peripheral roles to central, "A-team" status indicates the growing prominence of these positions within magazine work cultures. Increasingly, these individuals are expected to contribute to technological production practices as well as matters of content. Consequently, magazine editors—the traditional brand identity stewards—are facing off against media workers with very different skill sets and hierarchies of value.

Time Inc.'s decision to appoint digital advertising expert Laura Lang as chief executive officer of its magazine division in 2012 offers up a lesson about the trials of trying to fundamentally change "who we are as an organization." When she began her stint there, Lang had no previous experience in the world of magazine editing and publishing, hailing instead from the digital ad firm Digitas. In covering Time Inc.'s decision, the *Wall Street Journal* noted, "Laura Lang has never written a magazine story or sold a magazine ad. But she does understand the digital media landscape."[5] The significance of this departure from traditional discourses of magazine expertise cannot be overstated. Across the media landscape, today's leaders are expected to steer their organizations through change while maintaining continuity with the past; Lang, however, did not have the same sense of and commitment to the industry's uniquely rich history.

Against this backdrop, it is perhaps not surprising that Time Inc.'s choice was initially met with a blend of confusion and criticism. One company executive confessed to an *Advertising Age* reporter that many employees found the announcement "shocking." The problem, this individual continued, was not with Lang's lack of print experience per se, but rather with her insufficient understanding of magazine content and audiences: "She doesn't have much consumer experience. So I'm wondering if what Jeff [Bewkes] is thinking is let's bring her in to make the company more of a marketing services company. . . . I always thought if Jeff brought in someone from outside it would be someone with much broader experience, not just ad revenue experience. There's no advertising without consumers."[6]

And, indeed, it seemed Lang was unable to reverse Time's fortunes, for Bewkes announced in 2013 that she would be leaving her position as part of the magazine division spinoff (see chapter 2). As a reporter for *Adweek* summarized, "Lang's short tenure may be seen as a sign that hiring a CEO with zero publishing experience to run the No. 1 U.S. publishing company was a bad idea to start with."[7] The story of Lang's short-lived governance is both a cautionary tale and a telling case of the path on which many leading magazine companies are embarking, namely marketing services. In just the last few years, scrambling magazine companies have sought to make up for lost revenues by investing in marketing and creative service initiatives. In 2010, Meredith Corporation made headlines when it spun off a series of marketing partnerships, offering integrated campaigns for advertisers that once relied exclusively on traditional ad agencies. Condé Nast and Hearst, too, have aggressively pursued advertising clients by developing creative packages geared to the audiences they know best: their own consumers. Recall, for instance, *Seventeen* vice president and publisher Jayne Jamison's enthusiasm over her team's expanded offerings for clients; she was quite explicit about the magazine's movement into the "strategic marketing" arena. Momentarily sidestepping the ethical issues embedded in these partnerships, this trend indicates a dispersal of the magazine company's organizational identity (and resources) from its traditional placement within the media world into other forms of media and marketing.

In addition, the transformed circuits of magazine production and consumption are reconfiguring professional routines, practices, and structures. As the magazine *qua* magazine becomes less central to traditional publishers, worker's professional identities are being upended. Wolfgang Donsbach's account of the changing nature of newspaper journalism—where "what it means to be a journalist is no longer as clearly defined as in the past when journalists were reporters and editors working for newspapers, the broadcast media or wire services"—is an apt way to characterize the contemporary conditions and practices of magazine journalism.[8] Editors' and publishers' socialization and enculturation in the magazine business do not easily translate into a world of cross-platform practices, participatory media, and the politics of online search and syndication. Not only are print staffers forced to work closely with specialists from different professional orientations (e.g., search metrics, app development), but many are evolving into Jacks-and-Jills-of-all-trades. That is, they are increasingly expected to produce content for print as well as online, tablet, mobile, and social formats, all of which work together in synergistic harmony. This "juggling act of sorts," as one editor described it, is no doubt taking its toll on creative personnel who work within a professional field that is already considered precarious, contingent, and flexible. Demanding work conditions also filter down to matters of content quality. Accounts of unconfirmed, unedited, and "sloppy" stories circulating in the magazines' online spaces may reaffirm the saying "jack of all trades, master of none."

Threats to the professional identities of magazine workers are also coming from outside the industry as content channels spring up across the internet that offer the same kind of community, intimacy, and advice that long resided in the narrow domain of women's glossies. These interactive spaces range from bottom-up fashion, beauty, and women's interest blogs to top-down commercial websites such as iVillage, BlogHer, and SheKnows. Collectively, they purport to usher in a deprofessionalized internet economy in which "ordinary" individuals contribute to—and at times supplant—professional domains of expertise. However, as I have suggested, these narratives of power redistribution may be overstated in an effort to camouflage the ways in which producers are harnessing the resources of amateur content creators. Or, as critical media scholar Mark Andrejevic cautions, we should be cynical of the "all too familiar rhetoric that 'everything has changed.'"[9]

In the context of a gendered production site such as women's magazines, these shifting notions of organizational and professional identity are challenging deeply embedded discourses of gender identity. Magazine journalism has long been considered an inclusive space for females to work and, during times of social upheaval, pursue progressive politics. Recall from chapter 1 that female editors would hire other women for staff positions and fill the pages with the contributions of magazine readers. Now, I am not suggesting that women's work within the industry destabilized larger regimes of inequality; as Kathy Peiss explained in her historical study of the advertising and cosmetics industries, women often gained employment because of their exclusive ability to sell to other women.[10] Yet magazine work activities *did* provide nineteenth- and twentieth-century females with improved access to the cultural circuit and intimate discursive spaces for meaning-making activities.

Unfortunately, the shift toward digitization has the potential to undermine the role and status of women in the industry: if gendered assumptions about technological proficiency continue to guide hiring and managerial decisions, the demographic composition of women's magazines may shift as female leaders get displaced. In addition to influencing the actual number of women in the industry, this also implies a (re)gendering of work, which

Miranda Banks describes as "the terms of how a particular profession might be socially constructed through gender."[11] In the case of women's magazines, editorial positions have been structured by and through the imaginary dialogue between (female) creators and audiences. To unsettle this relationship would be a disservice to individuals in both social groups who find meaning in this structure and its symbolic history.

These identity-related shifts—from the movement of materials across media boundaries to audiences' encroachment on production activities to reconfigured social hierarchies—seem at first blush to fit neatly into contemporary narratives of convergence culture. After all, blurred boundaries—between technologies, between roles, between places, between media logics, and more—seem to have an inverse relationship to identity. However, while contemporary threats to the magazine industry are very real, I argue that that actual shifts taking place are much more nuanced than universal accounts about media convergence suggest. That is, while some traditional media boundaries are indeed collapsing, others are being remade to preserve historical and cultural identity articulations.

Ostensibly, producers are allowing the boundaries between business and editorial and between print and digital departments to break down in order to preserve essential aspects of their business, both material and symbolic. Another site of boundary collapse, which tends to fall below the radar in discourse about convergence, is that between companies/titles (e.g., *Glamour*) and the larger organization (e.g., Condé Nast). As in other genres, editors in the women's magazine business seem "increasingly under pressure to view their titles as merely one part of a carefully structured corporate portfolio rather than as stand-alone magazines."[12] Contemporary strategies such as pooled editorial, cross-pollinated content, and articles shared via syndicates further shift the focus to the institutional brand. For magazines that have been around for more than a century, this seems quite controversial, especially since there is little evidence to indicate that companies are articulating these institutional identities to consumers. I doubt that "Hearst" or "Condé Nast" has much resonance as a brand in the minds of individual consumers who might identify themselves as *Cosmo* girls or *Vogue* readers. Removing the exclusivity and perhaps the "personality" from the text is a direct threat to the organizational identity of particular titles. At the same time that these divisions are crumbling, producers are shoring up other boundaries. This includes their efforts to reassert the distinctions between different platforms (e.g., print content is different from web content is different from iPad content), between professional and amateur producers (especially fashion bloggers), and between individuals with and without technological training.

The ever-changing placement of these boundaries has stakes for both producers and consumers of magazine news, information, and entertainment content. Indeed, it is a sobering reality of the digital media environment that new technologies and flows of communication—internet, mobile, social media—are affecting the roles and routines of magazine professionals. Yet the nature and extent of this influence vary depending upon an individual's placement within the organization and embryonic divisions of labor. Many producers are forced to negotiate specialization with multi-skilled aptitude; yet this is ultimately a decision that is imposed upon them from above and is based on allocations of financial resources. There is also evidence that industrial changes are causing some producers to experience a loss of creative license as digital executives urge them to create more "search-friendly" and "advertiser-friendly" content. Far from reconciling the tension between creativity and constraint, new technologies and tools may mark a step in the direction of the latter.

In addition to the consequences of boundary shifts for media professionals and the organizations within which they work, those who consume magazine-branded content are also feeling the impact of changes. The implications can be structured around two main themes: the increasingly blurred boundary between advertising and editorial, and the emphasis on material with the greatest potential to flow easily across platforms. As noted earlier in this chapter, the incremental loss of revenues in the publishing industry has led many producers to seek out partnerships with advertisers. While editorial/advertising relations have long been considered problematic in women's magazines, the nature and extent of influence seems to be intensifying, particularly online and with the advent of tablet devices such as the iPad. The examples recounted earlier indicate that many magazine companies are moving into the territories of e-commerce and advertising services—quite unapologetically. As Carol Smith, the vice president and publisher of *Harper's Bazaar*, explained of the magazine's ShopBazaar e-commerce site (see chapter 6), "We read to dream and aspire, but also to acquire."[13] This mentality may foreshadow the accelerated movement of our mass media system toward more individualized, interactive, and above all advertising-friendly forms of entertainment.

Relatedly, the magazine content that audiences receive seems largely guided by the type of platform for which it is created. The variance will be discernible not only through the medium's material properties (e.g., temporality and spatiality), but also in the quality of content and editorial voice. To this end, consumers may be less apt to find "branded content" that they feel an emotional connection with as it gets outsourced to people in other departments, divisions, and organizations. Moreover, given the cross-platform mentality that drives editorial decision making, there is a chance that a story idea that fails to translate well across multiple platforms will be passed over. This confluence of factors could lead to very different forms of magazine content in both print and not-print forms.

A final issue related to consumer boundaries deserves critical attention: the rise of user-generated content. Findings suggest that despite the tendency among new media celebrants to conflate interactivity with empowerment, individuals' participation in magazines is limited to "formatted spaces of participation" that are 1) monitored, 2) commercially viable, and/or 3) direct feedback mechanisms for content creators.[14] That these participants are female further complicates the discursive construction of these commercial sites as interactive and community-oriented. As Liesbet van Zoonen concludes of the tendency for women to be targeted as online consumers, "The political (new) economy of the internet thus tends to reconstruct the common gendered distinction between consumption and production, between entertainment and information."[15]

With respect to the category of individuals who self-identify as "fashion bloggers," those who stand to profit the most from the digital media economy are the "Pro-Ams" who "deploy . . . publicly accredited knowledge and skills, often built up over a long career, which has involved sacrifices and frustrations."[16] Indeed, only a handful of fashion bloggers have been able to achieve traditional, economic-based measures of success; the rest reside at the margins of the cultural circuit, where they experience little more than flash-in-the-pan fame. The celebration of the former—articulated via the success stories of Bryanboy, Tavi Gevinson, and the like—obscures the practical realities of blogging: it is a creative and entrepreneurial activity that requires considerable time and resources. As such, blogger practices may be symptomatic of work in a post-Fordist, precarious labor economy. Of course, these are the very same practices and structural conditions of work in other creative industries—including magazines.

The picture that emerges from this cacophony illustrates that production boundaries are not wholly collapsing, nor are traditional hierarchies flattening. Rather, the shifts that are taking place enable producers to maintain some sense of their identities while responding to the exigencies of the digital media environment. Importantly, I do not mean to suggest that "convergence" is merely rhetorical—a seductive term deployed to corroborate the study of new media or harness cross-media content. Instead, I argue for a more nuanced interpretation of participatory media than those couched within totalizing theories of interactivity as *either* empowering *or* exploitative. Relatedly, we should be wary of the siren song of digital democracy, especially when such celebratory statements are the province of media corporations.

It also seems to me that some of the convergence foci are misplaced and thus obscure some entrenched patterns within media industries. In particular, I think the continued slippage between editorial and advertising content is just as culturally meaningful as the collapsed distinction between producers and consumers. The former is a longtime issue (problem?) that may get swept aside in favor of "new" media issues. As Lynda Dyson usefully points out, "[Contemporary] forms of promotional activity contribute to a very profitable and rapidly expanding media 'ecology' in which advertorial is becoming ubiquitous as lifestyle discourses give shape to consumer culture as a 'whole way to live.'"[17] The calculated evolution of magazines into "brands" provides compelling evidence of this commoditized media ecology. It thus makes sense to pause to consider other indexes of industrial and social change that have been overlooked within an era of digitization, participatory media, and technological convergence.

Indeed, much of the recent scholarship devoted to understanding media and cultural convergence tends to disregard the social positioning of gender and other collective identity markers.[18] In contrast to the vibrant body of literature at the nexus of gender, digitization, and *consumerism*, the role of female *producers* gets fundamentally overlooked, or is addressed through blanket assertions about "flexible work practices," which have failed to make significant inroads into gender inequality.[19] I believe there is much to be gained by bringing feminist media studies into dialogue with production-oriented research on digital cultural industries. This could entail interventions into male-dominated work cultures and grounded studies of creative labor that take seriously issues of identity politics. Let me be clear: I do not mean to suggest that the demographic composition of a workplace is akin to female empowerment. Rather, female production roles are merely the most visible benchmark of women's social positioning within a rapidly evolving media landscape.

The dust from these issues has yet to settle, and many more challenges are surely on the horizon. It therefore seems important to close by acknowledging that this study of the women's magazine industry is set within a moment of profound uncertainty and flux. It is quite conceivable that many of the trends and implications I have highlighted are transitional, and that the industry will continue to evolve until a new identity equilibrium is reached. It is equally possible that many aspects of the situation just described will endure. Thus, a structured answer to the question "What is a magazine?" seems premature, if not myopic. Yet a lesson from the history of another traditional medium—film—may help us find one answer. In the years of the Russian Revolution, when film stock was in short supply, legendary director Lev Kuleshov taught courses on "films without film," where the stage could be used to utilize the visual language of cinema. For those within the women's magazine industry who are working tirelessly to remake their processes and products, it perhaps makes sense to focus on making *magazines . . . without the magazine.*

Notes

Preface and Acknowledgments

1. Van Zoonen, *Feminist Media Studies*, 3, 127.

2. See, for example, Banet-Weiser, *Most Beautiful Girl*; Ballaster et al., *Women's Worlds*; Ang, *Watching Dallas*.

3. Ballaster et al., *Women's Worlds*, 1. Angela McRobbie argues that changes in feminism can be understood alongside changes in women's magazines from the 1970s to the 1990s (and I would extend this through today). McRobbie, "*More!*," 190.

4. Currie, *Girl Talk*, 7; Winship, *Inside Women's Magazines*, xiii; Walker, *Shaping Our Mothers' World*, xvii.

5. Van Zoonen, *Feminist Media Studies*, 7.

6. The term "productive tension" comes from McRobbie, who used it to describe the relationship of feminism within the pages of women's magazines. "*More!*," 200.

Introduction: Questioning Media Identity in the Digital Age

1. Constanza, "Magazine Is an iPad."

2. Sonderman, "To a One-Year Old," para. 1.

3. This was a comment from user "ladyauroraıca" posted under the YouTube video "A Magazine Is an iPad That Does Not Work."

4. Jenkins, *Convergence Culture*, 27.

5. See, for example, Bruns, *Blogs, Wikipedia*; Jenkins, *Convergence Culture*; Postigo, "America Online Volunteers."

6. Quoted in Hartley, "From the Consciousness Industry," 234. See also Andrejevic, "Watching Television," and Turow, *Niche Envy*, for arguments that user-generated activities can be considered a form of exploited labor and/or are used as justification to learn more about consumers' online activities.

7. See Jenkins, *Convergence Culture*; Deuze, "Convergence Culture in the Creative Industries"; Deuze, *Media Work*; Grant and Wilkinson, *Understanding Media Convergence*.

8. Deuze, "Professional Identity," 103.

9. Moses, "Irreplaceable You," para. 6.

10. Elliott, "Report Details Rise," paras. 2–3.

11. Stableford, "Magazine Executives Call Meeting."

12. Chozick, "Time Warner Picks New Head," para. 5.

13. Green, "Why Do They Call It TV?," 95.

14. For discussions of media specificity, see Brzyski, "New Media, Old Media"; Doane, "The Indexical"; and Krauss, "Reinventing the Medium."

15. Jenkins, "Cultural Logic," 37.

16. Lawson-Borders, *Media Organizations*, 5.

17. In 1985, Albert and Whetten published "Organizational Identity." Whetten reopened the discussion more than a decade later in "Albert and Whetten Revisited."

18. Hsu and Hannen, "Identities, Genres," 476.

19. See van Zoonen, "Professional, Unreliable, Heroic Marionette," for a discussion of the significance of organizational identity within journalistic cultures, which she describes as "the interface between structure and subjectivity" (137). Her approach differed from organizational identity writings within the management and organizational sociology fields. Yet from this departure, she productively distinguished organizational identities from organizational roles, the latter of which is close to my definition of professional identity.

20. Tripsas, "Technology, Identity, and Inertia."

21. Ibid., 455.

22. In Kreiner et al., "On the Edge of Identity," the authors use individual and professional identity somewhat interchangeably as part of their larger argument that identities are negotiated at different levels. Meanwhile, Cottle's review of sociological studies of news production seems to indicate that professional identities are constructed by and for the organization; *Media Organisation and Production*, chap. 1. De Bruin usefully differentiates them by arguing, "'Professional identity' refers to a wider frame of reference—an ideology—not so much carried by the members of a clearly identifiable organization, but rather by an imaginary community, that stretches across organizations. Moving out of a particular organization doesn't necessarily imply an ending of the professional identity; however, it usually does mean the end of a particular organizational identity." De Bruin, "Gender, Organizational and Professional Identities," 229.

23. Du Gay, *Production of Culture/Cultures of Production*, 291.

24. Deuze, *Media Work*.

25. See, for example, Curran, *Media Organisations*; Caves, *Creative Industries*; Deuze, *Media Work*; Neff, *Venture Labor*; Neff, Wissinger, and Zukin, "Entrepreneurial Labour."

26. Klinenberg, "Convergence," 55.

27. Jenkins, *Convergence Culture*, 19.

28. Deuze, "Towards Professional Participatory Storytelling."

29. Deuze explains how the rise of audience activity undermines professional identity. *Media Work*, 156.

30. De Bruin is one of the few scholars who have espoused an empirical approach that brings constructions of gender, professional, and organizational identity into dialogue. See "Gender, Organizational and Professional Identities."

31. Van Zoonen, *Feminist Media Studies*, 3.

32. See Butler, *Gender Trouble*.

33. Kathy Peiss explains how in 1935, *Fortune* magazine published a series of articles on "Women in Business" that focused on the lack of women in "vital industries." Yet even in the nineteenth century, magazine publishers hired women, realizing that they could better understand women readers and consumers. Peiss, "'Vital Industry,'" 218.

34. Acker, "Gender and Organizations," 177.

35. Peiss, "'Vital Industry,'" 219.

36. Byerly and Ross, *Women and Media*, 2.

37. Peiser, "Setting the Journalist Agenda."

38. De Bruin, "Gender, Organizational and Professional Identities."

39. See, for example, Gill, "Cool, Creative and Egalitarian"; Pitt, "Masculinities@ Work."

40. Gill, "Cool, Creative and Egalitarian," 88.

41. Banks and Milestone, "Individualization, Gender."

42. See Levine, "Toward a Paradigm"; Mayer, Banks, and Caldwell, *Production Studies*.

43. See, for example, Gans, *Deciding What's News*; Tuchman, *Making News*.

44. Cottle, *Media Organisation and Production*, 5.

45. Some of the most widely cited studies of entertainment include Ryan and Peterson, "Product Image"; Gitlin, *Inside Prime Time*; and Turow, *Media Industries*.

46. Levine, "Toward a Paradigm," 66.

47. Ibid.

48. See, for example, Hesmondhalgh, *Cultural Industries*; Holt and Perren, *Media Industries*; O'Connor, "Cultural and Creative Industries"; Mayer, Banks, and Caldwell, *Production Studies*.

49. Segers and Huijgh, "Clarifying the Complexity"; O'Connor, "Cultural and Creative Industries."

50. Havens, Lotz, and Tinic, "Critical Media Industry Studies"; Holt and Perren, *Media Industries*.

51. Mayer, Banks, and Caldwell, *Production Studies*, 5.

52. Hartley, "From the Consciousness Industry," 234.

53. Scholars pursuing this line of research have examined the challenge of balancing established notions of professionalism with nonprofessional audiences, constraints

to create news content that will flow back and forth between the printed page and other media platforms, and the economic issues structured into cross-platform news production. See, for example, Boczkowski, *Digitizing the News*; Singer, "Strange Bedfellows?"; Klinenberg, "Convergence"; Pavlik, "Sea-Change."

54. Caldwell, *Production Culture*; Deuze, *Media Work*; Mayer, *Below the Line.*

55. Deuze, *Media Work*, 53.

56. An exception is Hesmondhalgh and Baker's recent book *Creative Labour*, in which they draw upon interviews with professionals in the trade magazine and men's magazine industries. Yet aside from convergence-based research, magazines have generally been overlooked among media industries researchers.

57. Fosdick, "State of Magazine Research." A normative distinction that conceptually positions magazines outside the margins of journalism ("hard news") is one explanation for why the medium has been overlooked. Other scholars gesture toward the substantial methodological barriers to researching the publishing industry. During the same conference, industry veteran and professor David Sumner suggested that it may be more difficult to study magazines because many of the companies are privately held.

58. Kitch, *Girl on the Magazine Cover*, 4.

59. McRobbie, "*More!*," 190.

60. A magazine producer is broadly conceived as any professional who plays a key role in the creation, distribution, and exhibition of magazine-branded content, including editorial and advertising material.

61. Sender, *Business, Not Politics*, 244.

62. According to Gough-Yates, "Media professionals are understandably concerned about how they will be depicted in research and . . . the practitioners I approached seemed especially worried that I would criticize them for the ways their magazines depicted contemporary femininities." *Understanding Women's Magazines*, 23.

63. I began the study with a systematic analysis of *Folio: The Magazine for Magazine Management*, looking at content from January 2006 through summer 2010, when the interviews began. Using the EBSCO database, which provides full electronic access to *Folio*, I compiled all of the articles that dealt with the broad topics of digitization, technology, convergence, professions, and gender, as well as more specific ones on women's magazines and content. I also consulted a number of trade and mainstream news sources through subscriptions to three daily news brief services, Media Daily, AAF Smartbrief, and IAB Smartbrief. I examined more than two hundred additional articles and press releases. Not only did this provide me with a broad overview of media and advertising trends, it also pointed me to different sources with industry news relevant to my topic.

64. They are, she continues, "attempts by practitioners to organize their own understanding of what they do, and to represent it to other culture industry professionals. In other words, there is a politics of representation at issue that aims at modifying, reshaping and redirecting the relations not simply between the maga-

zines and their readers, but also between various colleagues, professionals and clients from the wider world of the commercial industry." Gough-Yates, *Understanding Women's Magazines*, 24.

65. Turow, "Challenge of Inference," 229.

Chapter 1. Making the Magazine: Three Hundred Years in Print

1. Dyson, "Customer Magazines," 636–37.

2. "Timeline: A History of Magazines," para. 2.

3. Beetham, *Magazine of Her Own*, 4, 19.

4. "Service magazines" are publications that provide women with guidance on their traditional domestic roles, such as cooking, home decorating, and family care.

5. Hesmondhalgh and Baker, *Creative Labour*, 14.

6. See, for example, Gough-Yates, *Understanding Women's Magazines*; Mendes and Carter, "Feminist and Gender Media Studies."

7. Steiner, "Would the Real Women's Magazine," 100.

8. Beetham, *Magazine of Her Own*, ix.

9. While many take the gender of the audience as a given, some scholars are very explicit about their definition of a women's magazine. For instance, in the introduction to *Victorian Women's Magazines: An Anthology*, the editors write: "What follows is not a history of the production of magazines. Its focus is rather on defining women's magazines through their consumption or readership. We define 'women's magazines' as those which were aimed specifically at women as readers" (3).

10. Through various theoretical and methodological prisms, scholars have addressed the role of women's periodicals in establishing guidelines for heteronormative femininity and domesticity (Ballaster et al., *Women's Worlds*; Shevelow, *Women and Print Culture*); in conflating gender with consumerism (e.g., McCracken, *Decoding Women's Magazines*); in perpetuating unrealistic standards of beauty and physicality (e.g., Wolf, *Beauty Myth*); and in opening up spaces for reader resistance, meaning making, and even pleasure (Hermes, *Reading Women's Magazines*; McRobbie, *Feminism and Youth Culture*; Winship, *Inside Women's Magazines*).

11. Friedan, *Feminine Mystique*, 133.

12. Ferguson, *Forever Feminine*.

13. "Introduction," in Davies et al., *Out of Focus*, 4.

14. See, for example, Hermes, *Reading Women's Magazines*.

15. For instance, after Ellen McCracken argued that women's magazines conflate desire with consumerism (*Decoding Women's Magazines*, 301), Amy Farrell critiqued her dismissal of the pleasure of individualist readers ("Desire and Consumption," 623–27).

16. As Hermes reflected on her analysis of magazine readers, "[There is] no essential meaning that can be actualized; nor is there an essential viewing mode or practice of meaning use." *Reading Women's Magazines*, 13.

17. Both Johnson ("Magazines") and Zuckerman (*History of Popular Women's Magazines*) have commented on the role of women in the early women's publishing industry.

18. Aronson, "Domesticity," 20–21.

19. See Cadwallader, "Ida M. Tarbell's 'Women in Journalism,'" for an overview and article excerpt.

20. Braitwaite, *Women's Magazines*, 46–47.

21. Benberry and Pinney Crabb, *Love of Quilts*, 326.

22. Waller-Zuckerman, "Old Homes," 732.

23. Gottlieb, unpublished ms., cited in Johnson and Prijatel, *Magazine Publishing*, 202–3.

24. Smith, "Scholar Speaks," para. 12.

25. Napikoski, "Ladies' Home Journal Sit-In."

26. Reed, *Women in Mass Communication*, 96.

27. Davies, "Women's Magazine Editors."

28. This comment was made at the 2009 "Top Women in Magazine Publishing" conference. Just a few years ago, the third edition of Creedon and Cramer, *Women in Mass Communication*, still heralded publishing as the only industrial site that offered "a good place for growth and stability for women" (7).

29. "How Women Leaders," para. 1.

30. "The Count 2012," www.vidaweb.org/the-count-2012.

31. Johnson and Prijatel, *Magazine from Cover to Cover*, 2nd ed., 17. See also Kitch, *Girl on the Magazine Cover*, 3.

32. All of these descriptions were taken from Amazon.com.

33. Waller-Zuckerman, "Old Homes," 728.

34. Zuckerman, *History of Popular Women's Magazines*, 205.

35. Carmody, "Identity Crisis," n.p.

36. Gough-Yates, *Understanding Women's Magazines*, 20.

37. Turow, *Breaking Up America*, 31.

38. Ettema and Whitney, *Audiencemaking*, 5.

39. Levy, "Future of Magazines."

40. Johnson and Prijatel, *Magazine from Cover to Cover*, 1st ed., 17.

41. Turow, *Breaking Up America*, 96–97.

42. Gough-Yates, *Understanding Women's Magazines*, 164.

43. Bok, *Americanization of Edward Bok*, chap. 16, sec. 7.

44. Ibid.

45. Illouz, *Cold Intimacies*, 10.

46. Braitwaite, *Women's Magazines*, 33.

47. Gough-Yates, *Understanding Women's Magazines*, 118.

48. Davies, "Women's Magazine Editors." Somewhat curiously, only one-third said they base assumptions about readers on their own interests. She suggests this is because they do a lot of research on readers.

49. McRobbie, "*More!*," 207.

50. Amy Aronson argues that in the days of Sarah Josepha Hale's editorship at *Godey's Lady's Book*, magazine communities provided readers with a feeling of belonging and the sense that they could collectively challenge male-dominated patterns. Aronson, "Domesticity."

51. Ballaster et al., *Women's Worlds*, 107.

52. Seeking Alpha, "Meredith CEO Hosts Analyst Meeting," Tom Harty sec., para 4.

53. Weekes, "Gloria Steinem Quotes," 21.

54. Waller-Zuckerman, "Old Homes," 75–56, brackets 1890–1916 as the period in which advertisers and women's magazines developed a symbiotic relationship; not only did they have huge circulations of female readers, but publishers began to insistently pursue advertising accounts.

55. Damon-Moore, "Magazines for the Millions," 15.

56. Edward Bok is known as the first editor to have "run editorial material through the advertisements traditionally segregated at the back of the magazine." Waller-Zuckerman, "Old Homes," 736.

57. Ibid., 755.

58. The symbiotic relationship between advertisers and women's magazines continued to escalate in the twentieth century, particularly during the postwar spending boom, when a culture of consumerism emerged. This is the time that is considered to be the birth hour of consumerism. Magazine historian Cynthia White explains that starting in the mid-1950s, "the balance of power between editorial and advertising departments began to swing in favour of the latter in response to increasing pressure from higher management." White, *Women's Magazines*, 157.

59. Bagdikian, *Media Monopoly*, 138.

60. Earnshaw, "Advertising and the Media," 411.

61. Steinem, "Sex, Lies, and Advertising," 18–20. In addition, McCracken defines "covert advertising . . . [as] a system of mutually sustaining techniques and themes that links the editorial material to the purchased adverting." McCracken, *Decoding Women's Magazines*, 63.

62. Steiner, "Would the Real Women's Magazine," 103.

Chapter 2. Transforming the Magazine: From Print to Bits

1. Kuczynski, "Merger Planned," para. 6.

2. With the acquisition, Hearst now oversees *Elle* and *Woman's Day*.

3. Turow, *Breaking Up America*, 115.

4. Johnson and Prijatel, *Magazine Publishing*, 182.

5. Gough-Yates, *Understanding Women's Magazines*, 48.

6. Randle, "Historical Overview."

7. McAllister, *Commercialization of American Culture*, 229.

8. Gough-Yates, *Understanding Women's Magazines*, 51.

9. Manly, "Newsstand for the Electronic Age," para. 3.

10. Miller, "Web Publishing," para 2.

11. Ingham and Weedon, "Time Well Spent."

12. Zebian, "Mass-Consumer Magazine Web Dilemma."

13. Swartz, "Time Spent."

14. Clifford, "Magazine Ad Pages."

15. Ives, "Online Ad Spending."

16. http://powerofmagazines.com/, April 2010.

17. Moses, "Can Personalized Ads Save Magazines?"

18. "Magazine Hot List 2010," paras. 1–2.

19. Barnes, "TV and Film."

20. Sass, "Majority of Readers," paras. 2–3. "While print still boasts impressive reach, digital consumption represents the fastest-growing segment of the total audience. . . . In comparison with the previous year, the number of digital users visiting magazine-branded social networks increased 5.7% to 30 million, and the number accessing magazine content via mobile devices, including smartphones and tablets, grew 6.2% to 35 million."

21. Wang, "Digital Ad Engagement."

22. Peters, "Why Magazine Publishers," para. 3.

23. Condé Nast Russia, "History of Condé Nast," http://condenast.ru/en/about/history/, accessed June 2011.

24. Moses, "Condé/Hearst Tale of the Tape."

25. Roberts, "Just How Much?"

26. The following circulation figures all come from http://www.magazine.org/insights-resources/research-publications/trends-data/magazine-industry-facts-data/2010-average-total.

27. Rushe, "Hearst Buys Elle Rights."

28. Hearst Magazines Digital Media website, www.hearst.com/magazines/hearst-digital-media.php, accessed March 2013.

29. Bosker, "Marie Claire Editor-in-Chief Joanna Coles."

30. Chozick, "Time Warner Ends Talks," para. 5.

31. Ives, "Time Inc. Tops List."

32. "Big Idea 2010."

Chapter 3. Production Tensions: New Positions, Routines, and Gender Roles

1. Mazzocchi, "'Running in Heels' Joins Stampede," para. 3, emphasis added.

2. Curran, *Media Organisations*, 34.

3. Lewis, "Tension," 836.

4. Deuze, *Media Work*, 56.

5. For a review of this literature, see Cottle, *Media Organisation*, and de Bruin, "Gender, Organizational and Professional Identities."

6. Mayer, *Below the Line*.

7. Hesmondhalgh and Baker, *Creative Labour*, 87.

8. Silber, "Behind the Wave," para. 8.

9. Peters, "In Magazine World."

10. Ibid., para. 8.

11. Ibid.

12. Chozick, "Time Warner Picks New Head."

13. "Are You a Legacy Editor?," sec. "From Editors to Brand Managers," para. 1.

14. Kaplan, "Magazine Publishers Scramble," paras. 1–2.

15. Kinsman, "Diluting the User-Gen Kool-Aid," para. 8.

16. Steinberg, "What's Condé Nast Doing," para 2.

17. Learmonth, "Old Media Decides."

18. Tuchman, *Making News*.

19. Forde, "Journalists with a Difference."

20. Boczkowski, *Digitizing the News* (e.g., 13, 77), and Singer, "Strange Bedfellows?" (e.g., 14–15), provide productive accounts of the ways in which the news industry is responding to convergent practices, including discussions of physical and sociocultural spaces.

21. This may have changed since the interview, given that another organizational restructuring has taken place at Condé Nast.

22. See Gill and Pratt, "In the Social Factory"; Lee, "Problematising."

23. Neff, Wissinger, and Zukin, "Entrepreneurial Labor." The authors go on to qualify their argument by noting, "although this [youth culture] may reflect the short history of the new media industry. Several factors, however, may encourage recruitment of more mature workers into new media. With a new emphasis on sound business plans, the integration of new and old media firms, and different criteria of capital investors, more experienced managers are being sought" (330).

24. Moore's immediate successor was Jack Griffin, who stepped down months later. The company was then overseen by an interim management committee, composed of Howard Averill, chief financial officer; Maurice Edelson, vice president and general counsel; and John Huey, editor-in-chief. Laura Lang was appointed in late 2011, but her future within Time's new structure is unclear.

25. Kinsman, "Gender Gap," para. 1.

Chapter 4. Rethinking Readership:
The Digital Challenge of Audience Construction

1. Elliott, "Glamour Campaign," paras. 9–10.

2. Quoted in Moses, "Meet the 'Glamour' Generation," para. 9.

3. As Ang argues, "the world of actual audiences is too polysemic and polymorphic to be completely articulated in a closed discursive structure." *Desperately Seeking the Audience*, 14.

4. Blumler, "Recasting the Audience," 100.

5. Williams, "Culture Is Ordinary," 98, emphasis added.

6. Ettema and Whitney, *Audiencemaking*, 14.

7. Ang notes that by the 1990s, "audience measurement ha[d] become a technologically-advanced practice in which enormous amounts of money and energy are invested." *Desperately Seeking the Audience*, 4. See, for example, Turow, *Breaking Up America*; Ettema and Whitney, *Audiencemaking*.

8. Dyson, "Customer Magazines," 637.

9. Seneca, "History of Women's Magazines," sec. 1, para. 11.

10. Quoted in Waller-Zuckerman, "Old Homes," 749.

11. Ward, *New Brand of Business*, 129.

12. Couzens, "Audience Measurement."

13. Napoli, "Audience Product."

14. Turow, *Breaking Up America*, 68.

15. Seeking Alpha, "Meredith's CEO Hosts Analyst Meeting," Tom Harty sec., para. 3.

16. "Magazine Measurement Initiative Update," para. 1.

17. Ibid., para. 6.

18. "Andrew Kirshenbaum," para. 5.

19. Ibid.

20. "Shape Survey."

21. Wilson, "Fashion Changes," para. 9.

22. All of these were available on the "Polls" page of *Glamour* in February 2012.

23. As of February 2013, the homepage of HootSuite, http://hootsuite.com/, included this quote from Mashable CEO Pete Cashmore.

24. Anderson and Wolff, "Web Is Dead."

25. Ambroz, "New Publishing Mandate."

26. McCracken, *Decoding Women's Magazines*, 14.

27. Turow, *Breaking Up America*, 96–97.

28. Money, "How Hearst Magazines Increased Website Traffic," para. 1.

29. Ibid., para. 6.

30. Kinsman and Botelho, "Business of Content," 29.

31. Hesmondhalgh and Baker, *Creative Labour*, 201.

32. LinkedIn profile: http://www.linkedin.com/in/sammydavis, accessed August 2012.

33. Segal, "Dirty Little Secrets," para. 21.

34. Blakley, "Social Media."

35. Shields, "Condé Uses 'Crowd Control,'" para. 4.

36. Anderson and Wolff, "Web Is Dead."

37. Ang, *Desperately Seeking the Audience*, 154–155.

38. Ibid., 155. In 2001, van Zoonen suggested that this was already beginning to take place in internet ratings: "Internet marketing research shares with television ratings

research strategic purposes and epistemological flaws; it is a means to sell advertising space, but it does not tell much about actual uses, meanings, need, practices and interpretations of internet users." "Feminist Internet Studies," 70.

39. Napoli, "Audience Product."

40. Hesmondhalgh and Baker, *Creative Labour*, 201.

41. Andrejevic, "Critical Media Studies 2.0"; Andrejevic, "Watching Television"; Pridmore and Zwick, "Marketing and the Rise."

42. Turow, Hennessy, and Bleakley, "Consumers' Understanding."

43. Andrejevic, "Critical Media Studies 2.0," 41.

Chapter 5. Inviting Audiences In:
Interactive Consumers and Fashion Bloggers

1. Rosen, "People Formerly Known," paras. 1–3.

2. Lichtenstein, "Content Still Matters," para. 4.

3. See, for example, Andrejevic, "Watching Television"; Zwick et al., "Putting Consumers to Work"; Turow, *Niche Envy*; Pridmore and Zwick, "Marketing and the Rise."

4. Smythe, *Dependency Road*; Smythe, "Communications."

5. See Fuchs, "Dallas Smythe Today," for an overview of this debate.

6. Contemporary critical researchers have argued that television producers cultivate audience participation on series' websites by creating spaces for feedback that doubles as unpaid market research. See, for example, Andrejevic, "Watching Television"; Johnson, "Inviting Audiences In."

7. Terranova, "Free Labor," 33.

8. Postigo, "America Online Volunteers," 464.

9. According to Postigo, passionate labor "describes the structural conditions of co-creative work, the subject positions of those doing free labor and the discourses and perspectives they make possible." Ibid., 467.

10. According to Meehan, "societal divisions of labor based on gender, plus prejudicial assumptions about gender, [have] played a significant role in defining and differentiating the commodity audience." "Gendering the Commodity Audience," 216.

11. Campbell, "It Takes an iVillage," 494.

12. Byerly and Ross, *Women and Media*, 8.

13. Campbell, "It Takes an iVillage"; Duffy, "Empowerment."

14. Seneca, "History of Women's Magazines."

15. Kinsman, "Diluting the User-Gen Kool-Aid," para. 2.

16. Kinsman, "Community Publishing."

17. Van Zoonen, "Feminist Internet Studies," 67.

18. Ibid., 68, 69.

19. Van Slyke, Comunale, and Belanger, "Gender Differences," 86.

20. Johnson, "Inviting Audiences In."

21. http://www.allure.com/contact, accessed February 2013.

22. Andrejevic, "Watching Television," 27.

23. Ambrosz, "New Publishing Mandate," paras. 12, 14.

24. Ibid.

25. Campbell, "It Takes an iVillage."

26. Kinsman and Voltolina, "Fame Awards 2009."

27. Elliott, "Glamour Promotes," para. 19.

28. http://www.generationglamour.com, accessed February 2013.

29. Serazio, *Your Ad Here*, 131.

30. Duffy, "Empowerment," 26. See also Carah, "Breaking into the Bubble."

31. Ives, "Ladies' Home Journal Lets Readers Write."

32. http://www.divinecaroline.comLHJ, accessed March 2012.

33. Andrejevic, "Watching Television," 43.

34. http://www.magazine.org/sites/default/files/Mark_Coatney_Tumblr-social2011
.pdf, January 14, 2011.

35. http://www.glamour.com/beauty/blogs/girls-in-the-beauty-department/2010/
07/the-cheapie-little-bacne-buste.html, July 2, 2010. "Bacne" is short for "back acne."

36. Johnson-Greene, "Hearst Launches 'Q&A Communities,'" para 4.

37. Holmes, "Fashion Week Tips Hat."

38. Givhan, "Everyone's a Fashion Critic," para. 3.

39. Brown, "Viewpoint," para. 3.

40. Adams, "Conde Nast Digital Loses Style.com," para. 2.

41. See, for example, Deuze, *Media Work*; Jenkins, *Convergence Culture*.

42. Corcoran, "Blogs That Took Over."

43. "New Survey Shows."

44. Heussner, "Survey," para. 6.

45. Testimonial from Tiffany Srisook, web.blogads.com/advertise/fashion_blogads
_network, accessed August 2012.

46. http://www.thebudgetfashionista.com/.

47. Gough-Yates, *Understanding Women's Magazines*, 118.

48. Harkin, "Luxury World."

49. Sozzani, "Editor's Blog," January 28, 2011, http://www.vogue.it/en/magazine/
editor-s-blog/2011/01/january-28th.

50. Mesure, "Fluff Flies," para. 7.

51. La Ferla, "Who Am I Wearing?," E1.

52. Jennine, July 12, 2008 (5:14 A.M.), *Independent Fashion Bloggers*, http://ifbu.blogspot
.com/.

53. Johnson and Prijatel, *Magazine Publishing*, 115.

54. Corcoran, "Blogs That Took Over."

55. Duffy, Liss-Mariño, and Sender, "Reflexivity," 308.

56. Peters, "Elle, Not Camera Shy," para. 21.

57. Lowrey, "Mapping."

58. Ambroz, "New Publishing Mandate."

59. Gambrell, "Key Players," para. 1.
60. Saunders, "News in the Age of Blogs," para. 2.
61. Ellis, "Glamour's Young and Posh Blogger Network," para. 1.
62. Lazzarato, "Immaterial labor," 133.
63. Campbell, "It Takes an iVillage."
64. See, for example, ibid.; Duffy, "Empowerment."
65. Müller, "Formatted Spaces," 60.
66. Bagdikian, *Media Monopoly*, 242.
67. Oates, "Designing Women's Magazines," 18.
68. Leadbeater and Miller, *Pro-Am Revolution*, 9.
69. Andrejevic, "Critical Media Studies 2.0," 47.

Chapter 6. Off the Page:
Medium-Specific Approaches to Content

1. "Top Women in Magazine Publishing."
2. Maras and Sutton, "Medium Specificity Re-visited," 98.
3. DiMaggio and Powell, "Iron Cage Revisited."
4. http://www.magazine.org/industry-news/speeches/nina-link-2010-american-magazine-conference, October 4, 2010, emphasis added.
5. Gillespie, "Politics of 'Platforms,'" 348.
6. Fletcher, "Sector Analysis."
7. Arvidsson, "Brands."
8. Petersen, "Q&A," para. 6.
9. Murray, "Brand Loyalties," 417.
10. Caldwell, *Production Culture*, 245.
11. Klinenberg, "Convergence," 54.
12. Navasky and Lerner, "Magazines and Their Websites," 18.
13. Clifford, "Glamour Puts on a Happy Face," para. 8.
14. Johnson and Prijatel, *Magazine Publishing*, 115.
15. Shields, "Mag Rack," paras. 1–2.
16. Kinsman, "Community Publishing," sec. titled "Can Pooled Editorial Work?"
17. Hesmondhalgh and Baker, *Creative Labour*, 221.
18. Maura Kelly, "Should 'Fatties' Get a Room? (Even on TV?)," October 25, 2010, 9:00 A.M., http://www.marieclaire.com/sex-love/dating-blog/overweight-couples-on-television.
19. Jill, "If Maura Kelly."
20. Byerly and Ross, *Women and Media*; Steiner, "Would the Real Women's Magazine."
21. Dyson, "Customer Magazines," 635.
22. http://www.magazine.org/asme/asme_guidelines/guidelines.aspx, January 2011.
23. Moses, "ASME Unveils New Guidelines," para. 4.

24. This interview took place as part of a separate project in October 2011. See http://www.asc.upenn.edu/newslink/Winter2011/Alumni_News_DuffyEisenberg.aspx.

25. This conversation was transcribed during the MPA: Association of Magazine Media conference, Chicago, October 2010.

26. Seeking Alpha, "Meredith CEO Hosts Analyst Meeting," Schimel sec., para. 26.

27. Russell, "Harper's Bazaar Introduces ShopBazaar," para. 3.

28. Indvik, "How the Fashion Magazine Industry Plans to Profit."

29. Peters, "Glamour's iPad Series," para. 6.

30. Kats, "MAC Cosmetics," para. 3.

31. Roberts and Campbell, "Click to Buy," para. 11.

32. Sivek, "Ethics," para. 9.

33. Johnson and Prijatel, *Magazine from Cover to Cover*, 2nd ed., 13–14.

34. Jenkins, "Cultural Logic," 37.

35. Boyd-Barrett and Newbold, *Approaches to Media*, 270.

36. Quoted in Deuze, *Media Work*, 110.

37. Roberts and Campbell, "Click to Buy," para. 3.

Conclusion: Remaking the Magazine

1. Heffernan, "Articles of Faith."

2. Albert and Whetten, "Organizational Identity."

3. Lotz, *Television*, 80.

4. Brzyski, "New Media, Old Media," para. 1.

5. Adams and Vranica, "Time Inc. Finds Its Future."

6. Patel and Ives, "Who Is Laura Lang?," paras. 11, 13.

7. Moses, "Lessons from Laura Lang's (Brief) Tenure," para. 5.

8. Donsbach, "Journalists," 43.

9. Andrejevic, "Critical Media Studies 2.0," 35.

10. Peiss, "'Vital Industry.'"

11. Banks, "Gender Below-the-Line," 88.

12. Forde, "Journalists with a Difference," 128.

13. Russell, "Harper's Bazaar Introduces ShopBazaar," para. 3.

14. Müller, "Formatted Spaces."

15. Van Zoonen, "Feminist Internet Studies," 68.

16. Leadbeater and Miller, "Pro-Am Revolution," 20.

17. Dyson, "Customer Magazines," 640.

18. The work of Vicki Mayer and Miranda Banks on "below the line" film and TV producers is a noteworthy exception. Mayer, *Below the Line*; Banks, "Gender Below-the-Line."

19. Pitt, "Masculinities@Work."

Bibliography

List of Interviewees

Lisa Arbetter, deputy managing editor at *InStyle*

Brianna Cox Brunecz, former advertising sales representative at *The Knot*

Debi Chirichella, senior vice president and chief financial officer at Hearst Magazines, formerly chief operating officer of Condé Nast Digital and chief financial officer of Condé Nast Publications

Joanna Coles, editor-in-chief of *Cosmopolitan*, formerly editor-in-chief of *Marie Claire*

Chuck Cordray, former senior vice president and general manager of Hearst Magazines Digital Media

Sammy Davis, former digital assistant at Hearst, owner of Sammy Davis Vintage blog

Lee Eisenberg, author and former consulting editor of strategic development at Time Inc.

Mark Golin, editorial director of the Digital, Style, and Entertainment and Lifestyle Groups at Time Inc., also former editor-in-chief of *Esquire* and editor of People.com

Devin Gordon, senior editor at *GQ*

Justine Harman, assistant editor at *Elle*, formerly of People.com and *People StyleWatch*

Tom Harty, president, National Media Group (Meredith)

Brennan Hayden, executive vice president and chief operating officer at Wireless Developer Agency

Jayne Jamison, vice president and publisher at *Seventeen*

Ellen Levine, editorial director of Hearst Magazines

Matt Milner, entrepreneur-in-residence at Hearst Magazines Digital Media, formerly Hearst Digital's vice president of social media and community; also the founder of Answerology

Hannah Morrill, formerly of InStyle.com and now an independent freelancer

Martha Nelson, editorial director at Time Inc.

Howard Polskin, executive vice president of communications and events at MPA—The Association of Magazine Media

Steve Sachs, former executive vice president of consumer marketing and sales at Time Inc.

Lavinel Savu, assistant managing editor at *InStyle*

Emily Masamitsu Scadden, former digital assets manager at *Marie Claire*

Vanessa Voltolina, former editor for *Folio: The Magazine for Magazine Management*, who is now at NBC Universal

Mark Weinberg, former vice president of programming and product strategy at Hearst Magazines Digital Media

Chris Wilkes, vice president of audience development and digital editions at Hearst Magazines, also vice president of Hearst's App Lab

Five anonymous contributors

Secondary Sources

Acker, Joan. "Gender and Organizations." In *Handbook of the Sociology of Gender*, edited by Janet Saltzman Chafetz, 177–93. New York: Kluwer Academic, 2006.

Adams, Russell. "Conde Nast Digital Loses Style.com." *Wall Street Journal Online*, October 25, 2010. http://blogs.wsj.com/digits/2010/10/25/conde-nast-digital-loses-stylecom/.

———. "Conde Nast Restructures Digital Ad Sales." *Wall Street Journal Blogs: Digits*, October 27, 2010 (1:43 P.M.). http://blogs.wsj.com/digits/2010/10/27/conde-nast-restructures-digital-ad-sales/.

Adams, Russell, and Jessica Vascellaro. "Google Digital Newsstand Aims to Muscle in on Apple." *Wall Street Journal*, January 2, 2011. http://online.wsj.com/article/SB10001424052748704543004576051800714082180.html.

Adams, Russell, and Susan Vranica. "Time Inc. Finds Its Future in Digital Ad Executive." *Wall Street Journal Online*, December 1, 2011. http://online.wsj.com/article/SB10001424052970204012004577069971240704762.html.

Albert, Stuart, and David A. Whetten. "Organizational Identity." *Research in Organizational Behavior* 7 (1985): 263–95.

Ambroz, Jill. "Magazine Production's New World Order." *Folio: The Magazine for Magazine Management*, January 20, 2010. http://www.foliomag.com/2010/magazine-productions-new-world-order#.UV2OC5jhumM.

———. "Marketing to Millennials: Gen Y Is Changing the Way Magazines Interact with Readers across All Platforms." *Folio: The Magazine for Magazine Management*, June 1, 2008. http://www.foliomag.com/2008/marketing-millennials#.UV2OLJjhumM.

———. "The New Publishing Mandate: Anywhere, Anytime." *Folio: The Magazine for Magazine Management*, August 31, 2009. http://www.foliomag.com/2009/new-publishing-mandate-anywhere-anytime#.UV2OyJjhumM.

———. "The Promise of Print Technologies." *Folio: The Magazine for Magazine Management*, May 29, 2007. http://www.foliomag.com/2007/promise-print-technologies#.UV2O65jhumM.

Anderson, Chris, and Michael Wolff. "The Web Is Dead. Long Live the Internet." *Wired*, August 17, 2010. http://www.wired.com/magazine/2010/08/ff_webrip/.

Andrejevic, Mark. "Critical Media Studies 2.0: An Interactive Upgrade." *Interactions: Studies in Communication and Culture* 1, no. 1 (2009): 35–51.

———. *ISpy: Surveillance and Power in the Interactive Era*. Lawrence: University Press of Kansas, 2007.

———. "Watching Television without Pity." *Television and New Media* 9, no. 1 (2008): 24–46.

"Andrew Kirshenbaum: Director of Database Marketing, Hearst Magazines." *Folio: The Magazine for Magazine Management*, March 31, 2010. http://www.foliomag.com/2010/andrew-kirshenbaum#.UG8MJvnuU40.

Ang, Ien. *Desperately Seeking the Audience*. New York: Routledge, 1991.

———. *Watching Dallas: Soap Opera and the Melodramatic Imagination*. London: Methuen, 1985.

"Are You a Legacy Editor?" *Folio: The Magazine for Magazine Management* 35, no. 3 (March 2006): 12–13. *Business Source Premier* (20294726).

Aronson, Amy. "Domesticity and Women's Collective Agency: Contribution and Collaboration in America's First Successful Women's Magazine." *American Periodicals* 11 (2001): 1–23.

Arvidsson, Adam. "Brands: A Critical Perspective." *Journal of Consumer Culture* 5, no. 2 (2005): 235–58.

Bagdikian, Ben. *The Media Monopoly*. 5th ed. Boston: Beacon Press, 1997.

Ballaster, Ros, Margaret Beetham, Elizabeth Frazer, and Sandra Hebron. *Women's Worlds: Ideology, Femininity and the Woman's Magazine*. New York: Macmillan, 1991.

Banet-Weiser, Sarah. *The Most Beautiful Girl in the World: Beauty Pageants and National Identity*. Berkeley: University of California Press, 1999.

Banks, John, and Mark Deuze. "Co-creative Labour." *International Journal of Cultural Studies* 12, no. 5 (2009): 419–31.

Banks, Mark, and Katie Milestone. "Individualization, Gender and Cultural Work." *Gender, Work and Organization* 18, no. 1 (2011): 73–89.

Banks, Miranda. "Gender Below-the-Line: Defining Feminist Production Studies." In *Production Studies: Cultural Studies of Media Industries*, edited by Vicki Mayer, Miranda Banks, and John Caldwell, 87–98. New York: Routledge, 2009.

Barnes, Brooks. "TV and Film, from Condé Nast." *New York Times*, October 9, 2011. http://mediadecoder.blogs.nytimes.com/2011/10/09/tv-and-film-from-conde-nast/.

Beetham, Margaret. *A Magazine of Her Own? Domesticity and Desire in the Woman's Magazine, 1800–1914*. London: Routledge, 1996.

Beetham, Margaret, and Kay Boardman, eds. *Victorian Women's Magazines: An Anthology*. New York: Manchester University Press, 2001.

Benberry, Cuesta Ray, and Carol Pinney Crabb. *Love of Quilts: A Treasury of Classic Quilting Stories*. St. Paul, MN: Voyageur Press, 2004.

Bermejo, Fernando. "Audience Manufacture in Historical Perspective: From Broadcasting to Google." *New Media and Society* 11, no. 1–2 (2009): 133–54.

"The Big Idea 2010." *Folio: The Magazine for Magazine Management*, August 1, 2009. http://www.foliomag.com/2009/big-idea-2010#.UV2PF5jhumM.

Blakley, Johanna. *Social Media and the End of Gender*. Filmed December 2010. TED-Women video. Posted February 2011. http://www.ted.com/talks/johanna_blakley _social_media_and_the_end_of_gender.html.

Blumler, Jay. "Recasting the Audience in the New Television Marketplace?" In *The Audience and Its Landscape*, edited by James Hay, Lawrence Grossberg, and Ellen Wartella, 97–112. Oxford: Westwind Press, 1996.

Blumler, Jay, and Elihu Katz. *The Uses of Mass Communications: Current Perspectives on Gratifications Research*. Beverly Hills, CA: Sage, 1974.

Boczkowski, Pablo. *Digitizing the News: Innovation in Online Newspapers*. Cambridge, MA: MIT Press, 2005.

Bok, Edward. *The Americanization of Edward Bok: The Autobiography of a Dutch Boy Fifty Years After*. New York: Charles Scribner's Sons, 1932.

Bosker, Bianca. "Marie Claire Editor-in-Chief Joanna Coles on Apple's 'Sexy' iPad, Women in Tech, and More." *Huffington Post*. First posted October 29, 2010, updated May 25, 2011. http://www.huffingtonpost.com/2010/10/29/editor-in-chief-joanna-co _n_775604.html#s167794.

Botelho, Stefanie. "Condé Nast, Other Publishers Look to Standardize Metrics in Digital Editions." *Folio: The Magazine for Magazine Management*, August 8, 2011. http:// www.foliomag.com/2011/conde-nast-other-publishers-look-standardize-metrics -digital-editions#.UR5PdfL5Qcs.

Boyd-Barrett, Oliver, and Chris Newbold. *Approaches to Media: A Reader*. New York: St. Martin's Press, 1995.

Braithwaite, Brian. *Women's Magazines: The First 300 Years*. London: Peter Owen, 1995.

Brown, Caitlin. "Viewpoint: Amateur Fashionistas Blog Their Way to the Top." *Centretown News Online*, March 25, 2011. http://centretownnewsonline.ca/index.php ?option=com_content&task=view&id=2272&Itemid=1.

Bruns, Axel. *Blogs, Wikipedia, Second Life, and Beyond: From Production to Produsage*. New York: Peter Lang, 2008.

Brzyski, Anna. "New Media, Old Media, Inter-Media, Trans-Media: A Historic Perspective." *Journal of the New Media Caucus* 4, no. 1 (Spring 2008). http://www.newmedia caucus.org/html/journal/issues.php?f=papers&time=2008_spring&page=brzyski.

Butler, Judith. *Gender Trouble: Feminism and the Subversion of Identity*. New York: Routledge, 1990.

Byerly, Carolyn M., and Karen Ross. *Women and Media: A Critical Introduction*. Oxford: Wiley-Blackwell, 2006.

Cadwallader, Robin L. "Ida M. Tarbell's 'Women in Journalism.'" *Legacy* 27, no. 2 (2010): 412–15.

Caldwell, John Thornton. *Production Culture: Industrial Reflexivity and Critical Practice in Film/Television*. Durham, NC: Duke University Press, 2008.

Campbell, John Edward. "It Takes an iVillage: Gender, Labor, and Community in the Age of Television-Internet Convergence." *International Journal of Communication* 5 (2011): 492–510. http://ijoc.org/ojs/index.php/ijoc/article/view/531.

Carah, Nicholas. "Breaking into the Bubble: Brand-Building Labour and 'Getting in' to the Culture Industry." *Continuum: Journal of Media and Cultural Studies* 25, no. 3 (2011): 427–38.

Carmody, Deirdre. "Identity Crisis for 'Seven Sisters.'" *New York Times*, August 6, 1990. http://www.nytimes.com/1990/08/06/business/identity-crisis-for-seven-sisters.html.

Caves, Richard E. *Creative Industries: Contracts between Art and Commerce*. Cambridge, MA: Harvard University Press, 2000.

Chozick, Amy. "Time Warner Ends Talks with Meredith and Will Spin Off Time Inc. into Separate Company." *New York Times*, Media Decoder Blog, March 6, 2013. http://mediadecoder.blogs.nytimes.com/2013/03/06/fate-of-four-time-inc-magazines-are-an-issue-in-talks-with-meredith/.

———. "Time Warner Picks New Head for Time Inc. Magazine Unit." *New York Times*, November 30, 2011. http://mediadecoder.blogs.nytimes.com/2011/11/30/warner-said-to-pick-new-head-of-time-inc-magazine-unit/.

Clifford, Stephanie. "Glamour Puts on a Happy Face to Attract Ads." *New York Times*, September 8, 2009. http://www.nytimes.com/2009/09/09/business/media/09adco.html.

———. "Magazine Ad Pages Continue to Drop." *New York Times*, April 9, 2010. http://mediadecoder.blogs.nytimes.com/2010/04/09/magazine-ad-pages-continue-to-drop.

Condé Nast Russia. "History of Condé Nast." Accessed October 2012. http://condenast.ru/en/about/history/.

Constanza, Jean-Louis. "A Magazine Is an iPad That Does Not Work." YouTube video, 1:26. Posted by "UserExperienceWorks," October 6, 2011. http://www.youtube.com/watch?v=aXV-yaFmQNk.

Corcoran, Cate T. "The Blogs That Took Over the Tents." *Women's Wear Daily*, February 6, 2006, 30.

Cottle, Simon. *Media Organisation and Production*. London: Sage, 2003.

Couzens, Michael. "Audience Measurement: Inching toward a Solution." *Folio: The Magazine for Magazine Management* 17, no. 4 (April 1988): 84–88. *Academic One File* (A6552013).

Creedon, Pamela J., and Judith Cramer. *Women in Mass Communication*. 3rd ed. London: Sage, 2007.

Curran, James. *Media Organisations in Society*. London: Arnold, 2000.

Currie, Dawn H. *Girl Talk: Adolescent Magazines and Their Readers*. Toronto: University of Toronto Press, 1999.

Damon-Moore, Helen. *Magazines for the Millions: Gender and Commerce in the "Ladies' Home Journal" and the "Saturday Evening Post," 1880–1920*. Albany, NY: SUNY Press, 1994.

Davies, Kath, Julienne Dickey, and Teresa Stratford, eds. *Out of Focus: Writings on Women and the Media*. London: Women's Press, 1987.

Davies, Kayt. "Women's Magazine Editors: Story Tellers and Their Cultural Role." PhD. diss., Edith Cowan University, 2009.

de Bruin, Marjan. "Gender, Organizational and Professional Identities in Journalism." *Journalism: Theory, Practice and Criticism* 1, no. 2 (2009): 217–38.

Deuze, Mark. "Convergence Culture and Media Work." In *Media Industries: History, Method, and Theory*, edited by Jennifer Holt and Alisa Perren, 144–56. Malden, MA: Wiley-Blackwell, 2009.

———. "Convergence Culture in the Creative Industries." *International Journal of Cultural Studies* 10, no. 2 (2007): 243–63.

———. *Media Work*. Cambridge: Polity Press, 2007.

———. "The Professional Identity of Journalists in the Context of Convergence Culture." *Observatorio* 2, no. 4 (2008): 103–17.

———. "Towards Professional Participatory Storytelling in Journalism and Advertising." *First Monday* 10, no. 7 (July 4, 2005). http://firstmonday.org/htbin/cgiwrap/bin/ojs/index.php/fm/article/view/1257/1177.

DiMaggio, Paul J., and Walter W. Powell. "The Iron Cage Revisited: Institutional Isomorphism and Collective Rationality in Organizational Fields." *American Sociological Review* 48, no. 2 (1983): 147–60.

Doane, Mary A. "The Indexical and the Concept of Medium Specificity." *Differences* 18, no. 1 (2007): 128–52.

Domb, Ana. "Misplacing Medium Specificity." *Futures of Entertainment Blog*, March 10, 2008. http://www.convergenceculture.org/weblog/2008/03/misplacing_medium_specificity.php.

Donsbach, Wolfgang. "Journalists and Their Professional Identities." In *The Routledge Companion to News and Journalism*, edited by Stuart Allan, 38–48. New York: Routledge, 2009.

Du Gay, Paul. *Production of Culture/Cultures of Production*. Thousand Oaks, CA: Sage Publications, 1997.

Duffy, Brooke E. "Empowerment through Endorsement? Polysemic Meaning in Dove's User-Generated Advertising." *Communication, Culture and Critique* 3, no. 1 (2010): 26–43.

Duffy, Brooke E., Tara Liss-Mariño, and Katherine Sender. "Reflexivity in Television Depictions of Media Industries: Peeking behind the Gilt Curtain." *Communication, Culture, and Critique* 4, no. 3 (2011): 296–313.

Dunn, Anne. "Medium Specificity and Cross-Media Production: Developing New Narrative Paradigms." Paper presented at the Australia and New Zealand Communications Association Annual Conference, Brisbane, Australia, July 8–10, 2009.

Dyson, Lynda. "Customer Magazines: The Rise of 'Glossies' as Brand Extensions." *Journalism Studies* 8, no. 4 (2007): 634–41.

Earnshaw, Stella. "Advertising and the Media: The Case of Women's Magazines." *Media, Culture and Society* 6, no. 4 (1984): 411–21.

"Editors Share Best Practices for Twitter." *Folio: The Magazine for Magazine Management*, October 10, 2011. http://www.foliomag.com/2011/editors-share-best-practices -twitter.

Elliott, Stuart. "Glamour Campaign Tries to Claim a Generation." *New York Times*, September 9, 2012. http://www.nytimes.com/2012/09/10/business/media/glamour -magazine-campaign-tries-to-reach-millennials.html.

———. "Glamour Promotes Its Brand and Its Readers." *New York Times*, September 7, 2010. http://www.nytimes.com/2010/09/08/business/media/08adco.html.

———. "Letting Consumers Control Marketing: Priceless." *New York Times*, October 9, 2006. http://www.nytimes.com/2006/10/09/business/media/09adcol.html.

———. "Report Details Rise of Social Media." *New York Times*, September 11, 2011. http://mediadecoder.blogs.nytimes.com/2011/09/11/report-details-rise-of-social -media/.

Ellis, Keisha. "Glamour's Young and Posh Blogger Network." *Socialtik*, February 4, 2011. http://www.socialtikmag.com/glamour-launches-young-posh-blogger-network/.

Erdal, Ivar J. "Cross-Media (Re)production Cultures." *Convergence: The International Journal of Research into New Media Technologies* 15, no. 2 (2009): 215–31.

Ettema, James S., and D. Charles Whitney, eds. *Audiencemaking: How the Media Create the Audience*. Thousand Oaks, CA: Sage, 1994.

———. *Individuals in Mass Media Organizations: Creativity and Constraint*. Thousand Oaks, CA: Sage, 1982.

Farrell, Amy E. "Desire and Consumption: Women's Magazines in the 1980s." Review of *Decoding Women's Magazines: From "Mademoiselle" to "Ms.,"* by Ellen McCracken. *American Quarterly* 46, no. 4 (1994): 621–28.

Fell, Jason. "Print Lay Out, Digital Edition: Design Done Side-by-Side." *Folio: The Magazine for Magazine Management* 39 (January 2010): 27. *Academic OneFile* (A216847887).

Ferguson, Marjorie. *Forever Feminine: Women's Magazines and the Cult of Femininity*. London: Heinemann, 1983.

Fiol, C. Marlene. "Capitalizing on Paradox: The Role of Language in Transforming Organizational Identities." *Organization Science* 13, no. 6 (2002): 653–66.

Fletcher, Mike. "Sector Analysis: Magazines." *Mediaweek* (UK), February 29, 2012. http://www.mediaweek.co.uk/news/1119858/Sector-Analysis-Magazines/.

Forde, Eamonn. "Journalists with a Difference: Producing Music Journalism." In *Media Organisations and Production*, edited by Simon Cottle, 113–31. London: Sage, 2003.

Fosdick, Scott. "The State of Magazine Research in 2008." *Journal of Magazine and New Media Research* 10, no. 1 (2008): 1–4.

Friedan, Betty. *The Feminine Mystique*. New York: Dell, 1963.

Fuchs, Christian. "Dallas Smythe Today—The Audience Commodity, the Digital Labour Debate, Marxist Political Economy and Critical Theory." *tripleC—Cognition, Communication, Co-operation* 10, no. 2 (2012): 692–740.

Fuery, Kelli. *New Media: Culture and Image*. London: Palgrave Macmillan, 2009.

Fusco, Serafina, and Marta Perrotta. "Rethinking the Format as a Theoretical Object in the Age of Media Convergence." *Observatorio Journal* 7 (2008): 89–102.

Gambrell, Evonne. "Key Players." *Teen Vogue*, February 2, 2009. http://www.teenvogue .com/industry/2009/02/teen-fashion-bloggers.

Gans, Herbert J. *Deciding What's News: A Study of "CBS Evening News," "NBC Nightly News," "Newsweek," and "Time."* New York: Pantheon, 1979.

Garfield, Bob. *The Chaos Scenario*. Nashville, TN: Stielstra, 2009.

"The Gazillion Dollar Question: So What Is a Media Company?" *Economist*, April 20, 2006, 13–15. http://www.economist.com/node/6794282.

"Getting Bloggers to Generate Content and Revenue for You." *Folio: The Magazine for Magazine Management*, July 3, 2007. http://www.foliomag.com/2007/getting-bloggers -generate-content-and-revenue-you#.

Gill, Rosalind. "Cool, Creative and Egalitarian? Exploring Gender in Project-Based New Media Work." *Information and Communication Studies* 5, no. 1 (2002): 70–89.

Gill, Rosalind, and Andy Pratt. "In the Social Factory?" *Theory, Culture & Society* 25, no. 7–8 (2008): 1–30.

Gillespie, Tarleton. "The Politics of 'Platforms.'" *New Media and Society* 12, no. 3 (2010): 347–64.

Gitlin, Todd. *Inside Prime Time*. Berkeley: University of California Press, 2000.

Givhan, Robin. "Everyone's a Fashion Critic." *Harper's Bazaar*, August 10, 2007. http:// www.harpersbazaar.com/fashion/fashion-articles/fashion-critic-givhan-0907.

Gottlieb, Agnes H. "Grit Your Teeth, Then Learn to Swear: Women in Journalistic Careers, 1850–1926." *American Journalism* 18, no. 1 (2001): 53–72.

Gough-Yates, Anna. *Understanding Women's Magazines: Publishing, Markets and Readerships*. New York: Routledge, 2003.

Grant, August E., and Jeffrey S. Wilkinson. *Understanding Media Convergence: The State of the Field*. New York: Oxford University Press, 2009.

Green, Joshua. "Why Do They Call It TV When It's Not on the Box? 'New' Television Services and Old Television Functions." *Media International Australia* 126 (2008): 95–105.

Gregg, Melissa. "The Normalisation of Flexible Female Labour in the Information Economy." *Feminist Media Studies* 8, no. 3 (2008): 285–99.

Griffen-Foley, Bridget. "From Tit-bits to Big Brother: A Century of Audience Participation in the Media." *Media, Culture and Society* 26, no. 4 (2004): 533–48.

Grindstaff, Laura, and Joseph Turow. "Video Cultures: Television Sociology in the 'New TV' Age." *Annual Review of Sociology* 32, no. 1 (2006): 103–25.

Grossberg, Lawrence, Ellen Wartella, D. Charles Whitney, and J. MacGregor Wise. *Mediamaking: Mass Media in a Popular Culture*. Thousand Oaks, CA: Sage, 1998.

Harkin, Fiona. "The Luxury World after Web 2.0." *Financial Times*, February 19, 2008. http://www.ft.com/intl/cms/s/0/9bc1724c-de90–11dc-9de3–0000779fd2ac. html#axzz2KzAJpgDY.

Hartley, John. "From the Consciousness Industry to the Creative Industries: Consumer-Created Content, Social Network Markets, and the Growth of Knowledge."

In *Media Industries: History, Theory, Method*, edited by Jennifer Holt and Alisa Perren, 231–44. Oxford: Wiley-Blackwell, 2009.

Hatch, Mary Jo, and Majken Schultz. "Relations between Organizational Culture, Identity and Image." *European Journal of Marketing* 31, no. 5/6 (1997): 356–65.

Havens, Timothy, Amanda Lotz, and Serra Tinic. "Critical Media Industry Studies: A Research Approach." *Communication, Culture and Critique* 2 no. 2 (2009): 234–53.

Heffernan, Virginia. "Articles of Faith." *New York Times*, December 30, 2010. http://www.nytimes.com/2010/01/03/magazine/03FOB-medium-t.html.

Hermes, Joke. "Media, Meaning and Everyday Life." *Cultural Studies* 7, no. 3 (1993): 493–506.

———. *Reading Women's Magazines*. Cambridge: Polity Press, 1995.

Hermida, Alfred, and Neil Thurman. "Clash of Cultures: The Integration of User-Generated Content within Professional Journalistic Frameworks at British Newspaper Websites." *Journalism Practice* 2, no. 3 (2008): 343–56.

Hesmondhalgh, David. *The Cultural Industries*. London: Sage, 2002.

Hesmondhalgh, David, and Sarah Baker. *Creative Labour: Media Work in Three Cultural Industries*. New York: Routledge, 2011.

Hesmondhalgh, David, and Andy C. Pratt. "Cultural Industries and Cultural Policy." *International Journal of Cultural Policy* 11, no. 1 (2005): 1–14.

Heussner, Ki Mae. "Survey: Women Trust Pinterest More Than Facebook, Twitter." *Adweek*, March 14, 2012. http://www.adweek.com/news/technology/survey-women-trust-pinterest-more-facebook-twitter-138930.

Holmes, Elizabeth. "Fashion Week Tips Hat to Blog Site." *Wall Street Journal*, February 9, 2011. http://online.wsj.com/article/SB10001424052748703313304576132221659118068.html.

Holmes, Tim. "Mapping the Magazine." *Journalism Studies* 8, no. 4 (2007): 510–21.

Holt, Jennifer, and Alisa Perren, eds. *Media Industries: History, Theory, Method*. Oxford: Wiley-Blackwell, 2009.

"How Women Leaders at Niche Publications Carve Out Territory in the Competitive World of Magazine Publishing." *Knowledge @ Emory*, January 10, 2007. http://knowledge.emory.edu/category.cfm?CID=12&startRow=26&maxrows=15.

Hsu, Greta, and Michael T. Hannan. "Identities, Genres, and Organizational Forms." *Organizational Science* 16 (2005): 474–90.

Huang, Edgar, Karen Davison, Stephanie Shreve, Twila Davis, Elizabeth Bettendorf, and Anita Nair. "Facing the Challenges of Convergence: Media Professionals' Concerns of Working across Media Platforms." *Convergence* 12, no. 1 (2006): 83–98.

Huang, J. Sonia, and Don Heider. "Media Convergence: A Case Study of a Cable News Station." *International Journal on Media Management* 9, no. 3 (2007): 105–15.

Illouz, Eva. *Cold Intimacies: The Making of Emotional Capitalism*. Malden, MA: Polity, 2007.

Indvik, Lauren. "How the Fashion Magazine Industry Plans to Profit from Digital This Fall." *Mashable*, July 20, 2010. http://mashable.com/2010/07/20/fashion-mags-digital-fall/.

———. "Pinterest Becomes Top Traffic Driver for Women's Magazines." *Mashable*, February 26, 2012. http://mashable.com/2012/02/26/pinterest-womens-magazines/.

Ingham, Deena, and Alexis Weedon. "Time Well Spent: The Magazine Publishing Industry's Online Niche." *Convergence: International Journal of Research into New Media Technologies* 14, no. 2 (2008): 205–20.

Ives, Nat. "Ladies' Home Journal Lets Readers Write the Magazine." *Ad Age*, January 9, 2012. http://adage.com/article/media/ladies-home-journal-lets-readers-write-magazine/231966/.

———. "Online Ad Spending to Pass Print for the First Time, Forecast Says." *Ad Age*, January 19, 2012. http://adage.com/article/media/emarketer-online-ad-spending-pass-print-time/232221/.

———. "Time Inc. Tops List of Digital Earners; Ad Age Analysis Shows Whole Mag Business Has a Lot of Web Work to Do." *Advertising Age*, January 19, 2009. http://adage.com/article/media/time-tops-list-digital-earners-publishing/133873/.

Jenkins, Henry. *Convergence Culture: Where Old and New Media Collide*. New York: New York University Press, 2006.

———. "The Cultural Logic of Media Convergence." *International Journal of Cultural Studies* 7, no. 1 (2004): 33–43.

Jhally, Sut, and Bill Livant. "Watching as Working: The Valorization of Audience Consciousness." *Journal of Communication* 36, no. 3 (1986): 124–43.

Jill. "If Maura Kelly Doesn't Like Seeing Fat People, Perhaps She Should Get a Room and Not Leave It." *Feministe*, October 27, 2010. http://www.feministe.us/blog/archives/2010/10/27/if-maura-kelly-doesnt-like-seeing-fat-people-perhaps-she-should-get-a-room-and-not-leave-it/.

Johnson, Derek. "Inviting Audiences In." *New Review of Film and Television Studies* 5, no. 1 (2007): 61–80.

Johnson, Sammye. "Magazines: Women's Salary and Status in the Magazine Industry." In *Women in Mass Communication*, 3rd ed., edited by Pamela J. Creedon and Judith Cramer, 134–53. Thousand Oaks, CA: Sage, 2007.

Johnson, Sammye, and Patricia Prijatel. *The Magazine from Cover to Cover: Inside a Dynamic Industry*. Lincolnwood, IL: NTC Publishing Group, 1999.

———. *The Magazine from Cover to Cover*. 2nd ed. New York: Oxford University Press, 2007.

———. *Magazine Publishing*. Lincolnwood, IL: NTC/Contemporary Publishing Group, 2000.

Johnson-Greene, Chandra. "Hearst Launches 'Q&A Communities' on Its Teen-Oriented Web Sites." *Audience Development*, April 1, 2009. http://www.audiencedevelopment.com/2009/hearst+launches+qa+communities+its+teen-oriented+web+sites#.UIDHRmnuU4o.

Kaplan, David. "Digital Head Sarah Chubb Leaving Condé Nast after 20 Years." *paidContent*, February 8, 2011. http://paidcontent.org/2011/02/08/419-sarah-chubb-leaving-conde-nast/.

———. "Magazine Publishers Scramble to Streamline Their App Production." *paidContent*, April 20, 2011. http://paidcontent.org/2011/04/20/419-magazine-publishers-scramble -to-streamline-their-app-production/.

Kats, Rimma. "MAC Cosmetics Targets Affluent Vogue Readers via iPad Sponsorship." *Mobile Commerce Daily*, February 24, 2011. http://www.mobilecommercedaily.com/ mac-cosmetics-targets-vogue's-affluent-customers-via-ipad-sponsorship.

Kinsman, Matt. "Can Pooled Editorial Work?" *Folio: The Magazine for Magazine Management*, November 26, 2008. http://www.foliomag.com/2008/community-publishing -next-new-hope.

———. "Community Publishing: The Next New Hope?" *Folio: The Magazine for Magazine Management*, November 26, 2008. http://www.foliomag.com/2008/ community-publishing-next-new-hope.

———. "Diluting the User-Gen Kool-Aid." *Folio: The Magazine for Magazine Management*, April 6, 2007. http://www.foliomag.com/2007/diluting-user-gen-kool-aid #.UV2PgpjhumM.

———. "Gender Gap in Publishing Pay Is Growing Wider." *Folio: The Magazine for Magazine Management*, January 7, 2010. http://www.foliomag.com/2010/gender- gap-publishing-pay-growing-wider#.

———. "Men Still Earn Significantly More Than Women in Publishing." *Folio: The Magazine for Magazine Management*, December 23, 2009. http://www.foliomag.com/ 2009/men-still-earn-significantly-more-women-publishing#.UV2PvZjhumM.

———. "2006 Consumer-Magazine CEO Survey." *Folio: The Magazine for Magazine Management*, September 28, 2006. http://www.foliomag.com/2006/2006-consumer -magazine-ceo-survey#.UV2P45jhumM.

Kinsman, Matt, and Stefanie Botelho. "The Business of Content." *Folio: The Magazine for Magazine Management*, August 8, 2011. http://www.foliomag.com/2011/ business-content#.UV2QIJjhumM.

Kinsman, Matt, and Vanessa Voltolina. "Fame Awards 2009." *Folio: The Magazine for Magazine Management* 38, no. 4 (April 2009): 56+. *Academic OneFile* (A198289166).

Kitch, Carolyn L. *The Girl on the Magazine Cover: The Origins of Visual Stereotypes in American Mass Media*. Chapel Hill: University of North Carolina Press, 2001.

Klinenberg, Eric. "Convergence: News Production in a Digital Age." *Annals of the American Academy of Political and Social Science* 597, no. 1 (2005): 48–64.

Klinenberg, Eric, and Claudio Benzecry. "Introduction: Cultural Production in a Digital Age." *Annals of the American Academy of Political and Social Science* 597 (2005): 6–18.

Krauss, Rosalind E. "Reinventing the Medium." *Critical Inquiry* 25, no. 2 (1999): 289–305.

Kreiner, Glenn E., Elaine C. Hollensbe, and Mathew L. Sheep. "On the Edge of Identity: Boundary Dynamics at the Interface of Individual and Organizational Identities." *Human Relations* 59, no. 10 (2006): 1315–41.

Kuczynski, Alex. "Merger Planned for 2 Giants of Fashion Publishing." *New York Times*, first posted August 20, 1999, updated August 24, 1999. http://www.nytimes.com/1999/08/20/business/the-media-business-merger-planned-for-2-giants-of-fashion-publishing.html.

La Ferla, Ruth. "Who Am I Wearing? Funny You Should Ask." *New York Times*, September 12, 2012. http://www.nytimes.com/2012/09/13/fashion/new-york-fashion-week-street-style-is-often-a-billboard-for-brands.html.

Lawson-Borders, Gracie L. *Media Organizations and Convergence: Case Studies of Media Convergence Pioneers*. Mahwah, NJ: Lawrence Erlbaum, 2006.

Lazzarato, Maurizio. "Immaterial Labor." In *Radical Thought in Italy: A Potential Politics*, edited by Paulo Virno and Michael Hardt, 133–46. Minneapolis: University of Minnesota Press, 1996.

Leadbeater, Charles, and Paul Miller. *The Pro-Am Revolution: How Enthusiasts Are Changing Our Economy and Society*. London: Demos, 2004.

Learmonth, Michael. "Old Media Decides Digital Still Needs a 'Chief.'" *Advertising Age*, November 22, 2010. http://adage.com/article/digital/media-jobs-media-decides-digital-chief/147229/.

Lee, Hye-Kyung. "Problematising the Creative Industries Discourse: From a Perspective of Cultural Market and Creative Labour." *Review of Cultural Economics* 12, no. 2 (2010). http://www.kcl.ac.uk/artshums/depts/cmci/people/papers/lee/problematising.pdf.

Levere, Jane L. "Cosmo Campaign Puts Viewers in the Photo Shoot." *New York Times*, September 29, 2010. http://www.nytimes.com/2010/09/30/business/media/30adco.html.

Levine, Elana. "Toward a Paradigm for Media Production Research: Behind the Scenes at General Hospital." *Critical Studies in Media Communication* 18, no. 1 (2001): 66–82.

Levy, Dan. "The Future of Magazines Is Here: Q&A with Susan Currie Sivek." *Sparksheet*, March 25, 2010. http://sparksheet.com/the-future-of-magazines-is-here-qa-with-susan-currie-sivek/.

———. "What Is a Magazine?" *Sparksheet: Good Ideas about Content, Media and Marketing*, May 28, 2010. http://sparksheet.com/what-is-a-magazine/.

Lewis, Seth C. "The Tension between Professional Control and Open Participation." *Information, Communication, and Society* 15, no. 6 (2012): 836–66.

Lichtenstein, Stephanie. "Content Still Matters in the Evolving World of Online Advertising." *Yahoo! Scene*, June 9, 2011. Accessed September 1, 2011. http://scene.yahoo.net/iwny-2011/the-sessions/sessions/content-still-matters-in-the-evolving-world-on-online-advertising.

Loc, Tim. "Conde Nast Dips into the Digital Agency Game." *iMedia Connection*, April 22, 2010. http://www.imediaconnection.com/content/26558.asp.

Lotz, Amanda D. *The Television Will Be Revolutionized*. New York: NYU Press, 2007.

Lowrey, Wilson. "Mapping the Journalism-Blogging Relationship." *Journalism* 7, no. 4 (2006): 477–500.

"The MagaBrand Revolution: How Media Brands Are Finding Success on the Printed Page and Beyond." American Magazine Conference, Boca Raton, FL, October 29, 2007.

Magazine Death Pool. "Magazine Death Pool." Last modified November 5, 2010. http://www.magazinedeathpool.com.

"Magazine Hot List 2010." *Mediaweek,* March 29, 2010. http://www.adweek.com/news/press/magazine-hot-list-2010-top-10–115055.

"Magazine Measurement Initiative Update." *Magazine Publishers of America,* January 30, 2009. http://www.magazine.org/advertising/measurement/update-magazine -measurement-initiative.aspx.

Magforum. "Timeline: A History of Magazines." Last modified November 21, 2012. http://www.magforum.com/time.htm.

Manly, Lorne. "A Newsstand for the Electronic Age." *Folio: The Magazine for Magazine Management* 22, no. 16 (1993): 17. *Business Source Premier* (9312012593).

Maras, Steven, and David Sutton. "Medium Specificity Re-visited." *Convergence: The International Journal of Research into New Media Technologies* 6, no. 2 (2000): 98–113.

Marjoribanks, Timothy. "Strategising Technological Innovation: The Case of News Corporation." In *Media Organisation and Production,* edited by Simon Cottle, 59–76. London: Sage, 2003.

"Mastering Your SEO." *Folio: The Magazine for Magazine Management,* May 1, 2006. http://www.foliomag.com/2006/mastering-your-seo.

Mayer, Vicki. *Below the Line: Producers and Production Studies in the New Television Economy.* Durham, NC: Duke University Press, 2011.

Mayer, Vicki, Miranda J. Banks, and John T. Caldwell. *Production Studies: Cultural Studies of Media Industries.* New York: Routledge, 2009.

Mazzocchi, Sherry. "'Running in Heels' Joins Stampede of Fashion Reality-Shows: Marie Claire and Style Network to Follow Editors at Work and Home." *Advertising Age,* September 9, 2008. http://adage.com/article/mediaworks/running-heels -joins-stampede-fashion-reality-shows/130841/.

McAllister, Matthew P. *The Commercialization of American Culture.* Thousand Oaks, CA: Sage, 1995.

McChesney, Robert W. *The Problem of the Media: US Communication Politics in the Twenty-First Century.* New York: Monthly Review Press, 2004.

McCombs, Maxwell E., and Donald L. Shaw. "The Agenda-Setting Function of Mass Media." *Public Opinion Quarterly* 36, no. 2 (1972): 176–87.

McCracken, Ellen. *Decoding Women's Magazines: From "Mademoiselle" to "Ms."* New York: St. Martin's Press, 1993.

McLuhan, Marshall. *Understanding Media: The Extensions of Man.* Cambridge, MA: MIT Press, 1964.

McMullan, John, and Ingrid Richardson. "The Mobile Phone: A Hybrid Multi-Platform Medium." In *IE 2006: Proceedings of the 3rd Australasian Conference on Interactive Entertainment,* 103–8. Perth: Murdoch University Division of Arts, 2006. dl.acm.org/citation.cfm?id+1231910.

McPheters, Rebecca. "Why Circ-Based Measurement Is Anachronistic." *Folio: The Magazine for Magazine Management,* August 30, 2006. http://www.foliomag. com/2006/why-circ-based-measurement-anachronistic#.UR5vgPL5Qcs.

McRobbie, Angela. *Feminism and Youth Culture: From "Jackie" to "Just Seventeen."* New York: Macmillan, 1991.

———. *In the Culture Society: Art, Fashion, and Popular Music.* London: Routledge, 1999.

———. *"More!* New Sexualities in Girls' and Women's Magazines." In *Back to Reality: Social Experience and Cultural Studies,* edited by Angela McRobbie, revised ed., 190–209. Manchester: Manchester University Press, 1997.

Meehan, Eileen. "Commodity Audience, Actual Audience: The Blindspot Debate." In *Illuminating the Blindspots: Essays Honouring Dallas W. Smythe,* edited by Janet Wasko, Vincent Mosco, and Manjunath Pendakur, 378–97. Norwood, NJ: Ablex, 1993.

———. "Gendering the Commodity Audience: Critical Media Research, Feminism, and Political Economy." In *Sex and Money: Feminism and Political Economy in the Media,* edited by Eileen Meehan and Ellen Riordan, 209–22. Minneapolis: University of Minnesota Press, 2002.

Mendes, Kaitlynn, and Cynthia Carter. "Feminist and Gender Media Studies: A Critical Overview." *Sociology Compass* 2, no. 6 (2008): 1701–18.

Mesure, Susie. "Fluff Flies as Fashion Writers Pick a Cat Fight with Bloggers." *Independent,* January 31, 2010. http://www.independent.co.uk/life-style/fashion/news/fluff-flies-as-fashion-writers-pick-a-cat-fight-with-bloggers-1884539.html.

Mickey, Bill. "Glamorizing Brands: Glam Media Inc. Flips the Idea of 'Destination Site' on Its Head." *Folio: The Magazine for Magazine Management,* January 3, 2008. http://www.foliomag.com/2008/glamorizing-brands#.

———. "Time Inc. Names Rothenberg Chief Digital Officer." *Folio: The Magazine for Magazine Management,* December 13, 2010. http://www.foliomag.com/2010/time-inc-names-randall-rothenberg-chief-digital-officer.

Miller, Tim. "Web Publishing: A Primer." *Folio: The Magazine for Magazine Management* 28, no. 1/2 (1999): 233. *Academic OneFile* (A53557517).

Mitchelstein, Eugenia, and Pablo J. Boczkowski. "Between Tradition and Change." *Journalism* 10, no. 5 (2009): 562–86.

Money, Rachelle. "How Hearst Magazines Increased Website Traffic by 150% with SEO and Wordtracker." *Wordtracker,* February 1, 2009. http://www.wordtracker.com/academy/hearst-magazines-seo.

Moses, Lucia. "ASME Unveils New Guidelines for Magazine Web Sites." *Adweek,* January 25, 2011. http://www.adweek.com/news/television/asme-unveils-new-guidelines-magazine-web-sites-125535.

———. "Can Personalized Ads Save Magazines?" *Adweek,* December 15, 2011. http://www.adweek.com/news/press/can-personalized-ads-save-magazines-137134.

———. "Condé/Hearst Tale of the Tape." *Adweek,* January 16, 2011. http://www.adweek.com/news/advertising-branding/cond-hearst-tale-tape-125414.

———. "Irreplaceable You? These Condé Nast Editors in Chief Won't Be at Their Magazines Forever." *Adweek*, January 11, 2012. http://www.adweek.com/news/ press/irreplaceable-you-137379.

———. "Lessons from Laura Lang's (Brief) Tenure atop Time Inc." *Adweek*, March 6, 2013. http://www.adweek.com/news/advertising-branding/lessons-laura-langs -brief-tenure-atop-time-inc-147755.

———. "Meet the 'Glamour' Generation: Women's Monthly Embraces the Millennial Woman." *Adweek*, August 6, 2012. http://www.adweek.com/news/advertising -branding/meet-glamour-generation-142565/.

Müller, Eggo. "Formatted Spaces of Participation." In *Digital Material: Tracing New Media in Everyday Life and Technology*, edited by Marianne van den Boomen, Sybille Lammes, Ann-Sophie Lehmann, Joost Raessens, and Mirko Tobias Schafer, 49–64. Amsterdam: Amsterdam University Press, 2009.

Murdock, Graham. "Blindspots about Western Marxism: A Reply to Dallas Smythe." In *The Political Economy of the Media I*, edited by Peter Golding and Graham Murdock, 465–74. Cheltenham: Edward Elgar, 1978.

Murray, Simone. "Brand Loyalties: Rethinking Content within Global Corporate Media." *Media, Culture & Society* 27, no. 3 (2005): 415–435.

Napikoski, Linda. "Ladies' Home Journal Sit-In." Last modified April 9, 2012. http:// womenshistory.about.com/od/feminism/a/ladies_home_journal_sit_in.htm.

Napoli, Phillip M. "The Audience Product and the New Media Environment: Implications for the Economics of Media Industries." *International Journal on Media Management* 3, no. 1 (2001): 66–73.

Navasky, Victor, and Evan Lerner. "Magazines and Their Websites: A Columbia Journalism Review Survey." *Columbia Journalism Review*, March 2010. http://www.cjr.org/ resources/magazines_and_their_websites/.

Neff, Gina. *Venture Labor: Work and the Burden of Risk in Innovative Industries.* Cambridge, MA: MIT Press, 2012.

Neff, Gina, Elizabeth Wissinger, and Sharon Zukin. "Entrepreneurial Labour among Cultural Producers: 'Cool' Jobs in 'Hot' Industries." *Social Semiotics* 15, no. 3 (2005): 307–34.

"New Survey Shows That Blogs Are Two Times More Likely to Drive Beauty Product Purchases Than Magazines." *PRWeb*, January 11, 2011. http://www.prweb.com/ releases/2011/1/prweb8057896.htm.

Nixon, Sean, and Paul du Gay. "Who Needs Cultural Intermediaries?" *Cultural Studies* 16, no. 4 (2002): 495–500.

Oates, Caroline. "Designing Women's Magazines." Paper presented at the Design Culture Conference, Sheffield Hallam University and the European Academy of Design, 1999.

O'Connor, Justin. "The Cultural and Creative Industries: A Review of the Literature." Report for Creative Partnerships, Arts Council England, November 2007. http:// kulturekonomi.se/uploads/cp_litrev4.pdf.

Örnebring, Henrik. "Technology and Journalism-as-Labour: Historical Perspectives." *Journalism* 11, no. 1 (2010): 57–74.

Owen, Laura Hazard. "Condé Nast Will Give Advertisers More Metrics on Tablet Editions." *paidContent*, March 15, 2012. http://paidcontent.org/article/419-conde-nast -will-give-advertisers-more-metrics-on-tablet-editions/.

Patel, Kunur, and Nat Ives. "Who Is Laura Lang, Time Inc.'s New CEO?" *Ad Age*, November 30, 2011. http://adage.com/article/media/laura-lang-time-s-ceo/231274/.

Pavlik, John V. "A Sea-Change in Journalism: Convergence, Journalists, Their Audiences and Sources." *Convergence* 10, no. 4 (2004): 21–29.

Peiser, Wolfram. "Setting the Journalist Agenda: Influences from Journalists' Individual Characteristics and from Media Factors." *Journalism and Mass Communication Quarterly* 77, no. 2 (2000): 243–57.

Peiss, Kathy. "'Vital Industry' and Women's Ventures: Conceptualizing Gender in Twentieth Century Business History." *Business History Review* 72, no. 2 (1998): 218–41.

Peters, Jeremy W. "Elle, Not Camera Shy, Embraces Reality TV." *New York Times*, June 20, 2010. http://www.nytimes.com/2010/06/21/business/media/21elle.html.

———. "Glamour's iPad Series to Let Viewers Buy Clothes from Gap." *New York Times*, March 6, 2011. http://mediadecoder.blogs.nytimes.com/2011/03/06/glamours-ipad-series-to-let-viewers-buy-clothes-from-gap/.

———. "In Magazine World, a New Crop of Chiefs." *New York Times*, November 28, 2010. http://www.nytimes.com/2010/11/29/business/media/29mag.html.

———. "Why Magazine Publishers Like the Fire." *New York Times*, November 30, 2011. http://bits.blogs.nytimes.com/2011/09/30/why-magazine-publishers-like-the-fire/.

Peters, Jeremy W., and Eric Pfanner. "Hearst Agrees to Buy 100 Magazines from Lagardère." *New York Times*, January 31, 2011. http://www.nytimes.com/2011/02/01/ business/media/01lagardere.html.

Petersen, Laurie. "Q&A: David Kang of Hearst Magazines on Content Extensions." *Econsultancy: Digital Marketing Excellence*, March 22, 2011. http://econsultancy.com/us/ blog/7311-q-a-with-david-kang-hearst-magazines-new-point-person-on-content -extensions.

Pitt, Lisa. "Masculinities@Work: Gender Inequality and the New Media Industries." *Feminist Media Studies* 3, no. 3 (2003): 378–81.

Postigo, Hector. "America Online Volunteers: Lessons from an Early Co-production Community." *International Journal of Cultural Studies* 12, no. 5 (2009): 451–69.

Potts, John. "Who's Afraid of Technological Determinism? Another Look at Medium Theory." *Fibreculture Journal* 12 (2008). http://journal.fibreculture.org/issue12/ issue12_potts.html.

PriceWaterHouseCoopers (Netherlands). "The Medium Is the Message: Outlook for Magazine Publishing in the Digital Age." 2008. http://www.pwc.com/gx/en/ entertainment-media/pdf/magpub.pdf.

Pridmore, Jason, and Detlev Zwick. "Marketing and the Rise of Consumer Surveillance." *Surveillance and Society* 8, no. 3 (2011): 269–77.

Randle, Quint. "A Historical Overview of the Effects of New Mass Media: Introductions in Magazine Publishing during the Twentieth Century." *First Monday* 6, no. 9- (September 3, 2001). http://firstmonday.org/article/view/885/794.

Ravasi, Davide, and Johan Van Rekom. "Key Issues in Organizational Identity and Identification Theory." *Corporate Reputation Review* 6, no. 2 (2003): 118–32.

Reed, Barbara Straus. "'Be Somebody': Ruth Whitney of *Glamour*." In *Women and Media: Content/Careers/Criticism*, edited by Cynthia Lont, 87–97. Belmont, CA: Wadsworth, 1995.

Reinhard, CarrieLynn D. "Discourse Swings in Understanding Audiences: Case Studies on Hollywood's Cooptation of Audience Activity(s) as Emergent Discourse." Paper presented at the annual meeting for the International Communication Association Conference, Chicago, May 21–25, 2009.

Roberts, Andrew, and Matthew Campbell. "Click to Buy That Bag in *Vogue* as Magazines Become e-Tailers." *Bloomberg*, April 1, 2011. http://www.bloomberg.com/news/2011-03-31/click-to-buy-that-handbag-in-vogue-as-magazines-become-e-tailers.html.

Roberts, Johnnie L. "Just How Much Did Condé Nast Lose?" *Newsweek*, October 7, 2009. http://www.thedailybeast.com/newsweek/2009/10/07/just-how-much-did-conde-nast-lose.html.

Rosen, Jay. "The People Formerly Known as the Audience." *Press Think: Ghost of Democracy in the Media Machine*, June 27, 2006. http://archive.pressthink.org/2006/06/27/ppl_frmr.html.

Rushe, Dominic. "Hearst Buys Elle Rights in $651m Lagardère Deal." *Guardian*, March 28, 2011. http://www.guardian.co.uk/media/2011/mar/28/hearst-buys-elle-rights-in-lagardere-deal.

Russell, Mallory. "Harper's Bazaar Introduces ShopBazaar as Magazines' E-Commerce Push Grows." *Advertising Age*, September 12, 2012. http://adage.com/article/media/harper-s-bazaar-introduces-shopbazaar-e-commerce-play/237148/.

Ryan, John W., and Richard A. Peterson. "The Product Image: The Fate of Creativity in Country Music Songwriting." In *Individuals in Mass Media Organizations: Creativity and Constraint*, edited by James S. Ettema and D. Charles Whitney, 11–32. Beverly Hills, CA: Sage, 1982.

Saltzis, Konstantinos, and Roger Dickinson. "Inside the Changing Newsroom: Journalists' Responses to Media Convergence." *Aslib Proceedings* 60, no. 3 (2008): 216–28.

Santos, Filipe M., and Kathleen M. Eisenhardt. "Organizational Boundaries and Theories of Organization." *Organization Science* 16, no. 5 (2005): 491–508.

Sass, Eric. "Majority of Readers Access Digital Magazine Content, Ads." *Media Daily News*, November 21, 2011. http://www.mediapost.com/publications/article/162780/majority-of-readers-access-digital-magazine-conten.html?print#axzz2OMbQtojN.

Saunders, Stephen M. "News in the Age of Blogs." *Folio: The Magazine for Magazine Management*, December 1, 2009. http://www.foliomag.com/2009/news-age-blogs.

Schudson, Michael. "The Sociology of News Production." *Media, Culture and Society* 11, no. 3 (1989): 263–82.

Seeking Alpha. "Meredith's CEO Hosts Analyst Meeting." February 15, 2012. http://seekingalpha.com/article/367681-meredith-s-ceo-hosts-analyst-meeting-transcript.

Segal, David. "The Dirty Little Secrets of Search." *New York Times*, February 12, 2011. http://www.nytimes.com/2011/02/13/business/13search.html.

Segers, Katia, and Ellen Huijgh. "Clarifying the Complexity and Ambivalence of the Cultural Industries." Cemeso Working Paper, no. 8. Brussels: Centre for Studies on Media and Culture, 2007. http://www.vub.ac.be/SCOM/cemeso/download/cemeso-08-complexity%20ambivalence%20cultural%20industries.pdf.

Sender, Katherine. *Business, Not Politics: The Making of the Gay Market*. New York: Columbia University Press, 2004.

Seneca, Tracy. "The History of Women's Magazines: Magazines as Virtual Communities." http://besser.tsoa.nyu.edu/impact/f93/students/tracy/tracy_hist.html.

Sennett, Richard. *The Culture of the New Capitalism*. New Haven, CT: Yale University Press, 2006.

Serazio, Michael. *Your Ad Here: The Cool Sell of Guerrilla Marketing*. New York: New York University Press, 2013.

"The Shape Survey." *Shape*, October 2011, 21–22.

Shevelow, Kathryn. *Women and Print Culture: The Construction of Femininity in the Early Periodical*. New York: Taylor and Francis, 1989.

Shields, Michael. "Condé Uses 'Crowd Control' to Dig into Digital Audience." *Adweek*, January 23, 2011. http://www.adweek.com/news/technology/cond-uses-crowd-control-dig-digital-audience-125517.

———. "Mag Rack: A Short Life." *Mediapost*, September 9, 2004. http://www.mediapost.com/publications/article/19905/mag-rack-a-short-life.html?print#ixzz2A7OVI8tM.

Shimpach, Shawn. "Working Watching: The Creative and Cultural Labor of the Media Audience." *Social Semiotics* 15, no. 3 (2005): 343–60.

Silber, Tony. "Behind the Wave of CEO Departures." *Folio: The Magazine for Magazine Management*, November 17, 2005. http://www.foliomag.com/2005/behind-wave-ceo-departures.

Singer, Jane B. "Strange Bedfellows? The Diffusion of Convergence in Four News Organizations." *Journalism Studies* 5, no. 1 (2004): 3–18.

Sivek, Susan Currie. "The Ethics of Digital Magazine Advertising." *MediaShift*, April 28, 2010. http://www.pbs.org/mediashift/2010/04/the-ethics-of-digital-magazine-advertising-118.html.

Smith, Katlyn. "Scholar Speaks on Feminism." *Observer*, first posted March 19, 2008, updated September 12, 2012. http://www.ndsmcobserver.com/news/scholar-speaks-on-feminism-1.259060#.UT-_DZjhumM.

Smythe, Dallas. "Communications: Blindspot of Western Marxism." *Canadian Journal of Political and Social Theory* 1, no. 3 (1977): 1–27.

———. *Dependency Road: Communications, Capitalism, Consciousness, and Canada.* Toronto: Ablex, 1981.

Sonderman, Jeff. "To a 1-Year Old, Print Magazine Seems Like a Broken iPad." *Poynter*, October 14, 2011. http://www.poynter.org/latest-news/mediawire/149595/to-a-1-year -old-print-magazine-seems-like-a-broken-ipad/.

Sozzani, Franca. "Bloggers: A Cultural Phenomenon or an Epidemic Issue?" *Italian Vogue Magazine*, January 28, 2011. http://www.vogue.it/en/magazine/editor-s-blog/ 2011/01/january-28th.

Stableford, Dylan. "Magazine Executives Call Meeting to Decide 'What's a Magazine?'" *The Wrap*, April 21, 2010. http://www.thewrap.com/media/column-post/magazine -executives-call-meeting-decide-whats-magazine-16509.

Steinberg, Brian. "What's Condé Nast Doing Making Kenneth Cole Ads for Facebook and YouTube? Under Threat, Media Push Further into Agency Territory." *Advertising Age*, April 26, 2010, 52.

Steinem, Gloria. "Sex, Lies, and Advertising." *Ms.* 8 (1997): 18–28.

Steiner, Linda. "Would the Real Women's Magazine Please Stand Up . . . for Women." In *Women and Media: Content/Careers/Criticism*, edited by Cynthia Lont, 99–108. New York: Wadsworth, 1995.

Sumner, David E. *The Magazine Century: American Magazines since 1900.* New York: Peter Lang, 2010.

Swartz, Jon. "Time Spent on Facebook, Twitter, YouTube Grows." *USA Today*, August 1, 2010. http://www.usatoday.com/tech/news/2010-08-02-networking02_ST_N.htm.

Terranova, Tiziana. "Free Labor: Producing Culture for the Digital Economy." *Social Text* 18, no. 2 (2000): 33–58.

Thornham, Sue. *Women, Feminism and Media.* Edinburgh: Edinburgh University Press, 2007.

"Top Women in Magazine Publishing." *Publishing Executive*, May 2009. http://www .pubexec.com/article/i-publishing-executive-i-honors-leading-female-executives -helping-shape-industry-407203/1.

Tripsas, Mary. "Technology, Identity, and Inertia through the Lens of the 'Digital' Photography Company." *Organization Science* 20, no. 2 (2009): 441–60.

Tuchman, Gaye. *Making News: A Study in the Construction of Reality.* New York: Free Press, 1978.

Turow, Joseph. "Audience Construction and Culture Production: Marketing Surveillance in the Digital Age." *Annals of the American Academy of Political and Social Science* 597, no. 1 (2005): 103–21.

———. *Breaking Up America: Advertisers and the New Media World.* Chicago: University of Chicago Press, 1998.

———. "The Challenge of Inference in Interinstitutional Research on Mass Communication." *Communication Research* 18, no. 2 (1991): 222–39.

———. *Media Industries: The Production of News and Entertainment.* New York: Longman, 1984.

———. *Media Systems in Society: Understanding Industries, Strategies, and Power.* New York: Longman, 1992.

———. *Niche Envy: Marketing Discrimination in the Digital Age.* Cambridge, MA: MIT Press, 2006.

———. "The Organizational Underpinnings of Contemporary Media Conglomerates." *Communication Research* 19, no. 6 (1992): 682–704.

———. "Unconventional Programs on Commercial Television: An Organizational Perspective." In *Individuals in Mass Media Organizations: Creativity and Constraint,* edited by James S. Ettema and D. Charles Whitney, 107–30. Thousand Oaks, CA: Sage, 1982.

Turow, Joseph, Michael Hennessy, and Amy Bleakley. "Consumers' Understanding of Privacy Rules in the Marketplace." *Journal of Consumer Affairs* 42, no. 3 (2008): 411–24.

Van Slyke, Craig, Christie L. Comunale, and France Belanger. "Gender Differences in Perceptions of Web-Based Shopping." *Communications of the ACM* 45, no. 8 (2002): 82–86.

van Zoonen, Liesbet. "Feminist Internet Studies." *Feminist Media Studies* 1, no. 1 (2001): 67–72.

———. *Feminist Media Studies.* Thousand Oaks, CA: Sage, 1994.

———. "A Professional, Unreliable, Heroic Marionette (M/F)." *European Journal of Cultural Studies* 1, no. 1 (1998): 123–43.

Voltolina, Vanessa, and Matt Kinsman. "Developing the Edit Staff That Will Define Your Future." *Folio: The Magazine for Magazine Management,* June 1, 2009. http://www.foliomag.com/2009/developing-edit-staff-will-define-your-future.

Walker, Nancy A. *Shaping Our Mothers' World: American Women's Magazines.* Jackson: University Press of Mississippi, 2000.

Waller-Zuckerman, Mary Ellen. "'Old Homes, in a City of Perpetual Change': Women's Magazines, 1890–1916." *Business History Review* 63, no. 4 (1989): 715–56.

Wang, Alex. *Digital Ad Engagement: Perceived Interactivity as a Driver of Advertising Effectiveness.* University of Connecticut—Stamford Research Study, 2010. http://www.adobe.com/products/digitalpublishingsuite/pdfs/digital_magazine_ad_engagement.pdf.

Ward, Douglas. *A New Brand of Business: Charles Coolidge Parlin, Curtis Publishing Company, and the Origins of Market Research.* Philadelphia: Temple University Press, 2010.

Weekes, Karen. "*Women Know Everything!*" *3,241 Quips, Quotes, and Brilliant Remarks.* Philadelphia: Quirk Books, 2007.

Weeks, Linton. "Web Ads Tied to News Photos Pop Up More and More." October 20, 2010. http://www.npr.org/templates/story/story.php?storyId=130660759.

Whetten, David. "Albert and Whetten Revisited: Strengthening the Concept of Organizational Identity." *Journal of Management Inquiry* 15, no. 3 (2006): 219–34.

White, Cynthia L. *Women's Magazines, 1693–1968.* London: Michael Joseph, 1970.

Wilkinson, Jeffrey S. "Converging Communication, Colliding Cultures: Shifting Boundaries and the Meaning of 'Our Field.'" In *Media Convergence: The State of the Field*, edited by August S. Grant and Jeffrey S. Wilkinson, 98–116. New York: Oxford University Press, 2009.

Williams, Raymond. "Culture Is Ordinary." In *The Raymond Williams Reader*, edited by John Higgins, 93–100. Oxford: Blackwell, 2001.

Wilson, Eric. "Fashion Changes, and So Do the Magazines." *New York Times*, February 1, 2012. http://www.nytimes.com/2012/02/02/fashion/fashion-changes-and-so-do-the-magazines.html.

Winship, Janice. *Inside Women's Magazines*. New York: Pandora Press, 1987.

Wolf, Naomi. *The Beauty Myth: How Images of Beauty Are Used against Women*. New York: William Morrow and Company, 1991.

Zebian, Linda. "The Mass-Consumer Magazine Web Dilemma." *Folio: The Magazine for Magazine Management*, July 30, 2007. http://www.foliomag.com/2007/mass-consumer-magazine-web-dilemma.

Zuckerman, Mary Ellen. *A History of Popular Women's Magazines in the United States, 1792–1995*. Westport, CT: Greenwood Press, 1998.

Zwick, Detlev, Samuel K. Bonsu, and Aron Darmody. "Putting Consumers to Work." *Journal of Consumer Culture* 8, no. 2 (2008): 163–96.

Index

BROOKE ERIN DUFFY is an assistant professor in the School of Media and Communication at Temple University and the coeditor of *Key Readings in Media Today: Mass Communication in Contexts.*

The University of Illinois Press
is a founding member of the
Association of American University Presses.

Composed in 10.5/13 Adobe Minion Pro
by Lisa Connery
at the University of Illinois Press
Manufactured by Cushing-Malloy, Inc.

University of Illinois Press
1325 South Oak Street
Champaign, IL 61820-6903
www.press.uillinois.edu